Young people and leisure

International Library of Sociology and Social Reconstruction

Founded by Karl Mannheim

Editor W. J. H. Sprott

A catalogue of books available in the **International Library of Sociology and Social Reconstruction** and new books in preparation for the Library will be found at the end of the volume.

Young people and leisure

John Leigh

WITHDRAWN

London   Routledge & Kegan Paul
Humanities Press, Inc.

First published 1971
by Routledge and Kegan Paul Ltd
Broadway House,
68-74 Carter Lane,
London, EC4V 5EL
Printed in Great Britain by
The Lavenham Press Ltd
© John Leigh 1971

ISBN O 7100 7059 4

Abel

Contents

Tables

Acknowledgments

In the course of the three years of the North-East Derbyshire Project and the longer period of the preparation of this book I have received help and encouragement from many people. It is impossible for me to express adequately my gratitude to all those from whom help has been received. I should, however, like to acknowledge my debt to the following bodies and groups: The project management committee, the King George V Jubilee Trust, the development committee of the National Association of Youth Clubs, the youth service staff of north-east Derbyshire, the ten students from the youth work course of Matlock College of Education who conducted the survey in Minton in 1968.

I should also like to express my particular thanks to the following individuals: Mr D. Anthony, Mr E. Bourne, Lt Col. R. T. Brain, Mr M. Farrant, Mr E. Joyce, Mrs M. Leigh, Dr C. S. Smith, Mr B. Stewart, Dr W. D. Wall and to Mr John Haines, the consultant to the project.

J.L.

Author's note

The young people mentioned in the studies in this book are all given fictitious names and fictitious initials. In no case are the initials or names used those of the real young people with whom the studies were concerned. The names of the places in which special studies were conducted are also fictitious. If there are real places with these names they are not therefore the places referred to in this book.

J.L.

Introduction

Most of the practical work for this book was carried out during the years 1966-9 as part of a project sponsored jointly by the National Association of Youth Clubs and Derbyshire Education Committee with the financial backing of the King George V Jubilee Trust. The starting point for the project was concern over the increasing absence of young adults from youth service and adult education provision. I was appointed for three years with very wide terms of reference to examine this situation and to report fully to my employing bodies.

I should say immediately that this book is not a report of that project nor is it limited to a consideration of the youth service or a particular age group. Indeed the only discussion of the position of young adults in youth clubs occurs in the final chapter.

As I immersed myself in the problem I had been set I became increasingly aware of the whole range of factors which relate to leisure provision and the service making such provision. Questions about education and leisure are inevitably bound up with questions about the sort of society we live in and that to which we aspire. Such questions cannot be 'answered' but consideration of them must increasingly concern and involve all who work in schools, youth service and adult education. My aim in writing this book is to stimulate and add to the debate.

Throughout the period of the project and the writing of this book questions about leisure provision, 'continuing education' and community development have been very much in the air. It has been an exciting and stimulating period in which to be working in this field.

The work of the Schools Council is beginning to have an impact on the curriculum and style of work in secondary schools. An increasing number of schools are experimenting with school leaver courses and are looking towards developments of this work with the raising of the school leaving age. Some five hundred schools have youth tutors attached to their staffs and many others engage extensively in making social and recreational provision for their pupils or for the areas which they serve. In many areas the concept of the community school is being translated into reality, though rarely as much of a reality as those at the heart of such ventures would wish.

Despite financial setbacks there have been enormous developments too in adult education. Adult education has always been an area where exciting ideas have flourished, but with more training and more professional adult educators there are more places where these ideas are being carried forward into practice than ever before. The service is more conscious of its total community role and is more than ever searching in its philosophy and experimental in its methods and practice.

For much of the period the youth service has been working through a period of re-assessment and has been waiting for and considering the report *Youth and Community Work in the 70s*. This process has seemed to be, by turns, both stimulating and depressive. A service so diverse naturally finds much to argue about. But the overall picture is very encouraging. Besides the great volume of clubwork which has had a massive expansion in the last ten years there is a growing tide of experimental work in clubs, in non-institutional settings and in training.

Anyone taking this kind of global view of the situation must derive great comfort from it. A great deal that is stimulating and vital is being talked and written about and at least some of it is being translated into practice. On the face of it there are sound preparations being made for the future.

This rosy view of the situation can be contrasted with other less hopeful, and sometimes more difficult, views. For example, it is always worth stressing that the overall, general picture is of only passing interest to the consumer. He is concerned about what is available to him in his locality and it is of little consolation that something better exists, inaccessibly, somewhere else. For him the school, youth club or adult centre which is there is the one which matters. For all practical purposes the church hall down the road *is* the youth service and sometimes it is not a very adequate service. Despite the lavishly equipped, palatial Adult Education Centre twenty miles away, the total reality of locally available adult education may well be flower arranging at the local primary school. This is the simple argument for more provision, that is to say, for *more of the best of what we have already*.

Yet even apparently well provided areas still leave many people unprovided for and the overall proportion of the population who make use of the services available is not very high. Sometimes it can be shown that the existing resources are fully used and that what is needed initially is simple expansion, but quite often it is also argued that there is a realistic ceiling for use of the kind of provision which is made. Youth service and adult education can be defined in terms of being providing services which realistically have a limited appeal. As much as possible should be done to persuade as many as possible to enter the fold but the 'fold' itself is restricted not only by its physical limitations but also by its own basic nature. The argument is both 'what we have to offer will only appeal to a limited number', and 'only a limited number can, because of the circumstances of their lives, avail themselves of what we have to offer'.

Set against this is the increasingly common view that the emphasis of the services should shift from provision and recruitment towards help and influence; that the role of the services should be more broadly defined and that the services should 'involve' themselves with more people. There are difficulties here. 'Help' and 'influence' may not be the words used, but they are near enough to what is often implied in this argument. They are concepts which do not fit easily into administrative frameworks which have been concerned previously with membership, classes and attendance. In any case such words sometimes seem to carry unpleasant overtones of patronage and social control. The newcomer to the scene, community development, frequently provokes strong reactions simply because of its title. It sounds a meddlesome activity. It doesn't seem to have much to do with an already 'developed' society and, perhaps most important of all, it doesn't seem to fit in with any of the mainstreams of what is actually happening at the moment.

There is also the view that schools or youth service or somebody ought to be concerned about education *for* leisure as well as providing educational activities which can be undertaken in leisure time. Some teachers would argue that this is an area of work in which they are already engaged and certainly there has been some official encouragement to take up such work. However, this topic too raises some difficult questions. What are the aims of education for leisure and by what methods are they achieved? What sort of evaluation takes place or might be possible? In what ways does this 'subject' relate to the rest of the curriculum? What successes can we count up and with whom are we most successful?

The main theme of this book is leisure and the response of schools, youth service and adult education to making preparation for, or providing for the leisure time of the population. While this may seem a far cry from the starting point of young adults in youth clubs it was in fact that aspect of the work of youth service which prompted the lines of inquiry which run through the book. If any account is taken of the estimates of future leisure the theme is a vitally important one.

I have found it useful to examine the work of youth service and adult education and some of the activities of secondary schools in relation to the central theme of leisure and in relation to evidence about the real leisure lives of a small sample of the population. While this approach through the theme of leisure leaves many factors out of the reckoning it does provide a framework which allows for an interrelated view of many of the things which are happening (and not happening) at the moment in schools, youth service and adult education. One of the purposes of the book is to try to show that there is something more useful in this idea than a simple desire to find unity and interrelatedness in all things.

Much of the book was written during the same period that the report *Youth and Community Work in the 70s* was being prepared and it may be read as an extension of, and critical commentary on that report. The ground covered is by no means wholly the same, but there are some key issues in common.

Many kinds of practical work went into the making of the book but observation and interview were those most commonly used. In some cases observation of a particular group or organization extended over a period of some months as it was sometimes necessary to get to know people well before they could talk freely. I took special pains to learn as much as I could of both the provider's and consumer's views of the situation. Not surprisingly these often differed from each other and frequently both differed from the 'official' line of the organization concerned. This makes for a book which is sometimes untidy and is always a good deal more personal in its approach and less scientific in its method than I had originally hoped would be the case.

The actual plan of the book is straightforward. The first three chapters deal with education and provision for leisure and the problems of schools, youth service and adult education in relation to this. Chapter 4 deals briefly with a number of organizations which are particularly interesting because of their origins, aims or organizational methods. Chapters 5, 6 and 7 are an examination of the leisure lives of the eighteen to twenty-five age group in one small industrial village and this provides some illustration of the difficulties of providing for leisure in non-urban areas. Chapter 8 is a detailed account of a simple experimental project in non-institutional provision and Chapter 9 is the concluding chapter.

1 Education for leisure?

One of the purposes of this book is to examine the relationship which exists between the education services and the leisure time of the people they attempt to serve. At one level this relationship would seem straightforward; the more leisure people have the greater the concern of the education services with this aspect of people's lives. Throughout the education services it is not difficult to point to expressions of this concern. Non-vocational adult education and youth service are both leisure-based services which have developed with the increase in leisure time and which concern themselves very directly with the leisure of their customers, both as providers for the present and, hopefully, educators for the future. With colleges and universities, there is a massive investment in leisure provision in union buildings, playing fields and other facilities and the rightness of making such investment is rarely questioned. An increasing number of schools too deploy staff and resources in activities associated with the present or future leisure lives of their pupils. In all this we can see a simple quantitative relationship between leisure and the education services.

The real nature of the activities of the education services in relation to leisure is, however, often more difficult to determine. Distinctions between leisure provision for the present and education for the future are often blurred, assessments of effectiveness difficult to come by and statements about aims and objectives far from clear. It is these issues in relation to schools which are examined in this chapter. First, though, it is necessary to make some general points about leisure and about education.

The simplest definition of leisure is that it is not work; but it is very clear that for most purposes this definition is inadequate. Few of us would regard all our non-work activities as leisure. The French sociologist Joffre Dumazadier says, 'Briefly, and most emphatically, contemporary leisure is defined by contrast not just to one's job, but to all of the ordinary necessities and obligations of existence ...'[1] So leisure can be seen as that area of existence where within our individual circumstantial limits we exercise choice about the use we make of time. Popularly leisure is 'free' time, but, of course this 'freedom' is circumscribed by physical circumstances, local cultural expectations and the total limitations of the individual whether of skill, education, information or aspiration.

From this I would deduce that the broad educational aim in relation to leisure is to increase this freedom; *to increase both the true range of choices available and the ability of the individual to make effective and significant choices.*[2]

It is important to ask whether the way our education services behave leads to the achievement of this aim. I suggest that in many cases it does not, and this not simply, and understandably, that the services fall short of their objectives, but rather that in some cases they are on the wrong track ever to achieve them. So far as schools are concerned many of the ideas about leisure and leisure education which are in common circulation seem unhelpful.

There has always been some educational interest in leisure and a growing sophistication in non-academic secondary education, stemming from the 1944 Education Act, has accelerated this interest. There has been an increasingly wide recognition among teachers that for the majority in a mechanized and automated age 'labour' is not an aspect of life which is necessarily very dignified and with this comes the hope that leisure might be more so. Under the chapter title 'Objectives' and immediately following a quotation from Alan Sillitoe's *Saturday Night and Sunday Morning* the Newsom Report poses the following question: 'Before they can tackle the problem the schools have to be clear about their ultimate objectives. What ought these to be for our pupils? In any immediately foreseeable future, large numbers of boys and girls who leave school will enter jobs which make as limited demands on them as Arthur Seaton's: 'Can their time in school help them to find more nourishment for the rest of their personal lives than loony-coloured phantasies?'[3]

The implications of this question are interesting and the key phrase is 'the rest of their personal lives' in the final sentence. The implication here is of a directly compensatory activity; that the rest of life can make up for a job that is dull and unrewarding, that if work cannot provide 'nourishment', then perhaps leisure can. Yet it is surely something of a pipe dream to suppose that life can be compartmentalized in this way. If the total educational experience helps to formulate an exploratory spirit and a critical turn of mind, then these attributes are as likely to be focused on work as on any other aspect of life. Education, in any real sense of the word, can never be a process which fits people for an unquestioning acceptance of drudgery. The values of leisure and work are interrelated. The education which fits one for a real engagement in leisure activities is likely to make 'dull 'work not *more* bearable, but *less* so. On this score Dumazadier writes: 'It is, similarly, impossible to deal with the problems of leisure and work separately. Indeed, the humanization of work through the values of leisure is inseparable from the humanization of leisure through the values of work.'[4]

Newsom says that the schools have to be clear about 'their ultimate objectives', but I would suggest that in many cases they are at present a long way removed from any such clarity and my hypothesis is that teachers in schools, and in the other education services, have been very much influenced by the idea of leisure as a compensatory activity. In an age when the dull, dreary, routine occupations that are to be the lot of many of those passing through secondary schools seemingly offer little opportunity for individual self-fulfilment, leisure has seemed to offer an acceptable back door entrance to the education of the 'whole man'.

In the long run, it could prove to be just this, but before this is remotely possible it is necessary for teachers to affirm, and this most strongly, that education for leisure is concerned with total, not partial, values. In terms of 'ultimate objectives' one of the characteristics of the educated man is that he is opposed to those processes, wherever they occur, which in anyway tend towards dehumanization. Thus the philosophical basis for leisure education has to be one which is concerned with values which transcend work/ leisure divisions and some indication of these values must be reflected in day to day educational practice.

It is both difficult and dangerous to say much about the practical implications of a philosophy, but if I am right in my belief that in the fields of leisure provision and leisure education there has been a generalized acceptance of the compensatory theory then one of the consequences of this might be an undue emphasis on diversionary activities and the fostering of a pseudo-high seriousness about essentially trivial activities which leads in the long run, not to personal and social development, but to escapism. An emphasis on leisure as a compensatory activity seems to me to tend towards its relegation to the level of the 'soma' of Huxley's *Brave New World*: something which makes existence more bearable, but life less human.

Over the past few years demands that schools should do something about leisure have been growing. Probably the thing for which the Newsom Report, *Half Our Future*, will be remembered is that it brought to Government notice the desperate inequalities in the allocation of educational resources. On the side lines, however, it also gave powerful support to the idea of an educational concern

3

with leisure activities, and for anyone concerned with leisure, the Newsom Report is an important document. The terms of reference given to the Newsom Committee explicitly refer to extra-curricular activities and the report of the committee probably devotes more space to 'leisure' than any previous government report specifically concerned with schools.

The grounds for this increased concern with leisure are set out quite clearly in the report itself.

'In western industrialised countries, the hours which must necessarily be spent in earning a living are likely to be markedly reduced during the working lifetime of children now in school. The responsibility for ensuring that this new leisure is the source of enjoyment and benefit it ought to be, and not of demoralising boredom, is not the schools' alone, but clearly education can play a key part.'[5]

It seems likely that in the future, increasing attention will be paid to the business of leisure education. Richard Boston in an article in *New Society* (26 December 1968) quotes Edward Short, Secretary of State for Education as predicting that by the end of the 1980s most people would not be working until their middle twenties and would probably finish in their middle fifties and that during their working life they would probably have about three days leisure a week. In January 1969 when interviewed on television in connection with the raising of the school leaving age, Mr Short stressed the point that in part the extra year should be used to prepare people for the increased leisure of the future. This is re-emphasizing what Newsom says, but the intervening five years have added a certain urgency and popular appeal to what is called 'the problem of leisure'.

Put at its simplest the 'problem of leisure' is that we are wholly unprepared for an age when automation reduces working life and the working week to the sort of proportions suggested by Mr Short. In the article which I have already quoted, Richard Boston suggests that perhaps this leisure explosion is not quite so imminent as some commentators have suggested. He argues that the basis for predictions is usually the reduction of the working week and points out that this can be a misleading indicator. Increases in the amount of overtime worked and in the incidence of double jobbing have largely offset reductions in the official working week and 'average hours worked' were the same in 1938 and 1958.

Richard Boston's article is about the accuracy of some current predictions. He does not question the main premise and his final paragraph contains the following: 'The Age of Leisure is, then, still some way off. This does not mean that it isn't coming. Gabor aptly quotes none less than Marx on the subject of child labour: "A general prohibition of child labour is incompatible with the existence of large scale industry and hence an empty, pious wish"

4

(*Critique of the Gotha Programme*, 1875). Marx was wrong about child labour, and those who doubt that adult labour may also largely disappear may prove equally wrong.'

However, even if Richard Boston is right in suggesting that we are as yet someway removed from an Age of Leisure which will affect the mass of the population there is no doubt that for some people it has already arrived. The male workers in at least one Lancashire cotton town work a three-day week and pit closures in the contracting mining industry have already thrust many miners into a premature retirement. It is salutary to reflect that so far as the miners are concerned their school 'education for leisure' took place in the twenties when future leisure must have been the last issue to which people in mining communities gave any consideration.

If the 'problem of leisure', in the sense of there being enormous spaces of time to be filled, is not one which concerns the majority of people at the moment, there is another sense in which the problem of leisure is very much with us. If, as is held to be the case, a more leisured future is generally feared, is not this the most savage commentary possible on the quality of leisure life in the present? If present leisure is something that will not bear extension then I would argue that we might define 'the problem of leisure' not in terms of the future but, very definitely and very urgently, in terms of the present. The 'problem of leisure' is concerned with its quality in the present as with its quantity in the future and the best preparation for the increased leisure of the future is to ensure that it is possible to lead leisure lives which are satisfying and fulfilling now.

With this in mind, there are some questions which I think it might be useful to ask about the contribution made by schools to leisure education. In particular, I want to question the extent of their contribution, the sort of contribution they make and the sort of contribution they are encouraged to make. There can be no pretence that these questions can be satisfactorily answered or that my answers are more than broad and subjective generalizations. None the less, I hope to touch on issues which I think constitute a real cause for concern and which, while they may be disputed in detail, cannot, I believe, be wholly ignored.

In the last resort all education is education for leisure just as it is education for work or for the whole of life. What I want to deal with here are those activities which take place in schools and of which teachers and educationalists speak and write in terms which associate them with the present and future leisure lives of the pupils.

These activities may be part of the school curriculum and, of this group, perhaps sports and games are the most obvious examples. But all the 'practical' subjects have some relevance here and although subjects like woodwork, metalwork and technical drawing may have a vocational bias they also provide the necessary basic skills for much leisure activity; and this more than ever in a 'do it yourself' age. These sorts of examples are common to most secondary schools, but increasingly evident too are the sorts of courses, like those linked to the Duke of Edinburgh's Award scheme, which take special provision for both experience of a range of leisure activities and for instruction in their basic skills. Here the scope is limitless and activities like skiing and filming, skin diving and jewellery making take their place in the curriculum alongside history and geography, maths and English.

Also, there are the extra-curricular and extra-mural activities of which the above may be a part, but which include, too, the school clubs and societies. For my main argument, it does not much matter that these disparate sorts of activity are lumped together and in any case in practice the distinctions between the curricular and extra-curricular and between voluntary and non-voluntary can become blurred.

So far as the extent of the contribution made by schools to leisure education is concerned, there is little reliable information to go on. However, a glance at any of the teachers' papers, a round of school speech days or a reading of the literature about what ought to be happening can leave an impression of high levels of activity and participation. To this I think it is necessary to offer some corrective.

While good work can take place in the most unhelpful conditions, any realistic view of schools must make some reference to the physical circumstances in which they operate. The Newsom survey of secondary school buildings had this to say:

> Less than two thirds of the schools have a library room of more than 500 square feet; over half the schools have no provision of any kind for music; a third of the schools have no proper science laboratory; half the schools have no gymnasium ...
> There is a general shortage of teaching spaces and large class-rooms. In addition, a quarter of all the schools in the sample were both poorly accommodated indoors and seriously deficient in playing field provision out-of-doors.[6]

This is not a situation which allows room for complacency and if one adds factors like the four o'clock exodus made unavoidable by a wide catchment area, the pressing problems of over-crowding even in new buildings, then one sees there are many situations in which the schools cannot contribute very much.

In considering the extent of leisure education opportunities in schools, it is possible to be misled too, by an undue reliance on official pronouncements that such opportunities exist. On this the

Schools Council Enquiry into young school leavers has this to say:

According to the information supplied by the schools, over four-fifths of fifteen year old leavers were in schools which ran sports or athletic clubs and an equal proportion were in schools which had hobby societies of various kinds. Considerably smaller proportions of the youngsters themselves said that there were school clubs or societies of these types which they were personally entitled to attend if they wished; just over half said that there were school sports clubs and a third that there were hobbies societies.[7]

As the report points out, this discrepancy can be accounted for by the fact that, although the clubs and societies existed, they were not open to the early school leavers who were interviewed. But also, the situation described is an interesting reflection of that which I have found to be common in society as a whole. The official guide to almost any town in the country will list an incredible diversity of clubs and societies. For example, in Chesterfield, with a population of eighty thousand, I traced over one hundred and sixty organizations excluding those directly concerned with young people. However, so far as I could tell, this seemingly rich social/recreational life impinged very little upon the public consciousness as a whole. Only about four per cent of the adult population were actively involved in any way and my impression is that the great mass of people would be totally unaware of the existence of this provision.

In talking about the opportunities which exist in schools for learning about leisure, we are seemingly talking about opportunities which exist for only a minority. How small that minority is would only be revealed by extensive consumer surveys, but if sports clubs exist for only a half and other clubs and societies for only a third we might guess that the number of participants among the early school leaver group is very small indeed.

The real questions however, must relate to the type of experiences offered. How well equipped are teachers to help young people in this way and in what ways do the circumstances under which they operate help or hinder them? Although these are difficult questions, there are perhaps some generalizations which will bear scrutiny.

I think it is fair to say that not all teachers are equipped to help in this way and not all those who do, should. John Partridge, in his book, *Life in a Secondary Modern School*[8] recounts how one of his colleagues took his 'whacker' with him on the school continental holiday and caned boys in the hotel bedrooms. My own experience of secondary modern schools, which includes five years teaching in one, would lead me to suppose that there was nothing out of the way in this incident. Certainly, it seems quite unrealistic to suppose that all the teachers who engage in extra-mural activities have qualities which fit them for this role. An active interest in extra-mural activities is one of the ways to promotion in teaching and so for some teachers the interest of the youngsters will come a poor second to their wish to display that they can organize activities efficiently. So often discussion of school activities starts with the assumption that all such activities are valuable, that for the young people any experience in this sphere is better than none. It seems to me to be no disservice to teachers to suggest that with leisure activities, as with the teaching of classroom subjects, 'bad' teaching can have harmful results. It may be difficult to define the border lines of 'bad' teaching in this respect, but I think it is safe enough to put the methods of the 'whacker' user in this category.

While it is vital to stress that quality in informal education is as important as in any other educational activity, it is important too to draw attention to the particular difficulties which face teachers who try to work with children in school, but outside official school hours. For example, what are the limits of their responsibility? Are they still in' loco parentis' and how is this defined? Do they have to provide the same sort of supervision that is legally expected of them in their teacher role and if so, how do they interpret this to groups with which they are trying to work more informally? How do they relate to normal school discipline? Can pupils be allowed to behave on school premises in ways that would be unthinkable in school hours? Specifically, can they run down the corridor after stamp club, or put their arms around their girl friends in the drama group? And what happens when the caretaker sneaks to the head about cigarette ends in the urinal? Only in part are these questions ones which the individual can resolve for himself. There may be a role conflict for the individual and every teacher has to decide for himself in what ways he reconciles his classroom and his non-classroom behaviour. But quite apart from this, every teacher who undertakes after-school activities steps out onto the ground where his contractual and legal responsibilities are often ill-charted, and where a major incident, a girl 'interfered with' on the way home, or an 'unsupervised' accident on the premises or even a misunderstanding about exactly where Jenny was at half past five, could, under certain circumstances, have disastrous consequences for his career.

The sorts of pressures to which teachers are subject in this kind of work also need to be considered. Activities like drama and football especially, may be tied up with the whole question of school prestige. They can become matters too important to be left very much to the 'kids' and the teacher who undertakes such activities may be very aware that what is at stake for him is that his professional competence will largely be judged by the success of the school team or of the school play. It would be cynical to suppose that such pressures are always surrendered to, but unrealistic to suppose that they do not exist and that they do not influence. With prestige activities, one might also question how voluntary they really are for the pupils involved in them. We can perhaps assume that the majority of youngsters involved are there because they want to be, but when it is a question of playing or acting or, most recent in the prestige stakes, doing social service 'for the school' then there are a variety of pressures which can be brought to bear. I once saw a secondary headmaster blackmail a group of pupils into taking part in the school play by threatening to put an end to their out of school jobs if they did not comply. I am not suggesting that they necessarily suffered much from this experience, but it is fair to point out that in some schools the Kurt Hahn principle of 'impelling people into experience' is carried to extremes.

All this is, quite deliberately, the dark side of the coin and perhaps an aspect of the situation to which too little attention is drawn. As there is talk of the potential of schools to contribute to leisure education and as it seems likely that in future they may be expected, or even instructed, to contribute more, it seems to me to be helpful rather than otherwise to draw attention to the problems which relate to their contribution. Even in the more fortunate situations where the general problem of limited resources does not apply, the pressures to which I have referred are very real and very disturbing to many teachers. They may result either in inhibiting action which is anyway adventurous or compel towards action which is inappropriate. Inevitably staff in schools will be subject to pressures of one sort or another and the nature of the institution demands that it functions within certain prescribed limits. However, it seems to me essential that work towards the development of leisure education in schools includes a determined effort to resolve some of the problems I have cited. Exhortations simply to do 'more' are not enough.

There are three further points I should like to make about schools and leisure education.

First, I would like to consider the sort of contribution which schools are encouraged to make to leisure education. This encouragement as I see it is of two kinds; that which comes from public papers and government documents and that which comes from the recognition of results. By implication, I have already dealt with the latter and suggested that public recognition of results can be too narrowly conceived and too uncritical and can be instrumental in creating what I regard as unhelpful pressures. This may seem a glib dismissal, but as a generalization I maintain that public recognition of the

9

success of school events, the sports day or the school play for example, necessarily leaves a lot of important educational factors out of the reckoning. Government documents on the other hand encourage by providing an informative description of the situation, indicating broad, generalized aims, and by providing an illustrated commentary on how the situation might be improved. While there are often specific recommendations for action much of the matter of such documents is in very broad and general terms which can be related to a variety of local circumstances.

It is very clear that the report of the Newsom Committee encourages the schools to do something about leisure education. There is encouragement for the growth of extra-curricular activities as a part of school life and for the use of leisure activities in the curriculum. It is suggested that the range of opportunities offered should be as wide as possible and that young people at school should be encouraged to try a wide variety of activities. The objectives to be gained by all this are twofold. First, as the quotation I have used from the report indicates, there is concern about the future extent of leisure and the use pupils will make of it. Second there is the objective of achieving personal and social development through leisure activities. The point I would make here is that the emphasis throughout the report is on this second objective. Although there is an expression of concern about the future and although at one or two points in the report there is reference to how this or that activity might be carried over into the future leisure lives of the pupils, leisure activities in the main are treated as a means to liberal education. The emphasis is on education *through* leisure rather than education *for* leisure. The unwritten assumption seems to be that these two aspects are necessarily one and the same. This I would question.

My second point is a general one which applies to all the education services. It is this: so far as leisure activities are concerned, the educational emphasis is on the teaching of activity skills. Of course, there are all sorts of elaborations of this, but when a teacher is engaged to teach football or dressmaking or golf it is taken for granted that his central activity in relation to his pupils is concerned with the fostering of their skills in the performance of these activities. If he is a good teacher he will be concerned with all sorts of other things too, like the personal and social development of his pupils and their ever widening view of the activity upon which they are engaged. He may teach directly or indirectly or employ any number of sophisticated approaches, but in the last analysis it is the basic skills of his activity which are taken as being the medium through which he works. To put this another way, one might say that it is the acquisition of activity skills which occupies the key position in the leisure education curriculum.

My third and most important point follows from the two which have preceded it. If part of leisure education is supposed to be an education *for* leisure then this process must involve more than the teaching of activity skills. In practical social situations, it is not simply a taste for an activity or even some ability in it which enables one to pursue it. There is a whole range of other factors involved too. To follow an activity it may be necessary to join and participate in an existing organization of some kind or to join together, formally or informally, with other people. These things also involve skill and yet the teaching of such skill is omitted, to my mind with disastrous consequences, from the leisure education curriculum.

In a haphazard way, many people learn the skills of social organization because personal drives or social circumstances demand that they should, but it is a chancy and uneven process. By analogy it would be possible to teach golf by turning the beginners loose on a golf course with a set of clubs and the occasional opportunity to see other good, bad and indifferent players perform. Perhaps from such a situation the occasional champion might emerge, but many more would only learn to play very badly and many would acquire habits that would inhibit further progress. Still more, I imagine, would pack up and go home before they even found out what the game was about.

This is very much the situation so far as social organizational skills are concerned. Some, by chance, learn a great deal, some learn enough to manage, but the majority pack up and go home. Common observation of a range of adult clubs and organizations will reveal an enormous variety in their degrees of success; and success not in the sense of whether they play good cricket or produce good plays, but in the sense of the participation, commitment and enjoyment of the members, in the extent to which the aims of the organization are clarified and realized, in the social satisfactions membership affords, in recruitment, in the efficiency with which business is conducted. Popularly, success or failure in these areas are talked about as though they were the result of the personal attributes or deficiencies of the people involved; as essentially personality matters which brook no change. I would suggest that the variety which can be observed in these respects is, to a large degree, a reflection of the level of the social organizational skills of the people involved and that these skills are as liable to be improved by skilled teaching and controlled practice as is the golf swing or the racing dive.

It is fair to question realistically how far schools can progress along this particular road and some of the difficulties to which I have already referred can be seen as severe obstacles, but perhaps the biggest difficulty is the general indifference to the need to teach

11

social organizational skills at all. Either there is the assumption that it is already happening and that the existing educational environment already adequately fosters the development of these skills, or that it is not the sort of province which is properly the concern of the teacher anyway and that it is something that ought properly to be left to chance. My contention is that social organizational skills are the province of the teacher and that any real degree of freedom to choose depends upon their adequate development.

There is no reason why this development should not start in the secondary school as part of leisure education. To take the simplest possible example there is no reason why the school football teams, school, house or form, should not function as football clubs. By this, I certainly don't mean that they should ape the practices of business football, but that they should devise practices which suit their own circumstances. In this way it would be possible to begin to introduce the participants to the mass of negotiations which even school football demands. It cannot be supposed that this would be easy or that at the moment anything approaching this very often happens. In the first place, the balance between involving young people in a situation where they might learn the skills of organization and overburdening them with responsibilities they cannot support is a very delicate one. In the second place it demands staff who know what they are about and who are prepared to cope patiently with a good deal of chaos; it is not a process which will bring the Borough Football cup any nearer. In the third place it has to be conceived of in educational terms. It is always relatively easy to provide organizational experience for those who are already 'socialized' to the point where their organizational efforts are likely to take broadly predictable and acceptable forms; and of course it is this which 'happens already'. To widen these opportunities to include those whose actions may be neither predictable nor immediately acceptable and to do this in an educational environment which realistically allows failure, but prevents disaster, is an educational task of some complexity.

The social organizational skills which a teacher in such a situation is trying to communicate I see as being of two kinds. First, there are the skills which are related to the activity itself. There are a number of things which one needs to know and which one needs to be able to do in order to participate fully in the life of a football club and even more things are involved if one has to start a club. Here I am thinking of entirely mundane and practical matters like where referees come from, how one organizes transport, what things cost and how one arranges the best discount, how one communicates unambiguously with other teams. These things are the foundation of member participation even for the good player who is snatched up into a team where such matters are already taken care of. But for the group of sixteen year olds who want to play largely social football on Sunday afternoons, the possession of such information and skill is a vital ingredient in the pursuit of their chosen activity. Any school education *for* leisure must contain some reference to the *means* by which activities are continued beyond school.

Second, there are those skills which relate to groups of people whatever activity they are pursuing. Such skills have to be taught through a particular activity, but their application is general; what is taught in connection with football has at least some relevance to active participation in the union or the political party association. What the teacher has to communicate here is some sense of the possibility of social organization, that it doesn't all depend on 'sir'. He has to provide for the possibility of success and foster a sense of the enormous strength that reposes in united group action. At the same time, in order to teach skill, he has to illustrate gently the pitfalls and difficulties. Often these difficulties will relate to communication, aims and the allocation of responsibility; matters which are both complex in nature and often emotionally charged and there is no denying that to carry such theory into practice, with, say, 4C on a bad Monday afternoon, is something which requires a high degree of skill.

How widely such skill already reposes in the teaching profession as a whole is an open question. For the future it should be possible to look to the Colleges of Education to increase it both in measure and extent. An acceleration of current moves towards the inclusion of group studies in the general work of education departments is very much to be desired. More specifically the work of youth option courses in colleges and the increasing number of teacher/youth worker appointments are encouraging signs but the posts themselves are often very unsatisfactory and place the incumbents under considerable stress. Optimism on this front should be cautious. In addition some recent work[9] by Litwak, Meyer and Warren on the different values of teachers and social workers suggests that there might be a scant sympathy for the sort of approach I have indicated from secondary school teachers in general. What I suggest here is that for successful education for leisure such an approach is necessary. How immediately possible it is is another matter.

The main points which I stress about schools and leisure education are the following:

1   Membership of school clubs, societies or organizations is not part of the common, accepted experience of young people in secondary schools. It is probably an experience which is more

common among the more able, rather than the average or less able, pupils and it is probably also for the more able group that most opportunities exist. At least half those who leave school at fifteen have no *opportunities* at all of this kind and therefore actual *experience* among this group may be very limited indeed.

2 It is dangerous to assume that those who do take part in school clubs and societies necessarily participate very much either in the practical organization of the activity with which they are concerned or in the social organization of the group with which they are involved. There are factors which would seem to mitigate against this participation.

3 There is little evidence that conscious efforts are made in schools to teach pupils the skills of social organization nor, in general, that teachers regard it as any part of their job to provide such teaching.

4 Although there are certain privileged minorities, prefects, sixth formers and sports team captains for example, who are willingly or unwillingly thrust into leadership positions where they may haphazardly learn the skills of social organization, we cannot assume that the majority of young people at present leaving our schools have had experiences which are in any way helpful to them in this respect.

2 The youth service

The layman would expect that the youth service is the service to turn to in all matters affecting youth and the service has often fostered this expectation. In fact, as the report *Youth and Community Work in the 70s*[1] shows, only about 29% of the population aged between fourteen and twenty are attracted to youth service provision at any one time. None the less youth service provision in some form or other is part of the experience of most young people. For many the experience is fleeting and short lived; for some it is perhaps profoundly significant and for others unhelpful and unsatisfactory. But because it is part of the lives of young people, and because the title 'youth service' promises so much, it is important to say something here about its nature, its short-comings and its potential.

In writing about the modern youth service it is necessary to make some reference to its history. In origin the youth service was the expression of a concern on the part of adults for either the moral or physical condition of young people. It was also the service by the 'haves' for the 'have-nots'. Although since those early days the physical conditions of the service have changed as has the language and what Gibson and Davis[2] call the 'tone of voice' of those adults involved in the service it would be more difficult to affirm that attitudes have changed very radically. Within the service in recent years there has been a great deal of talk about the participation of the young in the management of their own affairs and about opportunities for their self-determination and decision making. However there is very little indication of these concepts being carried into practice and little evidence to suggest that 'participation' or 'member self-determination' is any more common in youth clubs today than it was twenty years ago. As the phrases themselves become an established part of the jargon of the service there is perhaps increasing unwillingness to examine the full implications of the concepts they embrace or for workers to examine the very real practical difficulties that the realization of such concepts entails.

The twin threats of paternalism and patronage are part of the historical heritage of the youth service. The case that the modern service has turned its back on this part of the heritage is certainly not proven and many illustrations in this book will show the continuing influence of these particular historical factors.

Another theme to be considered and developed is that of the aims of youth service. This is by no means unrelated to what has already been said because here too the influence of the history of the service is powerful. In considering youth service aims it is necessary to distinguish between the voluntary and statutory agencies. It may be that much of the practical work carried out by both kinds of agency is very similar and that the immediate aims of club leaders have much in common, but the global aims of the two kinds of agency tend to be expressed in different terms. Let us first examine some of the aims of some of the voluntary agencies.

In 1960 the National Council of Social Service published 'An account of Young People in Voluntary Youth Organizations' entitled *Young People Today*.[3] Appendix II of this booklet lists the Standing Conference of National Voluntary Youth Organizations and quotes the aims of the member organizations. A few examples will serve to illustrate the kind of terminology in common use.

Army Cadet Force Association
'To train and inspire the youth of the nation to serve their Queen and Country by developing the Cadet's character ... by teaching him the duties of a good citizen.'

Association for Jewish Youth
'To promote the mental, physical and spiritual well-being of young Jews and to foster the highest standards of citizenship and the spirit of loyalty to Queen, country and religion.'

The Boys' Brigade
'The advancement of Christ's Kingdom among boys and the promotion of habits of obedience, reverence, discipline, self-respect and all that tends towards true Christian manliness.'

Boy Scouts Association
'To provide opportunities for developing those qualities which make the good citizen ...'

Girl Guides Association
'The promotion of good citizenship by means of individual character training ...'

The Girls Friendly Society and Townsend Members Fellowship
'To give Glory to God by bringing girls and women into the full life and fellowship of the Church ...'

Girls Guildry
'To help girls be followers of the Lord Jesus Christ, to promote girls' discipline, self-respect, helpfulness and reverence.'

The Grail
'The re-Christianisation of society through the training of its members and through their influence on their surroundings.'

National Association of Boys' Clubs
'The promotion of the mental, physical and spiritual well-being of boys throughout the United Kingdom.'

The National Association of Mixed Clubs and Girls Clubs
'to develop their physical, mental and spiritual capacities that they may grow to maturity as individuals and members of society.'

The National Association of Training Corps for Girls
'To provide a training for girls so that they may become disciplined and responsible citizens ...'

In an article in *Youth Review*[4] Dr Cyril Smith summed up the aims of the voluntary organizations in the word 'integration' and he went on to say:

Youth must be encouraged, drilled or persuaded by such movements to see themselves as part of society. This is not to say that there is no room for encouraging individual growth in their philosophy but rather that the emphasis of their teaching has been on social responsibility. The universal tendency of the young to upset the status quo becomes a more serious threat to the fragile social order of modern societies so they must be taught how to behave. Furthermore their concern with enjoying themselves here and now has to be confronted by the responsibilities they will bear to-morrow. Whichever way they interpret them and most lay more stress on the problems of order than on those of social continuity these are the common concerns of the voluntary youth movements.

To this valuable statement of what voluntary youth organizations are about Dr Smith adds a more detailed categorization. His article continues.

Most voluntary youth movements can be seen as one of three kinds; reinforcing, reforming or recruiting. The Boy Scouts Movement provides the purest example of the first kind for the boys they deal with are already being successfully integrated into society by the home and the school and this movement reinforces their teaching and in particular the importance of individual achievement. The National Association of Boys Clubs by contrast is a reforming agency which takes boys from the poorest social backgrounds and offers them very different ideals. It is not concerned with recruiting boys into an adult organisation but only with preparing them for adulthood as 'fit' men. The recruiting movements also set out to give moral teaching but the importance it is given may vary widely from one extreme of the traditional church youth movements to the other extreme of the military cadet movements.

Dr Smith goes on to suggest a possible historical development here with the earliest established youth movements being concerned with reform, the second wave with recruitment and those formed most recently with reinforcement. He concludes:
'Some movements have changed from one type to another in the course of their history and all movements are tending to become "reinforcing" as what they teach and what is being taught in the home and the school come to resemble each other'.

I have quoted Dr Smith's article at some length because it provides an excellent and compact exposition of what the voluntary youth organizations are about, of the function they perform and in broad terms of the ways in which their particular aims are interpreted.

However, while it is useful to categorize voluntary organizations in this way, it is useful too, to recognize that their individual aims probably still have some influence in making them the sort of organizations they are and affect in a quite specific way the kind of membership they attract. In many cases the global aims of the organization are probably unknown to the average member but they will certainly be known by the adult workers of the organization whose attitudes will in turn affect the self-selection of the membership. After all, to take an extreme example, the 're-Christianization of society' is hardly a matter which one can keep under one's hat, nor presumably, which one wants to. The specific religious objectives of many voluntary organizations are certainly a factor which has to be taken into account.

Dr Milson has often pointed out that the youth service was not something invented by Lady Albemarle on a wet Sunday afternoon but there is no doubt that much of the inspiration of the service, and particularly on the statutory side comes from the Albemarle Report[5] which has been often referred to as the youth service Bible. There can be few workers in the service who have not read, had read to them or been invited to read, Sir John Maude's statement that it is the aim of youth service 'to offer individual young people in their leisure time, opportunities of various kinds, complementary to those of home, formal education and work, to discover and develop their personal resources of body, mind and spirit and thus better to equip themselves to live the life of mature, creative and responsible members of a free society.'[6]

The Report goes on to categorize three functions of youth service as being concerned with association, training and challenge. It is useful here to examine what is meant by these terms and to say something about some of the particular difficulties which attend the performance of these functions. First a definition of the terms:

Association

Providing for association means building meeting places or making buildings available in which people can meet. The word 'association' raises the point made in the Report that not all association is 'valuable' but it is probably the least ambiguous of the three terms.

Training

The training function of youth service is the educational function. The Report suggests that there should be opportunity for training related to hobbies and skills and the argument here is that the possession of skill increases feelings of individual worth. The Report also suggests that there should be 'preparation for adult life' by which the Report means informal education in such matters as public affairs, employment and marriage.

Challenge

As used in the Report the term challenge means that young people should be given the opportunity to have experiences which are stimulating and demanding. The Report illustrates this by suggesting three sorts of experience:

(i)   Experience which is physically demanding
(ii) Travel
(iii) Community service

This paraphrase is of course a gross over-simplification but it provides adequate definition for present purposes and having roughly defined the terms we can now look at some of the difficulties present in their translation into practice.

Association

Nationally, provision for association is the level at which youth service is most successful. There are thousands of clubs attended by tens of thousands of young people. Yet for the youth leader 'association' presents difficulties. Few youth leaders would see themselves solely as club managers and many are strongly attracted to other aspects of the work,[7] usually either to informal education (i.e. 'Training') or to a pastoral (counselling or advice giving) role. This is likely to be reinforced during training and for some is very strongly reinforced by seeing the real needs of young people through the working situation. About this I would make the following points:

(i) Provision for association is the least glamorous aspect of youth work. Club management suggests low status while alternative roles, hinting as they do, at possession of specialist skills in human relationships, suggest high status.

(ii) Achievement is measurable chiefly in terms of attendance and although in practical terms this is a valuable measure (at times of economic difficulties a high attendance club will survive while low attendance clubs close) high attendance on its own is not very highly regarded in professional worker circles.

(iii) It is difficult to report the achievements of association while it is easy to report the achievements of training (i.e. the success of the football team.)

(iv) The pressures from lay committees of all types are towards achievements of a recognizable kind. Lay committees are likely to reward by praise achievements in sport, education, art and particularly at the moment social service by club members. As a general rule they take for granted the leader's role in making provision for association (the business of managing the premises) and withhold praise from it. The notable exception to this general rule is where association provision is presented as being provision for particularly 'difficult' young people.

All this may lead to:

(i) The under-valuation of one important aspect of youth service.

(ii) Some confusion over aims among leaders arising from this under-valuation.

Training

At first sight the question of skills training raises no serious problems so far as aims are concerned. If people gain satisfaction from the acquisition of skills then it is a reasonable proposition that provision for the opportunity to acquire any socially acceptable skill is to the general good. However, the concept of skills acquisition leading to a heightened sense of individual worth and the social implications of this does give rise to educational, social and philosophical arguments of some complexity.

Preparation for life is rather more obviously a difficult matter. In theory educational preparation for life is concerned with the ability to make choices and to exercise judgment. In practice there tends to be fairly strong pressure on the part of the educator towards what, from his particular standpoint, or that of his agency, are the areas of right choices. This is nearly always the case on moral issues. Most people want their children 'taught what is right' and any system of public education is at the focal point of public morality. In schools it is expected that teachers should be concerned about the moral standards and behaviour of their pupils.

The lines along which moral pressure should be exerted are very largely predetermined and any striking deviation is not generally tolerated. All the value debates that are present in schools are present also in youth service and are present in a particularly stark form because what in school is a peripheral matter (good behaviour generally being secondary to 'getting a good education') is in youth clubs a central matter; the transference of values is likely to be one of the main centres of attention and debate.

In practice then, this part of the argument over aims often boils down to the argument over the imposition of or attempted transfer of standards of behaviour in such matters such as smoking, gambling, drinking, styles of dress, sexual morality, language and a host of other items. It is not surprising that there should be argument over such matters, nor is it surprising in view of the rate of change of our moral codes, that this should be an area of some confusion and conflict. However, because the training aim of youth service tends to be interpreted as transfer of values, confusion over values is likely also to be confusion over aims. This is heightened in an L.E.A. situation because although any L.E.A. officer might be hard put to it to list the values an education service is trying to transfer, the image projected by schools is of a high standard of morality and well-ordered behaviour and it is difficult for youth service staff not to be influenced by this.

The training dilemma also appears at a deeper level. Para. 136 of the Albemarle Report contains the following: 'He (the adolescent today) needs to develop his capacity for making sound judgements; he needs, to take only one instance, opportunities for realising that some things—slower and more hardly won—are more rewarding than the excitement offered by each day's passing show. This is to us the basis of the case for specific education and training within the Youth Service.'

The implication of deferred gratification in the above statement is

21

an essentially middle-class value. The transference of middle-class values is implicit in the whole of our educational structure but any attempt to translate the above into practice is likely to point the conflict in class values in a striking way. Certainly any leader of a club in a predominantly working class area is likely to be disappointed if he looks for major value changes of this sort. There is ample room here for a variety of confusions between the club leader and his members and between the club leader and his employing body or his lay management committee. The danger for the leader interpreting this section of the Albemarle Report is that unless he is equipped with at least a basic knowledge of the different value systems he is likely to encounter among his members, he is likely to set himself a series of totally unrealistic tasks.

Also the existence of an education aim in youth service raises the problem of how to assess the progress made along the particular educational path chosen. For the youth leader one criterion externally applied to his work is likely to be the practical achievements of groups within his club and sporting, artistic, or social service achievements rank high. Community pressures dictate that young people must be 'seen to be doing' and it is a very determined man who can, without support, work energetically to facilitate for his members if his members' requirements are, even in minor matters, at odds with those of the community with which he works. But although at ground level there are demands and expectations along predictable lines success or failure at this level give little ground for the assessment of an education programme ambitiously designed 'to prepare for life'. The obvious criterion is the ultimate one, that if people are adequately prepared for life, this fact will be evident from the better lives they are seen to lead. If a better life is taken as being a more law-abiding one then one criterion of success might be the good behaviour of club members and their non-involvement in criminal activity.

Whether it is a desirable state of affairs or not there seems little doubt that youth service is often linked in the public mind with social control and anti-delinquency measures. For the youth worker this is always a factor complicating his social educational work and an additional public expectation with which he has to cope.[8]

Challenge

Challenge is a highly emotive word and any interpretation of it is beset with difficulties. In educational contexts the word generally has connotations which might be summarized as follows:

(i) It is desirable that we should adopt a positive rather than a negative attitude towards adversity. We should be stimulated (i.e. 'challenged') by it rather than dismayed.

(ii) It is desirable to present young people with experiences which are challenging because such experiences lead to the discovery of previously unknown personal resources and increased self-awareness and triumph over adversity brings self-confidence.

(iii) An extension of this thinking is that there is extensive transfer of training between different kinds of situations; that overcoming the difficulties of the mountain equips one better to overcome other kinds of difficulty too. Direct references to such transfer of training have become far less common in recent years as have also claims for 'character training' with which, in the past, these references were often associated. None the less, the influence of such thinking is still very powerful. Even if it is rarely spelt out there is in much youth work the underlying assumption that taking part in team games will foster 'team spirit' and the ability to co-operate and that long walks, camping and mountain activities will foster individual resourcefulness, bring self-knowledge and help to 'build character'.

The particular danger with all of this is the emotional aura which tends to surround any discussions about 'challenge'. It is not an unreasonable hypothesis that experiences which are 'challenging' in the sense that they make heavy demands on an individual's personal resources may be experiences which have considerable educational potential. They may bring increased self-knowledge, they may lead to an increased self-confidence—at least in those areas of experience similar to the challenge which has been met. They may, by virtue of deeply felt experience, add new dimensions to the emotional and intellectual range of the individual and in this sense 'build character'. Having said this, however, there remain some enormous questions to be asked. What experiences are 'challenging' to which people under what kind of circumstances? What happens to those who are unable to meet the challenge with which they are faced? In what ways is their new self-knowledge valuable to them? It is the weakness of slogan words like 'challenge' that they inhibit the asking and answering of such questions.

This is not to say that to bring people to demanding experiences for educational purposes is not justifiable but what might be usefully suggested is that the skilful control and sensitive management of such situations is crucial if educational objectives are to be won. Such management is unlikely to be encouraged by emotive blanket terms like 'challenge' nor by describing certain kinds of experience as in themselves challenging. It is more useful to see the kinds of experience which the Albemarle Committee described as challenging as being training experiences which have the potential of bringing rich rewards to the individual but which because they are also potentially dangerous to the individual's physical or psychic well-being demand from the youth worker high degrees of skill and sensitivity in their management. Adult enthusiasm for 'challenging' the young is normally tempered with some regard for their physical safety. To regard such experiences as being essentially complex and demanding forms of 'training' would help to focus attention on the need to safeguard mental and emotional well-being also.

In the section above I have taken the theme of youth service aims and have used it to attempt to show something of the special place occupied by the service. All global aims in either the education or the social services throw up difficulties of interpretation and implementation but youth service warrants some special consideration by virtue of the extent to which in its aims it seemingly deals exclusively with intangible issues. The main stream of further or higher education has its systems of evaluation and much social work can often be interpreted in terms of case loads and results. Crude though these measures sometimes are they provide the roots from which can grow more refined evaluations of the work or they may provide focal points for criticism which can lead to more disciplined approaches. The case of the youth service is at least in degree more difficult. It is not easy to say what processes lead toward 'a true Christian manliness' or even those which better equip one to live the life of 'mature, creative and responsible members of a free society' and in detail there are very real problems about the interpretation of the Albemarle Report's triple aims of association, training and challenge. This being so one might expect the interpretation of aims both by workers and the individual agencies to be particularly rigorous and for there to be at local level constant efforts to assess and refine the work carried out. Yet in most instances this is certainly not the case and it is in fact often very difficult to see where and how many of the practical decisions (i.e. the interpretation of aims) in youth service are made. To understand this it is necessary to look at the organization of the service.

In organization as in other aspects youth service agencies vary considerably. As an example I have selected one agency, a local education authority, to illustrate the points I wish to make. It could not be said that the agency is 'typical' because the pattern throughout the country is too diverse to allow any such claim. However, the authority concerned has a considerable reputation for 'good' youth service provision and their pattern of organization has many features in common with other youth service agencies both statutory and voluntary.

The organization of youth service agencies is usually both

hierarchical and bureaucratic. In the case of the local authority youth service this bureaucracy is itself part of the larger bureaucracy which is the Education Service and the still larger one which is Local Government.

The particular weakness of bureaucracy is that it tends to cope ineffectually with matters which do not seem to be entirely the province of any one department or which are seemingly outside the scope of the organization as a whole. The bureaucracy's response to new situations is to set up new departments but in industry it is generally held that bureaucracies are inefficient in coping with periods of rapid change because they cannot set up departments swiftly enough to meet the new situations and when they attempt to do so the whole structure becomes too unwieldy for efficient management. Also in bureaucracies there is a tendency for the ends to become submerged by the means. The patterns of administrative procedure take on an importance of their own and in extreme cases can be observed almost ritualistically without reference to the objectives

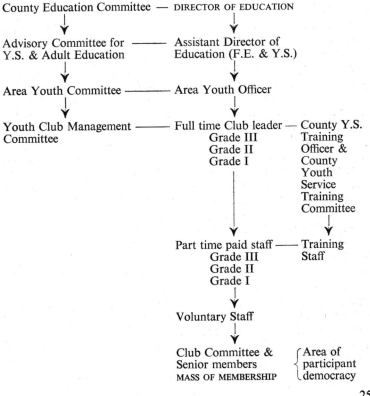

for which the administrative procedures exist. This may be particularly harmful when new projects with new objectives are subject to administrative procedures designed originally to serve other ends.

With a local authority youth service the vulnerability of the bureaucracy complicates the issues. The whole organization is subject to influence and control from lay committees operating at a variety of levels and although it may be in the best interests of the community that the organization is subject to these pressures, in terms of actual organizational efficiency they may constitute an interference which weakens the chain of command and reduces officers' willingness to fulfil their decision-making functions.

The actual organizational structure of the service I have selected as a model is best expressed diagrammatically. There are a number of points to be made about the diagram above.

The central pillar of the diagram is straightforward until we come to the Full-time Club Leader. Here the authority I am describing has instituted three gradings of staff who stand in hierarchical relationship to each other. This was a deliberate attempt on the part of the authority concerned to create a career structure for its full-time youth service staff. Grade III staff have responsibility for a main youth club and for subsidiary clubs in surrounding areas. In theory, rarely realized in practice, they should be supported by two other full-time workers. The Grade II leaders operate either as principal assistants to the Grade III leaders or are responsible for youth clubs either on their own or with the help of a Grade I assistant; the Grade I leaders are the new entrants to the profession who can normally look for promotion to a Grade II level after a period of eighteen months or two years.

The gradations of part-time staff are related directly to the amount of training they have received under the Authority's three year training scheme for part-time staff. There is also differentiation between the grades in the pay they receive. These staff do not necessarily stand in direct hierarchical relationship to each other but in some circumstances may do so.

The left-hand column shows the lay committees which are related to the service. Here the Education Committee is all-powerful but is a body likely to be strongly influenced by its principal professional officers. The Advisory Committee is a body with a large professional representation and one which can influence the broad policy of the Authority. On the other hand the Area Youth Committee is a body with such indistinct functions that unless the Area Youth Officer chooses to invest it with a particular job of work it hardly matters that it exists at all. The Youth Club Management Committee warrants more detailed attention.

Historically Management Committees existed because they were the body of adults who formed a club for the young people of the community. Their existence provided for the continuity of the provision and the Committee became the body concerned with the permanence of the provision having a controlling say in the finance and staffing of the club. Given a situation where the membership of youth clubs is composed of people with limited legal rights and the leader is a paid employee it has commonly been held desirable to have an adult body directly responsible for the affairs of individual clubs. Management Committees have collected other roles too. They are the body through which, in theory at any rate, the voluntary and statutory agencies communicate with the club and they are often responsible also for fund raising. They may be the group which provide for the youth leader the immediate adult community reaction to his plans for the club and they may be, at a much more refined level, the group which supports the leader in his work. In the Local Authority service Management Committee membership serves other extrinsic functions too. It is part of the process of local government and membership of Management Committees is one of the activities in which local and county councillors are involved.

How Management Committees behave in practice varies a very great deal. It is worth making the point however that they can be extremely powerful and influential and have profound effect upon what happens or fails to happen in particular clubs. They may operate along the traditional line of being the body responsible in the best sense of the word for the club and Mary Blandys book *Razor Edge*[9] gives one illustration of a Management Committee working in this way. On the other hand they may be very much 'the managers' of the club exerting a strong controlling influence directly over the staff and through them over the members. The results here are not always happy ones. Some leaders in north-east Derbyshire found their Management Commmittees both frequently ignorant of the issues at stake and unsympathetic towards them personally as club leaders. Many of the staff found Management Committee meetings unpleasant experiences, destructive rather than supportive and some leaders were actually physically ill prior to the meetings. Visiting meetings as an observer I was often shocked both by the ignorance which many Management Committee members displayed about matters on which it was within the encompassment of their duties to be well informed, and by the way in which they dealt with the staff.

As at a practical level much of the effectiveness of club work depends on the relationship which exists between the club leader, his staff and the club members, one cannot ignore the effect upon this relationship of the influence, for good or ill, of the club Management Committee.

The right hand column of this diagram shows the training wing of the agency. Here the influence is likely to be benevolent as training staff are not normally directly involved in the management of the staff in other departments. However the situation is much more complex than this very considerably simplified diagram of the organization reveals. Very often in youth service as in other fields status is gained by being involved in staff training and many of the training staff are also full-time staff of the agency. Staff who are 'good at training' and whose skill warrants their being given considerable responsibility in this field, may not always be those who occupy top positions in the central field work column of the agency. Given this basic premise it will readily be seen that innumerable complications and professional rivalries can ensue.

The arrows on the diagram indicate some of the main lines of influence but the diagram is a very simplified description of the organization and it would be taking a very dismal view to take it entirely at face value and conclude that all influence is downward. However it would not be unfair to say that this is the main direction of many forms of communication.

This discussion about the organization of the service started with questions about the interpretation of youth service aims and the account of the organization so far given does provide some of the answers. In the case of the Local Authority the County Education Committee, with advice from officers and from advisory sub-committees, decides such matters as the extent of the financial investment in the service and the kind of investment, buildings, equipment and staff, which is to be made. The principal officers and officers of the Authority, singly or jointly, make decisions which to a large extent affect the practice of the service. They decide about the siting of clubs and their staffing and equipment, the kinds of in-service and part-time worker training which are appropriate and the various supporting services to be made available to the youth clubs. All these decisions can be seen as interpretations of the broader aims of the service. They are decisions about the use of resources and statements about the kind of service which it is intended to create.

However all this still leaves an enormous number of 'decisions' in the sense of interpretations of aims still to be made and logically one might assume these to be the province of the youth leader whose job it is to interpret aims in the light of the needs of the locality in which he works and the resources at his disposal. In theory this is so but this theory is not easily translated into practice.

The leader is faced with an extremely wide brief and has to make decisions about which tasks he performs and which he leaves alone. Not all the possible tasks which face him are compatible. For

28

example, working with young people whose social behaviour is 'difficult' may not be compatible with the high standard of social provision for other club users, opportunities for counselling may not go hand in hard with efficient club management either because they demand different personality traits or more simply because there is not time for both. Emphasis on member government may mean that the club is less efficient in providing classes or sporting groups. The exact nature of the choices to be made depends on local circumstances but effective working demands that choices are made and that a consistent plan of campaign is followed towards the achievement of objectives in the areas of work selected.

In practice though, these conditions for effective working are very difficult to fulfil and there are two kinds of pressures to which many youth leaders are subjected; those which inhibit altogether the makings of some kinds of decision and those which are strongly influential on the kinds of decision which are made.

Foremost in the first category is the illusion common throughout the service that policy making is something which takes place elsewhere. Thus leaders look to their employers for a clear lead about what they ought to be doing while the officers look to the leaders for reliable information about what is happening in the field. Both are likely to look in vain; the former because although the policy of the authority constitutes some refinement of the global aims of national government this refinement still leaves, usually with deliberate intent, broad areas for more individual interpretations; the latter because the upward lines of communication are all too often those which will work least effectively and because often the leader sees little point in this sort of communication. Also there are considerable pressures on the leader from employers, from the community and through the training agencies to branch out into new fields of endeavour. Besides running a club with a wide range of social and educational activities, and running it in an orderly manner, he is encouraged to be actively engaged in social work and welfare activities, to be doing something about young immigrants, sex education, handicapped young people, the rowdies on the market place, counselling, the organization of the social service programmes, drug addiction, member participation and many other things as well. Thus it is not simply that the tasks of youth service are diffuse; if youth leaders concentrated on leisure provision they would still be that; but that the tasks upon which it is expected some effort is expended are so often irreconcilable and incompatible. Faced with this situation many youth leaders tend to devote their energies to the present and immediate and to work very largely on a day to day basis.

Youth leaders are often criticized for their lack of ability to conceptualize about their work but the truth of the matter may be that often there is nothing about which to conceptualize. The potential for specialized and detailed work always exists but cannot be realized if all the alternative and frequently conflicting options are also kept open. Put simply, the problem for the leaders is that they are under constant pressure to keep all the options open, to be all things to all men at all times, and they are given little encouragement to devise policies which would reduce their generalized availability even though the formulation of such policies would be the logical outcome of many of the particular demands made upon them. Although this is the source of considerable frustration, 'we never have time to do anything well', it is also the source of a perverse kind of pride.

A verse by A. H. Pearson in *Youth Service* (October 1967) contains the following:

'Juke-box mechanic, booker of groups, vetter of letters to
                      Marjorie Proops;
Programme planner, compiler of charts, fixer of feathers on
                      flights for darts;
Dresser of wounds, reliever of pain, sayer of sooths when all's
                      in vain;
Starter of races, stopper of fights, righter of wrongs and righter
                      of rights;
Buffer twixt the members and the police, riot act reader, and
                      keeper of peace;
Erector of tents and launcher of boats, driver of all the carnival
                      floats;
Counsellor, courier, maker of plans, dropper of bricks and
                      carrier of cans';[10]

The verse goes on to detail the rest of the leader's chores. It is part of the ethos of the service that it is, in intent at least, a comprehensive service providing all things and available to all young people.

This has profound implications for the future of the service because the obviously demonstrated need for a service which is as comprehensive in scope as the youth service tries to be, declines as other agencies (schools for example) take over aspects of the work. This makes the service extremely vulnerable, not necessarily because it is not needed, though there may be areas where this is the case, but because having developed on so broad a front it is, as a service, ill equipped to *justify* its existence.

Youth leaders are themselves aware of the situation and of the uncertain future of the service. The study by Watts and Whitworth[11] shows leaders saying that the 'present set-up won't last' and that the future is 'in the lap of the gods' and every member of the sample made some reference to impending changes. Doubts about the future of the service can sap the morale of those who work in it and may well help to stifle their exercise of initiative.

A good deal of this goes back to the structure of the service. Youth leaders are usually isolated workers subject to a variety of pressures and in many cases it seems that the structure within which they operate is an inappropriate one for the job which has to be done. The functions of some sections of the youth service organization (some management committees for example) no longer seem very relevant to the needs of the young people for whom the service exists. With some youth services it is possible that if serious consideration were given to the reorganization of the service the effectiveness of individual workers might be greatly increased. Clearly it is not possible to be dogmatic about this. In the youth service personality factors are strongly influential and the service is one in which to a remarkable extent workers select themselves for the work on their own assessment of their own suitability. However, given this existing situation it seems necessary to construct a system of organization which lays stress on the need for individual workers to examine local needs and maximizes their ability to make for themselves the decisions necessary to meet these needs.

It is useful too to make some real distinctions between the different functions the service performs and particularly between specialist functions like counselling and the more general function of creating and maintaining a leisure provision for young people. Not to make such distinctions is to devalue both kinds of function and at present the role of the service in making leisure provision is often seen mainly as a means to other ends; to 'education', to social control or to reformation and behaviour change. Of course providing for leisure may well be a means to providing opportunities to achieve these further ends but it is also an inestimably important and difficult job in its own right and one which demands, though it rarely receives, a similar quality of thought and a similar degree of serious attention as that more readily given to the closely defined specialist functions.

Having looked at the aims and organization of the service I shall now turn our attention to its *raison d'être*; the young people who make use of it. Here the picture is enormously varied and all kinds of young people join clubs and societies or make use of the services provided. However although it may be 'all kinds of people' it is clear that it is not all young people. At the time of the Albemarle Report it was estimated that 'provision of some sort has been made for the needs of one in three of young people between 15 and 21' (Paargraph 33). Later estimates suggest that the proportion of young people catered for by youth service agencies is 29% of the 14-20 year olds[12] though it would be difficult to say whether this reflects the disaffiliation of the young from the service or simply points to inaccuracy in the Albemarle estimate.

More important than the inaccuracy of the figures about the national youth service is the interpretation of these figures. Although we may say that roughly 29% of the young people in this country have some connection with youth service provision at any given time this certainly does not mean that 29% of the population remain members very long. There are probably comparatively few young people who have never had any contact with a youth service agency though in some cases this contact may have been extremely brief. Some youth clubs in north-east Derbyshire have an annual membership turnover of about two-thirds of their membership while in other clubs the membership is much more stable with a steady annual recruitment and loss. While it is probably true that a very brief membership is brief because it is unsatisfactory to the member concerned it may also be that a protracted membership is not always helpful to the individual. The transition from childhood to adulthood is not helped by a service which besides helping people during the transitional phase also conducts its affairs in such a way that it helps to extend this transitional period. It is an open question whether this is a fair charge to level at some sections of youth service but the real point is that a satisfactory criterion for the length of membership can only be established by reference to individual needs. There may be as many important critical questions to ask about those clubs which succeed in 'holding' their membership as there are about clubs where membership is usually of short duration.

For the great majority of young people youth service is what happens at the club down the road and for the young people of a particular neighbourhood the service is as good or as bad as is the solitary outpost of it they know so well. Ideas about 'good' county or regional service are essentially the concepts of the providers rather than the consumers.

The point about the diffuseness of youth service has been made already in relation to staffing and organization, but perhaps the most important aspect of this is the variety of kinds and intensity of experience which the youth service affords young people. So broadly based a service offers innumerable possibilities and this means that it is difficult to speak with confidence about the actual performance of the service; about what sections of the population attend youth clubs; about the length of their attendance or about the nature of the experience that this attendance affords. A statistical survey may provide some of these answers but deviations from the norm could hardly be interpreted as being 'the exceptions which proved the rule'. Rather they would be demonstrations of other, equally permissible, options being exercised.

32

In 1967 I conducted a questionnaire survey of some member attitudes in nine youth clubs in north-east Derbyshire. From what has been said already it will be clear that information from this survey should be interpreted with caution. For the purpose of this chapter the survey provides information for some simple general statements about some youth clubs.

Nine clubs were selected to take part in the project. At least one club from each Youth Club Committee area was included and the selection was random. Clubs with full-time, part-time and voluntary leadership were all included and three clubs in each category were included. Two boys and two girls from each age year of the youth service age range were randomly selected to complete the questionnaire. This would have given a complete sample of 252. One hundred and sixty-six useable returns were received and the discrepancy is accounted for mainly by the fact that not all the clubs had members in all years of the youth service age range and so a complete set of returns could not have been achieved. A second factor was that of attendance. Not all those selected to be respondents in fact attended their clubs during the period when the survey was being conducted. There were no refusals and only one or two partially spoilt returns.

Among the sample the peak age for youth club membership was 16-17 for boys and 15-16 for girls.

Most of the respondents attended or had attended secondary modern schools but grammar school pupils were well represented and the survey supported the popular supposition that academically more successful pupils (as indicated by grammar school selection) are more attracted to voluntary than to statutory organizations. Just under half the respondents said that they neither liked nor disliked school and on a five point scale there were rather more who weighed in on the positive than on the negative side of this statement.

Although a third of the boys and half the girls were still at school the majority of the sample were at work; most of the boys in skilled or semi-skilled manual occupations and most of the girls in clerical work or in the service trades. As with the Minton survey which is dealt with later the incidence of Saturday work showed up strikingly and of those at work two-thirds were regularly engaged in working either half a day or a full day on Saturday.

A number of statement questions were constructed to attempt to gauge something of the motives of club members in joining clubs and the nature of their club experience. While much of the information which emerged from this was detailed and inconclusive there was very strong support for the idea that for members the functions of clubs is expressive.[13] Overwhelmingly they joined because friends were already members or because they wanted to make new friends. They went to the clubs to meet their friends and what they 'liked most' about the club was that it afforded this opportunity. There was some criticism of club activities and of the club programme but the general picture was of a satisfied membership. A sizeable minority, about ten per cent, would have liked more say in the running of the club but this proportion represented considerably fewer people than those who had no criticisms about their club at all.

All this is very inconclusive but it does provide some general statements about the youth club, all of which can be questioned, refuted or amplified. To these statements I would add here some observations and impressions of my own which are based on many club visits and many hours of discussion with young people both in and out of youth clubs. They are offered as the observations of one person who was fortunate in being able to spend a considerable time looking impartially at a variety of youth clubs and organizations and talking with staff, members and non-members.

One of my strongest and most persistent impressions is of the discrepancy which often exists between the staff and member view of particular youth clubs and particular youth club events. Of course there are many staff who develop very sophisticated techniques for keeping their fingers on the pulse of the club and the reactions of their members, but many others seemed particularly prone to simple and extremely optimistic interpretations of what was going on and of the satisfactions they provided for their club members. Quite often I saw what I interpreted as a polite acquiescence on the part of members construed as enthusiasm by a leader who then went off to make plans for activities and events which had nothing to do with the real needs or requirements of the members. When the events themselves were poorly attended there were sometimes recriminations against the young people for their failure to 'support the club' and head-shakings over the contemporary lack of 'loyalty' and the difficulties of working with modern youth. Many youth workers will say that this is just poor leadership and of course in this they are right, but I came across examples frequently enough for this to provoke more fundamental questions about the state of the service.

It seemed to me that the service has fostered myths about its own performance which it strives perpetually to maintain. Members' committees in clubs are a good example here. Frequently I was told how the members 'ran the club' only to have this statement confounded both by my own observation of what occurred and by the words of the members who themselves took a very different view of the situation. Of course it is possible for members to run their own club and it is arguable that on social and educational grounds running the club is something members should have a hand in.[14] But under normal circumstances this is going to be something which is tremendously difficult for the leader to achieve. To create an environment in which it is possible for members to run the club will almost certainly demand more of the leader than would directing the operations of the club himself. Yet it is quite frequently claimed that it happens and this without particular pride and without reference to the difficulties which have had to be overcome. It is almost as though there has been a magical transformation from what is held to be desirable to what is. The implications of this are far-reaching and one of the most obvious of these is that staff can hardly devote their enthusiastic attention to achieving a state of affairs which is at the outset regarded as the norm.

However, members do not usually have these sorts of ideas and aspirations about their youth clubs. Most of the conversations I have ever had with young people about youth clubs have been characterized by a description of the expressive function of the club. Clubs are where you go to be with friends and have fun, or at least where you go when you have no money to go anywhere else and where you hope, not necessarily with much conviction, that you might have fun. Often I have listened to descriptions of clubs as being 'dead' and 'boring' from the very young people who have attended the club faithfully night after night for month after month. Youth clubs cannot under normal circumstances continually provide the exciting 'swinging' environment that many young people want to exist. Often the hold of membership is tenuous and the 'loyalty' of members more imagined and sought-after than real. Often too the member view of youth clubs is intensely realistic; the adult ballyhoo just does not work. In his play *Zigger-Zagger* Peter Terson displays this acutely in a scene where Zigger and Harry take two girl youth club members away from the youth club (from which Zigger and Harry have just been ejected) to join them in their world of the big match and the football terraces.

Harry: 'You won't come?'
Sandra: 'Why not?'
Harry: 'You in there with that drama, and that coffee bar that you've made yourself and them Belgian holidays.'
Sandra: 'That drama is one act plays for the worst festival ever, the coffee bar is just a piece of hardboard covered in ivy wall-paper, and it rained on the Belgian holidays last year.'[15]

For particular groups of members the youth club world assumes a special significance and the membership of club member committees, area youth committees and youth councils is composed of people for whom this world is important. Often membership of such groups gives both the social satisfaction of belonging to an 'in group' and the satisfaction of belonging to a task group with particular powers and status. The members of such groups, though, are often quick to point out their own dissimilarity from the mass of club membership and they are prone to align themselves with the adult view of the difficulty of engaging the interest and support of the mass of the membership.

Although I have suggested that I have found many young people unenthusiastic about youth club membership this does not seem to me to weaken the fundamental case for the youth club. Clubs can only be as good as their financial resources and leadership allow and the service as a whole is under-financed and inadequately staffed. Given existing resources it is hardly surprising that many clubs fail to meet the high aspirations of either young people or adults. But clubs do provide 'somewhere to go' for the majority of those who use them and so provide always the potential of significant experiences for a minority. Where leader and member views of the club seem most often to diverge is that what Peter Terson's Sandra describes as 'the worst festival ever' and 'ivy wall-papered hardboard' are items which have more significance for leaders than they have for the members who have been actively concerned with them. On the other hand the fact of the club's existence, its availability as a meeting-place, is often a matter of considerable importance to even the most disenchanted and outspokenly critical of the members while the staff see this as of secondary importance to activities, achievements, or the lasting relationships between adult staff and members.

If some members are in a general sense unenthusiastic about their club they often reveal considerable enthusiasm for particular events or particular aspects of club life.

Here again there are some differences between the attitudes of many leaders and of their members. Often to the adult the club is important and the functioning of the separate parts takes second place to the welfare of the whole. While less common than it was, it is still possible to find situations where attendance at certain 'social' events in the club programme is conditional upon proof of prior attendance at 'classes' or activity coaching groups. This practice of providing sugar coating for the 'educational' pill is no longer common in its original crude form but persists in the idea that members should 'support their club'; that they should earn their right to pursue their sectional interest by giving support to the parent whole by attending functions or events in which they have no personal interest. Needless to say such ideas run contrary to those held by many young people who want to do things (including 'doing nothing') with their friends at the times they want to do them and with as few strings attached as possible. Of course youth workers will always want to try to extend the experience of their members but the means they choose to employ are extremely important. In a later chapter I shall say why I believe emphasis on sectional interests to be of more educational value than emphasis on club.

Often the particular aspects of club life which fire the imagination and enthusiasm of members have nothing to do with the regular club programme. It is a particular outing or event or even a single conversation which seemingly remains in the memory as the most stimulating, exciting and significant event in the whole of an individual's club membership. This is not to say the 'programme' is unimportant but simply that members are conscious of particular and limited events of great importance to them. The question which must exercise those interested in informal education is whether such experiences are necessarily individual and accidental or whether it is possible to create an environment which increases the probability of their occuring. Certainly this latter possibility cannot be ignored.

The aspects of club life which I have found to evoke some of the strongest criticism from past and present club members are those which affront the young people's concepts of honest behaviour. Misrepresentation of events, the over-selling of the services offered, pseudo importance imparted to the trivial, committees which have no real function to perform, are all things which can arouse real anger in members. Yet because of the strong social satisfactions which membership of clubs affords it is only in extreme circumstances that members will exercise the only real voting right they often have; that of 'voting with their feet'. As an external observer in many clubs what struck me chiefly about this was certainly not deliberate dishonesty or even crude manipulation on the part of staff but a degree of self deception and lack of sensitivity to the power and influence that goes with being an adult in gatherings of people much younger. If some adults feel that clubs do not matter enough to their young members, then, as an observer, I sometimes felt that they mattered too much to many of the adults involved.

To garble Byron it sometimes seemed as if:

'The club to the member is a thing apart
'Tis the leader's whole existence.'[16]

These very personal comments arising from observation of clubs and discussions with members illustrate reservations about the practice of the service. Clearly anyone looking at any service will find something to criticize in its practice but the point I would make here is that in a general sense I have found what happens in clubs a long way removed from the client centred practice advocated by the spokesmen of the service. It is important to stress that the service has still a potential for development which is only partially explored. What the service might achieve, given not only more resources but also keener staff selection and better training, we can only guess, but it could well come closer to achieving its own highest aspirations and make a significant contribution to the social development of those young people for whom the efforts of other agencies have largely failed.

3   Education in leisure time

In this chapter I want to examine some particular aspects of the part played by youth service and adult education in making leisure provision for the present and providing education for future leisure.

The youth service

By way of summarizing some of the points from the last chapter one might say that it is very difficult to comment in general terms about what youth service is supposed to do. A glance through the literature of the service reveals a scope of activity which is almost limitless and the extension of possible inclusions has by no means ceased. In origin the service was much concerned with 'ensuring that the young grew into "full Christian manliness" together with training them to be "good citizens" and for "responsible roles in society" ', and these broad aims persist today, though possibly the first might be differently expressed. Some see the service as being broadly educational, others as 'social' provision, and still others as being primarily concerned with individual reformation and social change. Some want youth workers to be educators, some want them to be social workers and some want them to fulfil both roles. Popularly youth service has something to do with delinquency and it is seen as being concerned with reformation and as a massive preventitive bulwark. Wherever social problems occur, youth workers are likely to be exhorted to push a finger into the pie. The Albemarle Committee saw the service as helping 'to counteract the increasing educational and professional stratification of society'.[1] Today the emphasis might be on racial integration, drugs, the moderation of rebelliousness or community aid programmes.

So wide is the encompassment of the service that there are few educational or social matters to which some individual youth workers or units have not at some stage or other turned their attention and sometimes with great success. This richness and diversity is one of the strengths of the service, but one of the dangers inherent in this very richness is the variety of demands which are made of individual clubs and youth workers. Not all these demands can be met and as I have already indicated not all may be compatible. The individual club unit cannot be all things to all men and who decides what it 'ought' to be and on what basis such a decision is made is, as I have shown, a complicated question.

Although it is difficult to generalize about the varied objectives urged upon the service, it is possible to make some rational comments about what the main stream of the youth club service actually does. Whatever the youth club sets out to do, to preach, to educate or to reform, it does by first making a social provision, and it is the general nature of this provision which I want to examine here.

Youth clubs deal with a clientele which has some special characteristics. Most psychologists would agree that the need for peer group association is particularly strong in adolescence and there are a variety of theories to account for this From the point of view of my argument the most interesting of these is concerned with role, and the accomplishment of the massive role change which occurs between the states of childhood and adulthood. According to this theory the peer group provides support for the adolescent during this transition and provides for some avoidance of hurtful conflict situations with adults.

The youth club is one way in which this need for peer group association can be satisfied, and the age group with which youth clubs are mainly concerned have few other opportunities. There are special conditions which relate to the social lives of this age group and these I would summarize as follows;

1. The sum of money they have for discretionary spending is low compared with many other age groups and therefore they seek meeting places which are either free or cheap.

2. Many of the group are precluded by law from the use of cars or motor bikes and many of those who are old enough have insufficient means to own or use private transport. Equally frequent use of public transport for long journeys is beyond the financial resources of many. As a group, therefore, they are limited in the main to meeting places which are local.

3. The group as a whole is excluded by law or by parental restriction from many of the meeting places which exist for the adult community. Public houses are the most obvious example here, but parental restriction may embrace many other forms of provision too.

In very general terms it is young people between the ages of fourteen and eighteen who are subject to these conditions and it is for this age group that the youth club has most appeal. Certainly the conditions relating to the leisure lives of those over eighteen are usually very different. The sum available to them for discretionary spending is very much higher and in some cases higher than at any other period of life. They are not subject to parental restriction, nor yet to the later restrictions imposed by marital and family responsibility. Thus they are not limited in their choice of social provision to that which is cheap and local and has parental approval. There can be few forms of social provision from which they are legally excluded and though it might be argued that in terms of social provision they do not always fare very well it would be difficult to argue that they fare any worse than anybody else.

This distinction between those under and over eighteen seems to me a very important one. Of course eighteen is an arbitrary age selected because of its legal implications; but in general terms there is a younger and an older group between which it is possible to distinguish on the grounds of the social opportunities available to them. The case for making a generally available social provision for the younger group is fairly clear cut. If there are to be 'places for association in which young people may maintain and develop ... their sense of fellowship, of mutual respect and tolerance'[2] then, as the Albemarle Committee point out, these must be provided. But the older group have more or less the same opportunities for association as do the rest of the adult population.

Unlike the younger group they do not constitute a 'special case' so far as social provision is concerned and any argument in favour of working with them must be on grounds other than this.

Besides special needs for social provision it is also possible to distinguish between the younger and older group on the grounds of psychological development. Very roughly these two groups might be equated with early and late adolescence. In terms of role theory early adolescence would be the stage characterized by the withdrawal from adult conflict situations with its emphasis on the support of the peer group, while late adolescence would be characterized by an exploration of adult society and 'testing out' of adult roles in the context of that society.

Now it would be altogether too glib for me to suggest that the two groups which I have postulated exist as separate entities, happily distinguishable from one another by their different psychological and 'social' conditions. The role change process is best seen as a continuum as is, I would suggest, the move away from the younger group's 'special case' need of social provision. However, it is in no way stretching a point to say that the two factors are interrelated. It becomes possible to 'test out' adult roles fully only when the social provision of the adult world becomes accessible and by definition this is also the point when the need for a special 'non-adult' provision declines.

Certainly the behaviour of the mass of young people in relation to youth club attendance would support this theory. It would seem that membership rises to a peak at somewhere about sixteen or seventeen years of age and declines quite dramatically after eighteen. Members drift away, rather than leave, and the girls do this earlier than the boys. There are perhaps thousands of young adults who, for one reason or another, continue to gain satisfaction from youth club attendance after they are eighteen, but the mainstream of youth club work is concerned with a younger age group and it is this mainstream of work that I want to deal with here.

The question which I want to raise at this stage is whether youth clubs, any more than schools, help young people to provide for themselves. It is one of the key ideas of modern youth work that the young people should be active participants in the organization of their own activities and indeed in the total organization of the clubs to which they belong. However, it would be very difficult to determine to what extent this really happens and one of the difficulties is that the climate of opinion is so weighted in favour of this being what 'ought to happen' that whatever actually occurs tends to be presented in this light. This certainly leads to exaggerated claims being made for a level of democratic participation which in my experience does not often exist.

What I think is chiefly damaging about this is not so much that democratic opportunities do not exist, but that there may be a mis-education through participation in a system which is partly bogus. I have seen this happen with members' committees where tremendous staff effort has gone into the organization of democratic elections for a committee which, when in situ, has been encouraged to conduct its business with all the pomp and state of a city council and has finished up taking a peripheral part in the organization of a club dance. The active participation of members in the organization of their affairs is a desirable end, but such participation must be related to reality. In many clubs the opportunities for such participation are severely limited and 'reality' begins with an appreciation of the limitations of the framework within which one operates.

These limitations vary enormously from club to club but they are likely to include some of the following items.

1 The use of premises is conditional. There are limits on the uses to which premises can be put, the hours at which they may be used and the way the fabric of the building is treated.

2 Youth clubs operate within a framework of public accountability and general parental approval. Agencies must take steps to ensure

the moral and physical safety of members. So far as local authorities are concerned there are likely to be rules about such things as the use of gymnasia, the accompaniment of mixed parties, night hikes, accident insurance and the use of motor vehicles.

3 The financial affairs of youth clubs are not the sole concern of the members. The sponsoring agency has a concern for, at the very least, that measure of financial responsibility which will ensure the continuance of the provision.

4 There are a variety of public restraints upon the ways in which members behave. It is unlikely, for example, that at closing time a youth club would be allowed to indulge in the same quantity of noise and disturbance that is tolerated with public houses or dance halls. In addition, there is a general public concern for the moral behaviour of the young. Such matters as smoking, gambling, drinking, language, sexual morality and modes of dress come under a special degree of scrutiny when the young people enter into some formally recognized relationship with 'responsible' adults. Popularly, what the adults allow, they are held to encourage, and thus there are some fierce restraints upon what they can be allowed to 'encourage' in the area of moral behaviour.

Within these limitations there is still room for participation and for learning how to participate and the skilled worker may see his job as allowing for a realistic interpretation of this situation and the control of the intrusion of adverse external pressures to give the club members the maximum room for manoeuvre. But the sheer complexity of this task is generally underestimated. It is far too simple an explanation of youth club life to describe it in terms of free associations of young people who come together with 'understanding' adults who 'enable' them to clarify and achieve their group and individual aims. The club may be able to provide a more permissive environment than can the school, but it is still an environment subject to limitations and restraints very different from those which pertain in adult society or even in teenage society beyond the walls of club or school.

Inevitably clubs, like schools, are concerned with the twin tasks of personal development and socialization. It is fair to argue often, that it would be a happier state of affairs if they moved rather more in the direction of the former, made greater allowance for change and social deviance and were less morally judgmental and restrictive. But having said this it is difficult to see how any agency which stands in a directly managerial relation to its club can ever be anything other than super protective so far as the moral and physical welfare of club members is concerned and the acceptance of this responsibility imposes its own limitations on the actions of members and staff.

All this raises some big questions about the way clubs are run. Training in youth work at the moment lays emphasis upon democratic leadership and the value of working through groups. Yet in most of the clubs which I have seen it is difficult to see how the club could survive unless the youth worker adopted a fairly positive managerial role in relation to many aspects of club life, and if one accepts that the club provision is itself something of value then this is an acceptable way of dealing with the situation. In many cases it may be the only way. The worker who has to cope with a young club, shifting membership and limited resources can only give stability to the situation by taking the leadership into his own hands. The youth worker's first priority is concerned with the maintenance of a social provision which is realistically geared to the needs of young people in the community in which he operates. To achieve this is in itself a difficult and worthwhile objective. More sophisticated educational aims can really only come into the picture when this has been achieved, and the staff turnover alone, to give but one of many factors, makes this a comparatively rare situation.

To say this is not to counsel despair but to counsel realism. Unrealistic ideals about what clubs 'should be' can militate against the full exploration of the possibilities which exist within their realistic limits and lead instead to their adopting the form of the 'ideal' without ever realizing its substance. This is what I suspect often happens with 'democracy' and member participation. The ideal seems to be of the club as a member participative, organizationally democratic institution. However, the reality of the situation is surely that clubs are a compromise between what young people want and what adults want them to have. They do not operate simply within the bounds of what is legal, but within the much narrower confines of what is, in adult terms, desirable. There is room for consultation here between the young people and the adults concerned, but to dress up this consultation as a full-blown decision-taking democracy is a misrepresentation. What is perhaps far more useful is the sort of consultation which sets out clearly the limits within which the club operates and the areas that are open for negotiation and I am attracted by the suggestion in Davies and Gibson's book *The Social Education of the Adolescent*[3] that such negotiations might be conducted on union/management lines between club members and the adult management committee. This at least allows for the possibility of a realistic exploration of the conflict and misunderstanding which may exist between the generations and could be a learning situation for both parties. There is no easy solution along these lines, but as an ultimate goal it offers a situation more real and more related to the community than that afforded by a protected democracy where many of the determing factors are hidden from the participants.

While in varying degrees the organization of the whole club may offer to some members some opportunity to learn something of the skills of social organization it is not here that I would see that its main potential lies. Rather I would consider that the more frequent opportunity for young people to learn the skills of social organization might come through the smaller groups operating within the club. It is perhaps dangerous these days to see youth clubs very much in terms of activity groups. Many of the larger clubs particularly may offer a general, rather anonymous, recreational provision in which organized activity groups play a comparatively small part. None the less it is this part, large or small, which I think offers opportunity.

It is an opportunity which is often not realized. Most youth workers would support the idea that activity groups in clubs should have the opportunity to learn about the activity and to practise it and should very largely run their own affairs along their own lines. The stereotyped ideal of the traditional youth worker is of a person who has both skills in working with people and activity skills. His contact with a group of people enables him to introduce them to new experiences and activities. Some of the people so introduced are motivated towards a further exploration of the activity and the youth worker is able to help them both with the extension of their technical ability and with the group organization of their activity. He works deliberately and consciously towards their self sufficiency and his own withdrawal from the situation. He moves from the position of being a stimulator and initiator, through a supportive teaching role to the position where he provides only such advice and support as is asked for. Finally, having enabled the group to form necessary external links with other agencies and individuals in the community he withdraws from the situation altogether.

Of course this does happen in clubs, but I doubt whether it happens very often and there are some new factors in the situation which are in some respects disturbing. The 'ideal' which I have presented presupposes a high degree of skill and naturally enough such skill is always rare. However, with the extensions over the past ten years in both professional and part-time youth leader training there are some grounds for assuming that in some measure it ought to exist. But whether the skill exists or not it is perhaps not much exercised in the way which I have just described, and there are a number of reasons why this may be so.

The job which is in the main open to the full-time professional youth leader is that of managing a large and expensive piece of recreational provision. This does not necessarily preclude him from working in the way I have described with small groups of members but it does mean that the time he can devote to this is limited and he certainly has the option of electing an entirely managerial role if this is what he wants. In most cases the smooth running of the establishment is the first priority of his employers and therefore must be his too. It is after all a reasonable priority.

In some areas the training of part-time staff is sophisticated enough to enable them to fulfil the sort of function which I have described, although there are all sorts of practical difficulties which may prevent them ever doing so, like the staffing ratio, and the ever present need to deploy staff to protect premises. But what also has to be borne in mind here is that while staff training may be very adequate, selection is often non-existent and the way of working indicated by the training may have little impact upon those whose fundamental attitudes are alien to its acceptance. None the less, it is upon the shoulders of part-time and voluntary staff that most of the small group work done in clubs must rest and the arguments for extending the training opportunities available to them and for encouraging wider recruitment and selection, are powerful ones.

In practice though, the same difficulty which I mentioned in connection with schools has some relevance so far as youth clubs are concerned; this is the emphasis on instruction in activity skills. Increasingly youth clubs make use of an instructional staff to look after the needs of activity groups. In a large centre a common deployment of staff might be: a senior worker who takes overall responsibility and who 'manages' the provision, the part-time youth workers who 'man' the centre and who attempt to work with those who use the general recreational provision, and the instructional staff who work with activity groups. Probably in most circumstances the instructors confine themselves to technical instruction in their activity and this is what they are briefed to do. They are concerned with technical competence and personal development through this. The more complex social role which I have ascribed to the youth worker is foreign to them and they have not been trained to work in this way. The youth workers may initiate activities and if these are social in nature and related to short term projects they will probably carry them through with the group concerned. However, if they are activities which involve a technical competence these are likely to be passed on to instructional staff where this is possible. There are all sorts of reasons why this happens. There are good educational reasons for bringing a variety of adults into the club and it is fair to assume a need for technical competence. Also, with perpetual under-staffing it is one practical way of increasing the staffing ratio to cope with the members not engaged in activities.

What I am suggesting here is that clubs afford far fewer opportunities for young people to learn social organizational skills than might seem to be the case. In fact instead of learning how to run the activity for themselves the young people can easily come to rely on the institution for the continued provision of the activity. The activity is 'laid on' so long as there is a demand for it and the progression is towards expertise rather than independence.

I think this progression towards a reliance on institutions is also a feature of other educational services. At this point I want to leave youth service and take a brief look at adult education. Here there are some similarities with youth service, but consideration of adult education also leads to new questions and provides some fresh perspectives.

Adult education

The adult education which I am concerned with here is the non-vocational adult education which takes place under the auspices of the local education authority. Section forty-one of the Education Act of 1944 states that it is the 'duty of every local education authority to secure provision for their area of adequate facilities for further education, that is to say ... leisure-time occupation in such organised cultural training and recreative activities as are suited to their requirements, for any persons over compulsory school age who are able and willing to profit by the facilities provided for that purpose.' There are a variety of ways in which such provision might be made and indeed an exciting diversity in which the provision is made, but its commonest expression is through the classes and activities of the evening institute and the Adult Education Centre.

Here the emphasis is on instruction in leisure activities. The judo, pottery, flower arranging, dressmaking, car maintenance which make up the evening centre programme is likely to be parcelled up and labelled, 'Leisure with a Purpose', or 'Learning for Leisure', and it is under such titles that it is advertised. A complex of motives will attract people towards the centres, but few will doubt that instruction will form the basis of the period they spend in formal attendance.

The commonly expressed educational objectives are straight-forward. It is intended that there should be development of personal skill and resources in relation to the subject of study and in addition it is hoped that the teaching will be such that the student comes to see the particular subject of study in some wider social context and that his personal interests will grow commensurately. The educator builds on existing wants but is also concerned to 'present what is worth wanting in such a way that it creates new wants and stimulates new interests'.[4]

The resources available to fulfil these aims vary enormously, but in many areas adult education is the cinderella of the education services struggling in unsuitable premises, with limited materials and an often inexperienced part-time staff to establish the very foundations of a service. On the other hand, new adult centres often provide accommodation that by school or youth service standards is lavish; though it is interesting to note that the creation of such provision has in some cases preceeded the establishment of any scheme of training for part-time staff. Looking at adult education resources no one could grumble at lack of diversity or shortage of seeming contradictions and inconsistencies.

The question I would ask in relation to adult education is 'What is the nature of the vision?', and by this I mean, what is the service there to do, and what would life be like if its most imaginative aims were suddenly and magically achieved? Of course, such questions are impossible to answer except in the broad global terms which leave the individual free to define his own Utopia, but it is not wholly unreasonable to look for answers in terms of extensions of present practice. But when I do this, I find some grounds for concern, and this concern is not related to those practices which arise from the understandable deficiencies of a developing service, but rather to practices which relate to some of the 'best' examples of the mainstream of the service.

The particular danger which I see here is that while the centres concentrate on the teaching of activity skills they are likely to become the main community source of a certain kind of leisure provision. This is fair enough, and certainly we want more and better institutions, but I think also we have to be very clear about the way such institutions serve their local communities. The greater the extent to which the centre becomes seen as the place which 'delivers the goods' the greater the degree of dependence upon that institution. If we project much of present practice into the future what we see is more, more and yet more institutions with each one building upon the demands created by its predecessor, becoming increasingly sophisticated and yet continuing self-contained and insular.

Of course, there are certain sorts of provision which can only be made institutionally, but what is surely questionable is whether the main stimulus of local education authority institutional provision should be geared towards the self feeding process of increasing demands for more provision of the same kind. The key question should be not 'what happens at the centre?', but, 'what happens in the community as a result of the centre being there?', and in some cases the answer to this second question might be very disturbing. In fact, it is quite possible for a 'new' adult centre to establish itself and to thrive by doing very little more than re-housing and taking over classes and activities which are already going concerns in the community. By the time the centre has re-housed the evening classes which previously occupied the junior school, taken the local drama group and the silver prize band into associate membership and let off rooms to other already existing organizations, the centre's 'programme' is full. Of course, improved facilities for all these groups are needed and are valued, but provision in this sense does not necessarily produce any very significant growth in the leisure opportunities for the community as a whole, though, dangerously, it can create the impression of having done so. Similarly, with evening institute activity classes, it is surely fair to ask whether such classes lead to the external practice of the activity with which they are concerned or whether the classes constitute the only practice of the activity in the locality. It is natural that the distinction between instruction in an activity and the practice of that activity should become blurred, but it is important that it should not become so blurred as to obscure the very necessary distinction between people who want teaching and people who want access to gymnasia or workshop facilities. Some authorities are beginning to draw this distinction by introducing two separate fee structures, but in other areas the only way access can be gained to the physical provision managed by the L.E.A. is by joining an instructional class.

It is possible to offer some positive suggestions as to how the institutional emphasis of adult education might be modified, but at root it depends on how we choose to look at the adult centres. Do we look at how full they are or do we look at the effect they have on the lives of people in the communities they serve? At present, I suggest, we tend to do the former and have pious hopes about the latter. However, should we choose to assume that part of the job of adult education centres is to stimulate leisure activities in the community then there are certain corollaries to this proposition and some of these I have indicated below.

In part, at least, the assessment of the effectiveness of the institution must be related to its community role. Naturally this could not be done with any subtlety, but to count the heads of people associated with the institution through its community contacts is no harder than counting the heads of those attending classes. The resulting information would be no more, or no less valuable. It would probably be strenuously argued that the class returns at present submitted by centres is information of an administrative and not an evaluative nature, but so long as the bulk of the information asked for has to do with what happens at the centre then there remains a very real pressure on the staff of centres to concentrate their efforts there.

With teaching there would be a concern for the teaching of the skills of social organization as well as with skills instruction of other kinds. If people come to a centre to learn a skill then it is reasonable to assume that besides wanting the complex satisfactions of class attendance some of them will also want to practise the skills they have come to learn. The teachers would explore with their students the possibilities for the continuance of the activity. They would help them to join groups or help them to form new ones. If the centre's specialist provision were involved then they would examine with their students, who are, after all the part owners of the provision, the possible circumstances under which they might make a non-instruction-based use of it.

All this, it may be argued, puts the class teacher out of a job and one cannot realistically expect adult teachers to work towards a condition of their own unemployment. But this is true only so long as the unit of employment is the class; the problem very largely disappears the moment one considers there being other employment opportunities besides those involving class teaching. In addition, in the long term a stimulated community will always make more direct educational demands of institutional provision than can be met and more often it is the insular institution in the culturally deprived community which perpetually struggles for survival.

The institution's concern with the community might be expressed in a variety of ways. There are a number of services which could be offered to existing specialist groups; short term coaching course for the sports clubs, and lectures, film shows and demonstrations for some of the others. There is no difficulty here because these are precisely the services which many centres already provide, but I would suggest that there is a tremendous difference between providing a service at the centre in relation to some known local interest, and actually offering such a service to a particular club as something which they could arrange on their terms. The first service is public provision by a public authority, the second service is club provision, the precise and apt nature of which is the subject of negotiation between the members of the club and the adult education centre staff. In the second case, there are new educational factors in the situation. The discussion about what sort of event it is which is needed is in itself an educational process, both in the short term in helping the club members to think about their club needs and in the long term in helping them to see how they can best use the educational resources of their community.

Even beyond this though I would see a more sophisticated role which I would like to see some adult education staff able to fulfil. I have written about the skills of social organization and although I have not been able to define these very closely I have tried to make it clear that I regard the acquisition of such skills as a process quite apart from either learning how to organize from a position of established leadership, or the normal processes of socialization which enables one to 'get along with people'. My hypothesis is simply that some of the difficulties which clubs, societies and organizations run into arise through lack of skill on the part of the members. To suggest that there are some cases in which the adult education teacher might be able to help is not to suggest that he ought to turn himself into a community worker. All I am suggesting is that if he means business about 'learning for leisure' then he has to concern himself with issues other than simply offering skills instruction.

The ways in which he might help are best illustrated by giving one example. One of the difficulties which face many clubs is that of recruitment. In theory most clubs want to recruit new members; but in practice there are many clubs which though technically open for recruitment would not welcome the disruption which new members might bring. However, when I wrote to a large number of clubs in Chesterfield, I received in reply a number of unsolicited letters which made reference to the need to recruit members and the writers asked about the possibility of being put in touch with young people who might like to join their organization. This I would imagine is a fairly common situation.

Obviously, though, the business of recruitment is nothing like as simple as this. The small club which sets out to recruit new members is probably in the position that the established social relationships in the club are an effective barrier against recruitment and recruitment would only be possible if the established club members were prepared to modify their behaviour quite considerably. The lack of skill comes in not recognizing the factors in the situation and it is here that the adult education teacher, in his broadly advisory pastoral role in relation to the adult clubs and organizations in his area, might be able to help. He can initiate discussion that focuses attention on the cost of recruitment and the extent of the changes it would bring. If the club really is open to recruitment on realistic terms then technical advice on how to set about it is quite easily given if it is needed; the real difficulty is in clarifying the nature of the decision which has to be made.

I have had some little experience of functioning in this way, with established adult organizations and perhaps one instance is worth recounting. This was with a swimming club which had made a number of unsuccessful attempts at recruitment. The nucleus of the club was made up of a group of people who were mainly concerned with competitive swimming. As what they wanted was to recruit a number of fully fledged competitive swimmers it was hardly surprising that, in a small community, they did not recruit at all. The expectations with which new members came to the club were so at odds with those of the existing members that they attended only a few nights before deciding that it was not for them. However, as the club was

51

moving towards extinction point there was a strong motive towards recruitment. The choice for the club was change or die, but what it is important to stress is that though this seems childishly obvious from the analysis which I have given here it was not the issue which was ever discussed by club members. They were concerned with the survival of the club as they had experienced it, and their emotional energy went into bemoaning the declining interest in competitive swimming.

As an outsider any solution I offered would certainly have been resented and rejected. Through discussion with the members it was possible to bring into the reckoning some of the factors which had previously been ignored. However, I would stress that I was not in the position of knowing things about the club which the members did not know. I simply asked the questions which led the members to the analysis of the situation which I have given above and I did not start this process from the point of having an answer or even of knowing precisely the nature of the problem. My contribution was really that I presented to the group the idea that the sort of problem with which they appeared to be wrestling was one which might be resolved by critical discussion, In the event the 'happy ending' was that the members weighed up the factors involved in change and completely altered the nature of their club, giving over the bulk of their club time to the training of new members. Recruitment was massive and maintained over a period of certainly two years, and as an unforeseen bonus the opportunities for competitive work increased rather than declined. In a sense though, it would have been an equally happy solution had the members all agreed to give up the frustrating business of unsuccessful recruitment and settled down to enjoy the last seasons of the club on their original terms. What they decided was their affair; my concern was simply to provide the technique by which a decision could be made and it is this role which I imagine adult education teachers could in many cases fulfil.

Nothing which I have suggested is wildly unrealistic in terms of the manpower and resources available, limited though these are, and little, if any, is outside the ideals of the adult education service. It does, however, constitute a shift of emphasis from an institution based to a community based service and there are grounds for looking with caution at any claims that it 'is all already happening'.

The particular potential of the adult education service is that the staff of the service can negotiate on grounds of equality with the people in the community the service is there to serve. Unlike schools and youth service its workers are not constrained to adopt protective or moralistic attitudes towards the people with whom they deal. Yet so often in practice the service slips into the same paternalistic, protective role in relation to its users as that which characterizes the other two services. The educational posture adopted is still often that of the nineteenth century; the 'haves' providing for the 'have nots' and although there may be marginally more participation on the part of the users, the rules of this participation are still laid down by the providers. That today the providers may be a democratically elected education committee makes very little practical difference to the would-be participant who wants to change the rules relating to the terms on which adult education is available to him in his local community.

A community-based service is one which gives to the educator the maximum opportunity to subject himself to community pressures. He reacts to these pressures in relation to the educational disciplines in which he has been trained and he is not solely concerned with those other rules and other pressures which relate to institutional provision. Such an approach may mean that the educator finds himself working in physical situations which are very different from those in which he now spends most of his time and a concern with social organizational skills means that he broadens the scope of activities. However, I would stress that the educator remains an educator and to suggest that he might be a community-orientated educator is to do no more than to suggest that his main concern is with people rather than with places.

Although in this chapter and the ones which preeceded it I have raised a number of issues, there are two which predominate. These are the teaching of social organizational skills and the development of non-institutional approaches by the education services. My thesis here is that the development of leisure education demands from the educator new techniques and new approaches. Traditionally education provides for personal development and the growth of the individual and although this concept seems all embracing it is certainly one which can be interpreted very narrowly. Educators are very quick to shun the role of 'social engineer' claiming that their concern is simply with the development of individual abilities. But in practice the education services have a large measure of control over physical resources, skill and information and the social implications of the use, or lack of use, of these resources cannot be shrugged off as a matter of no consequence.

In the case of leisure time education services the argument is particularly pointed and education in leisure time brings the educator face to face with new questions and new issues. There is little room for miscalculation about what is at stake here and some writers[5] about future leisure have placed it for comparison alongside such world problems as destruction by nuclear holocaust and extinction by overpopulation. More hopeful views stress the possibility of new forms of social participation and of new life styles.

53

Playing for such stakes it is impossible not to ask for the extension of the education services and upon this point Dumazadier comments:

Educators have to solve the most difficult question in the whole history of education: the constant improvement of the levels of culture of all layers of society in terms of ever more complex needs for development and by means of the most ambiguous activities, those of leisure. Only a common front of professional educators, popular leaders, information specialists, and social service workers can master this problem.[6]

But realistically and immediately is it not reasonable to ask of the existing services themselves that they should extend their sphere of influence; that they should seek ways of making limited resources as widely available as possible; that they should consciously extend help to clubs, societies and organizations wherever they happen to meet; that they should deliberately help people to participate and to organize and should foster engagement in political, social and cultural life in whatever legal forms it takes and, above all, that policy, training and research should be directed towards these ends?

4 The leisure organizations of some young adults

There are many services and organizations which cater for young people which are not 'youth service' in the commonly accepted sense of that term. There are even some organizations which are a recognized part of 'youth service' in some parts of the country, but not in others. In this chapter I want to look at one or two particular movements and organizations which are limited to, or seem specially attractive to young adults. This is not a survey and the organizations and movements mentioned are simply examples chosen to illustrate particular ways of going about things. A great part of the chapter is taken up with the examination of one organization, the Federation of Eighteen Plus Groups. Although this is quite a small organization and one which probably 'exists' for only a small section of the population it does have a number of interesting features which deserve to be more widely known. Commercial organizations, which perhaps make the most important contribution to the leisure of most people, are not mentioned here at all, but are dealt with in relation to local studies in the chapters which follow.

The National Federation of Young Farmers' Clubs

Young Farmers' Clubs are commonly accepted as part of the youth service although the closeness of their relationship with other branches of the service, through S.C.N.V.Y.O. or the L.E.A., varies a good deal from area to area. Although they are 'in' the youth service they are frequently regarded as being on the periphery of it or at least as being different from the organizations which comprise its main core.

One of the features of Young Farmers' Clubs which is often remarked upon is the extent to which the members seem to have achieved the kind of democratic participation at which the rest of the youth service is aiming. Individual Young Farmers' Clubs elect their own officers who run the club. The officers are also members of the county executive who order the affairs of the county federation and this is also the body which employs the county organizing secretary. At this level at least I have found little evidence of generation conflict and the organization is generally accepting of and accepted by the adult community.

It is interesting too that the organization has a wide age range, 10 or 11 to 25, at a time when in the main stream of the service it is generally held that organizations with a wide age range do not work. It is also interesting that at a time when most youth organizations have a dearth of senior members over half the membership of Young Farmers' Clubs are over eighteen.[1]

All this is different enough to deserve comment. Young Farmers' Clubs provide a useful illustration of what is possible. It is possible to have a youth organization and with an extended age range. It is possible for a youth organization to maintain a strong senior membership. It is possible for a youth organization to work harmoniously, co-operatively and on equal terms with the rest of the adult community. It is not that there are not other clubs which illustrate this also, but here is a whole organization in which these characteristics are clearly discernible. By way of explaining this situation there are two main factors to consider. One is the rural setting of young farmers' clubs and the other is the composition of their membership.

While young farmers' clubs are by no means exclusively agricultural they are still rural and exist within the ethos of the agricultural industry. It is the tendency in villages for contact between the generations to be more common and more accepting than is usually the case in urban areas. Also in farming real responsibility goes to the young. There are still many schoolboys who go home to the farm to do a real job of work and who have to behave responsibly towards livestock and valuable farm machinery. The essential nature of their contribution is recognized and rewarded. This is the background against which the Y.F.C. functions.

In membership the Y.F.C. movement is different from many other youth organizations. While a third of the membership have little connection with agriculture, those who do come from farming backgrounds tend to come from the larger farms. Thus they come from the most prosperous and influential sections of their own communities. Among those who stay long in membership and achieve influential positions in the organization a high proportion are in, or have benefited from, some form of higher education. These factors are undoubtedly very important ones in enabling the organization to conduct its affairs in the way it does.

The National Federation of Eighteen Plus Groups

What is now the National Federation of Eighteen Plus Groups originated from the work of the Carnegie Trust which in 1939 published a report[2] of a survey they had conducted into the leisure time activities of the eighteen to thirty age group. The report concluded that 'young people do not mix well with their seniors' and that 'young people demand the opportunity of making immediate contribution to practical affairs'.

Following the report a panel was set up to find out what kind of provision would meet the needs of young people over the age of eighteen and with a small grant from the Carnegie Trust an experiment was launched which involved the setting up of Eighteen Plus groups in a number of towns and suburbs up and down the country. By 1943 the Federation comprised 24 groups with an approximate membership of 350. The scatter of the groups, Aberdeen to Shoreditch, meant that there was little contact between many of them and wartime conscription did not aid the building up of a stable membership. In 1947 the organization persuaded the Carnegie Trust to make a second grant and this allowed for the appointment of a paid organizer for the Manchester area for a period of three years. As a result of this appointment a large number of groups were formed in the north-west region.

During all these years, however, it seems that despite the opening of many new groups overall development was slow. In 1948 national membership was 390 and by 1954 still only 480. The main development came in the sixties and by 1963 membership exceeded a thousand. In 1969 national membership was estimated at 8,000.

There are two points worth stressing about the Federation of Eighteen Plus Groups as a national organization.

1 It came into being as the result of a survey.
2 Its creation involved very little financial outlay.

(The first grant of £2,000 was for five years, the second of £1,500 was for three years. A third grant was made in 1967 by the Department of Education and Science to allow the Federation to employ a full-time assistant secretary.)

Thus with very little money from external sources the organization has developed into its present complex form as a National Federation with a large membership and scores of active voluntary officers at national, regional and local levels.

During 1967 and 1968 I spent some time looking at some of the Eighteen Plus groups in the Midlands and during that period I formed some impression of the organization.

My first impression, and one which subsequent experience has done little to modify, was that the organization was predominantly middle class in membership and predominantly social in its function. Some groups in some towns have the reputation among other young people of being snobby, elitist and cliqueish. However, many of the groups I visited were very accepting in their membership and the larger groups particularly seemed well able to absorb people from very different kinds of backgrounds. Among members I found a wide range of educational levels, both early school leavers and graduates, and quite a wide range of occupations, though with a predominance of those from retailing and the service industries.

The main function of the organization seemed to be to provide the opportunity for people to meet in a social context. The meetings I attended were neither particularly frivolous nor were they characterized by any real engagement in serious concerns of any kind. Some were mildly but uncommittedly educational, others were straightforwardly and uncomplicatedly social. I rarely had any doubts that both kinds of meetings were valuable to and valued by the members. I stress the strong social content of the programme, however, because what I observed in this respect seemed to be a little at odds with the avowed aims of the organization, which suggest more serious purposes. The aims are:

The Federation seeks to assist people between the ages of eighteen and thirty to:

a Understand and appreciate life
b Develop a personal philosophy
c Acquire experience in public affairs
d Act in co-operation for the benefit of the community
e Provide opportunity for cultural, social and recreational activities.

While I think it is unlikely that the organization in fact contributes much to meeting all its own stated aims and objectives I have no doubt at all that it is an organization which is very valuable to its members and one which has very many interesting features.

A typical Eighteen Plus group programme would mean little to the uninitiated. A section of it might well look like this:

JUNE
Thurs.	2	Fair Game
Sat.	4	Home with X
Sun.	5	To the Woods!
Mon.	6	Bowling Tournament
Thurs.	9	Join Up
Fri.	10	Swimming Evening
Sat.	11	Dance Date!
Sun.	12	Area Conference

Thurs. 16 Treasure Trail
Sun. 19 Ramble into Derbyshire
Tues. 21 Sun Worshippers Evening

The pattern which many groups seem to follow is that of having a regular weekly meeting at which there is a talk or a discussion or a film and which is also the business meeting for the week. Many of the talks I attended were broadly educational and dealt with such topics as town planning, 'the work of the police' or 'medicine today'. In addition to visiting speakers, members often talk about their hobbies, interests or their work. Some of the members' talks I heard were very good but even when they were bad they were tolerantly received.

The business side of the weekly meeting was really just a question of finalizing the arrangements for any events occurring during the following seven days. Some of the larger groups might well have something going on every night of the week. These activities would not involve all the membership but they would be advertised and available. Often what the 'programme' amounted to was that Bill's group were going swimming on Tuesday and Sandra's group were going bowling on Friday. But the invitations to join in were open and genuine. There was always the impression of a lot going on, of being part of a scene where things were happening. The weekly meetings gave people the opportunity to recruit for their own particular interests. Sue would want the names of those prepared to help in some community service activity, Henry would be canvassing for a group to share the cost of transport to Brands Hatch and Joe would get up and advertise the forthcoming attraction at his folk club. Thus an important part of the programme is not what Eighteen Plus provides itself, but what it enables its members to enjoy through the information and companionship which it affords.

In matters of organization Eighteen Plus groups have a number of interesting features. The officers are elected for one year only. At its best this means that leadership opportunities occur fairly frequently and that there are usually a number of people in the group who know from personal experience the difficulties of being Chairman or Secretary and who are likely to be sympathetic and helpful to the current officers. Some groups have Social Representatives who try to introduce newcomers to the members. The existence of such posts indicates that members are conscious that new members need special attention of some kind. I sat in on one meeting where after lengthy discussion it was decided that the posts of Social Representative should not be filled on the grounds that it was everyone's responsibility to welcome new members.

Of particular interest is the Federation's method of opening new groups. New groups are opened by existing groups who 'invade' the town where the new group is to be established and conduct a publicity campaign. This campaign leads to a public meeting and the new group is launched with temporary officers from the parent group. The parent group pays the rent of the room in which the newly formed group meets and covers all the initial costs. After a short period, often only three weeks, the new group is regarded as established and elects its own officers.

Naturally on this basis some new groups founder, but the success of the Federation in recent years indicates that many survive. I saw the formation of two new groups. In one case attendance at the initial meeting, including those attending from the parent group, was sixteen. In the other case it was over a hundred. The smaller group flourished and expanded while the large one waned and after about eighteen months expired completely. While there are a number of reasons why this was so it was very evident that the organization was not geared to dealing with so large an initial response and this was outside the previous experience of all the officers and members whom I met.

The success of individual Eighteen Plus groups varies a good deal and in examining this I felt that size, ease of communication with other groups and leadership were all important factors. One of the satisfactions of belonging to an Eighteen Plus group is the opportunity it affords to meet other people and particularly other people of the opposite sex. The best opportunities were afforded by the large groups and those where numerous events were organized in association with neighbouring groups. The sponsorship method of development means that there is always a good chance of there being a good working relationship between neighbouring groups, but a good deal depends also upon the ease or difficulty of the journey between group meeting places, the traditional lines of communication and the transport situation. Survival for the small and isolated group seemed to me to be always in the balance as here the social satisfactions arising from membership were least evident. Large groups too seemed to have the best chance of throwing up people with good organizing ability and traditions of good leadership existed where groups had been established for some time.

Another important factor in the success of the group was the opportunity for social activities afforded by the local environment. While the Eighteen Plus groups I saw did some things for themselves they also relied to a considerable extent upon the opportunity to do things together; to visit commercial provision of all kinds. Eighteen Plus groups rely upon the richness of existing leisure provision and they are likely to thrive best in areas well provided with swimming baths, skating rinks, cinemas, bowling alleys and restaurants. In under provided areas Eighteen Plus groups tend to function by bringing the commercial provision of nearby towns within the reach of more people by organizing parties to visit the provision. My impression is that groups only survive where this remains a realistic proposition in terms of the money and time which need to be expended.

During my examination of Eighteen Plus groups I did not conduct a survey of the membership. With this organization as with many others this would be an extremely rewarding exercise though it was one which was beyond my resources. However I met members from more than six groups and conducted formal interviews with some of them. While my main interest lay in the organizational features of the organization I was struck very forcibly by its ethos. I found it, to a quite unusual extent, to be an organization which mattered to its members. This is best illustrated in their own words in their own account of their experiences of school, of youth clubs, of joining Eighteen Plus groups and of the satisfactions they gained from membership.

School

'(I went) to an all girls school and when I was fifteen I started work in an office and I've been there ever since.'

'I went to school at ———. After that I went to a college of further education still doing nothing much, so I started work and still mixed with the same people.'

'I had a very mixed schooling ... I went to an infants school the same as everyone else, then I had an illness ... I went to Juniors for about nine months, then I went away to a special school 'till I was twelve then I went back to my local school, a secondary modern. I didn't do too well there.'

'I was school librarian and chess club and Oh everything else. You know you like to fill your life with school and this is what I did and it seemed quite empty afterwards.'

'I just went to an ordinary secondary school. I'm not bright. No G.C.E.s or anything.'

'I went to a secondary school. There was nothing particularly exciting about it. I'm not particularly brilliant or anything like that.'

'Went to school. It was a comprehensive school. It was going to be a big thing but I'm not very clever so I left at sixteeen without taking any exams.'

Youth Club

'Rambling Association, the guides, youth groups, church youth groups, a study group and a record club. Some of the things have just packed up or I got fed up with them.'

'I belonged to the Guides, but that was about it ... a few bits here and there but ... (shrug) ... I think I left really because I was one of the oldest there (at sixteen) and the others ... they all seemed very young.'

'I was a Scout until I was fifteen and then I left.'

'I tried a club but it wasn't very well run and so I didn't bother any more.'

'Many years ago when I was at school ... this was a Church organization. They had a committee there and I was elected onto it. It was a good club. It was quite all right but there again it catered up to about fifteen or sixteen and that was your lot and when you were over that you wandered round like everyone else.'

Joining Eighteen Plus

'It was an article in the '*Post*. It was just saying about the entertainment going on and that it (Eighteen Plus) has been going on for about four years in ———.'

'(On her first visit) Diane dragged me along; she wouldn't come on her own so I had to come as moral support. I'm impressed. I definitely think I'd like to come again.'

'Well, I was wandering about the town, about Easter time this year and I looked into the bank on the Square and I saw this notice about Eighteen Plus and I thought it's just the sort of thing I'd like to get involved in because I've never been one for youth clubs or anything like that.'

'I was the first person there which I think is usual for new members. Well, Eighteen Plus, you saw it tonight, people roll up late. A few people wandered in and just kind of stood a few feet away from you, you know ... The first few meetings I went to I didn't really become part of it.'

'How old was I? Nineteen almost twenty. It was just before Christmas and a friend at work asked me to go to the anniversary dance which was a few weeks before Christmas and I couldn't go, but I asked him what it was connected with and he told me about this club he went to—you know—and I told him I had been looking out for some type of club to join ... The thing that struck me most of all was that people actually came up to me and started talking to me and this overwhelmed me—honestly, it did really ... Everybody seemed friendly and you weren't shut out at all.'

The satisfactions of being a member

'All I want of Eighteen Plus is the chance to get to know people and to mix in with people.'

'For me at present, what happens here is more interesting than the people. But in time that might be different.'

'Well I came over to ... from ... about '63, at the beginning of the winter and I joined the bank over here. But it's not the kind of atmosphere in a bank to make friends ... The first six months or so I was here I was very lonely ... I wanted to do something interesting ... Well now I just haven't the time to do all the things I want to do.'

'Pressure groups pushed me into chairmanship and from then on it was all go.'

'I've hardly missed a time. You soon get dragged into these things.'

'I was naturally shy going somewhere and not knowing anybody at all but you find in Eighteen Plus, when I say everybody's your friend—I don't mean buddies and mates and that sort of thing—but people will talk to you. I know a number of people in Eighteen Plus who are a bit on the snobby type, but they will talk to you all the same.'

As I said at the outset my main reason for writing about Eighteen Plus is that it is interesting in its organizational features, but there are one or two more general points I would make by way of summary.

Eighteen Plus functions within clearly defined limits. It is, in the main, middle class, conformist and respectable. It is not a socializing agency and it could not survive if it recruited many who were not already conforming members of society. Neither is it a training agency and for its survival Eighteen Plus needs to recruit a high proportion of those who already have social and organizational skills, though it may provide a context in which such skills can be practised and refined.

It is interesting that Eighteen Plus exists at all. It runs on little money (the annual subscription is ten shillings) without premises of its own and without an obvious central activity interest. It caters for the age group, effectively 18 to 23/24 whose absence from other organizations is often remarked on. It has a considerable membership turnover, but recruits members on a minimum of publicity. I mentioned earlier the Eighteen Plus group initial meeting which attracted well over a hundred people. Those attending on this occasion did not find what they were looking for, but they were presumably looking for something, for the scant publicity had promised them very little. The existence of Eighteen Plus raises the question of how many people in towns and cities all over the country are looking for a social organization of some kind.

The Underground

The Underground is an umbrella term used to cover a large number of very diverse activities associated with a new kind of movement which attracts young people. Because the movement is new and in some respects genuinely different it cannot easily be measured against longer established movements with different conventions. It means something to those who are associated with it; very little to those who are not. It breaks surface through its artistic expressions; pop concerts and the Underground cinema and these manifestations of its existence are well known because of the press coverage they frequently receive.

The Underground is a network rather than an organization. In so far as it can properly be called a movement it is concerned with life style, with values, with being an alternative society. Its vices and excesses are well publicized in the popular press; for its virtues, tolerance, pacificism, self-help and self-expression it has to be its own publicist. It is impossible at this stage to form much impression of how strong the movement is or, in the long run, how important its existence will prove to be. It is fair to guess, however, that to the vast majority of young people the Underground means nothing and the mass of young people in Bootle or Blackburn or Newcastle will even be unfamiliar with the term. Most of the activities associated with the Underground are centred in London, though the readership of the *International Times* is national and estimated at 20,000. The movement has given rise to two organizations which I want to mention briefly here.

Release

Release is an organization which exists to help those charged with drug offences and its aim is to reform the way in which those concerned with offences under the dangerous drugs act are dealt with. As an organization it is well known, at least by name, as its staff have inevitably been involved in much of the mass media discussion about drugs during recent years.

Release operates on several levels. It publishes advice on what to do if arrested.[3] It provides a twenty-four hour service of help to those who are arrested. It documents the treatment of those arrested and publicizes it in ways designed to secure better treatment for others who are charged in the future.

By any standards Release is a remarkable venture. It is a self-help organization which besides meeting the immediate demands of an often desperate situation has also shown up the deficiencies in the system and has become a respected, if not always welcomed, voice on behalf of those in need. What needs to be said about Release is perhaps best said by Michael Schofield in his postscript to the Release Report.

> Why has it been left to them and other people in the Under-ground? The way some adults revile the young, particularly those in the Underground, the very existence of this report should be a surprise. I hope these people will learn that there is much activity and much useful work going on among the young, and I am not talking about the Duke of Edinburgh's Award Scheme. This report has not only demonstrated the inadequacies of the system, it has also shown there is no other channel for pointing out these faults. Furthermore one should be ashamed that it has been necessary for the young people in the Under-ground to organise their own self help organization.[4]

BIT

Bit is the smallest unit of information dealt with by a computer and the organization which bears this name was started in London in the summer of 1968 as an information service. John Hopkins of the *International Times* was its originator and Paul McCartney of the Beatles provided some of the initial capital. The service was developed and run by Peter Polish.

The service deals with about 1,200 enquiries a week ranging from the trivial to the tragic. Being what it is where it is Bit is on the wavelength to help many who cannot or will not be helped by other services. It helps the homeless, the jobless and the addicted. Some phone in simply to find out what is on at Middle Earth, others call in desperate straits. Bit deals with everything from pregnant girls to men with sick dogs, from what's on at the cinema to what's happening in British communes.

Services of information and help are not in themselves unusual. They are part of the system. What is different about Bit is partly that it is part of an alternative system. It belongs to the Underground. But its striking difference is in its methods. It is a network and much of its work is personal as well as voluntary. While it makes some use of official channels much of what it does it can only do because the network exists. The temporarily homeless stay with friends or with the friends of friends. The 'helped' tend to be drawn in and themselves to become, in whatever ways are appropriate, the helpers.

Of course neither Release nor Bit are organizations directly concerned with leisure provision though some of Bit's services are certainly concerned with leisure activities. The Underground, however, is a phenomenon of a leisured society and it is from this that both Release and Bit have sprung. As organizations they are interesting in their own right; in what they do and how they do it. They are interesting too in their origins and in the youth of their staff and their associates. Wider knowledge of their existence might well prove a shock to the complacent superiority of much of the 'adult' world. Even among those professionally involved with young people the capability of the young seems not to be easily accepted. General distinctions about capability tend often to be made in relation to age groups rather than in terms of differences between groups of people irrespective of their ages.

This chapter has provided some examples of organizations in the hands of capable young people and many more could have been given. The examples here are quite different from each other. In simple terms Eighteen Plus and the Underground might be seen as lying at the opposite ends of the conforming/non-conforming continuum. Whatever one thinks about how the organizations behave it is evident that they are run by people who possess social and organizational skill. It is with this concept of skill in mind that I wish to conclude this chapter.

I would suggest that while there is no necessary virtue in joining things there are very definite advantages in possessing, or being associated with people who possess, the kinds of skill which often find their most recognizable expression through organizations. Most leisure activity, whether serious or frivolous, involves other people and involves organization in some form. Only the isolate lacks the ability to meet other people and to organize himself in relation to others. Most people possess social and organizational skill to some degree; but the degree varies very widely indeed.

In the earlier chapters I have dealt with the role of the education services in relation to the learning of the kind of social and organizational skills which are useful in leisure. In schools the academically more able are advantaged in this, as in other respects. There are more clubs and societies for the upper school than for the early school leaver, and rich opportunities for social learning await those who go on to higher education. As I suggested earlier this is a system which produces losers. It might be seen as the role of youth service and adult education to provide a compensatory social education for these, but often instead these services patronize their customers and encourage their dependence. Despite this many people manage well enough because other experience, through family, friendship groups or other organizations provide for the growth of social skills. Others though seem not to have managed so well, seem to have missed out completely on the kinds of experiences which have helped them learn how to function in co-operation with other people. A group described in Chapter 8 were like this and were often destructive of their own collective efforts to achieve a richer social life. This is, I suggest, a very common state of affairs and a critically important one in certain social situations.

In the next chapter I want to move into a very different world from the one which has occupied the majority of space in this chapter. Eighteen Plus is middle class and largely an organization of the towns or their suburbs. The Underground belongs in the main to the mobile and the articulate. Young Farmers' Clubs are run by those with social and educational advantages. The predominantly working class industrial village sprawl is very different from all this.

5   Young adults, work and leisure in Minton: part I

How much leisure do people have and how do they spend it? These questions lie near the heart of any consideration of services concerned with leisure provision. In this chapter and the ones that follow I try to answer these questions so far as the 18-25-year-olds in a mining village in north-east Derbyshire are concerned. The basis of these answers is a survey I conducted in that village in the winter of 1968.

One of the assumptions I made when I attempted this survey was the common-sense one that there are enormous variations in the amount of leisure available to people and in the ways in which they spend it and that in general terms there are local as well as individual variations. Just how widely applicable is the picture which emerges from the Minton study is a matter of debate. Certainly I would make no serious claims for the typicality of Minton. Superficially it seems not unlike thousands of other villages which make up the industrial village sprawl which stretches across the north Midlands, into Yorkshire and beyond. One might guess that so far as leisure is concerned the lives of the people in these villages generally have more in common with each other than they do with the lives of people in the rural village or the big city. More than this it would be unreasonable to suggest. Common-sense tells us that leisure life in a Derbyshire mining village may have little or nothing in common with leisure life in Stornaway or South Kensington. But although in this sense there can be no generally applicable findings I would still hope that detailed analysis of the specific can help to illuminate our understanding of the whole; if only to reinforce us in our distrust of generalized statements about young adults and what they do.

The survey was conducted by interview and dealt mainly with straightforward and practical issues which can be summed up by the two questions, 'How much leisure?' and 'How is it used?'. The answers, mainly in table form, appear throughout the next two chapters. To this numerical information I have tried to add another perspective by including descriptions and impressions to form a more rounded picture of the village and the lives of some of its residents.

Minton is a mining village situated in the north-east tip of Derbyshire and in the heart of the Derby, Nottingham, Yorkshire coalfield. The nearest town is Worksop to the east while some miles south is Mansfield, with Chesterfield roughly the same distance to the west. The surrounding countryside is undulating and often heavily wooded; an attractive landscape only partly devastated by the eruptions of slag heap and pit head and the pervading grime of the coal industry.

Like many such villages Minton does not begin and end neatly. At its extremities it slips unobtrusively into other communities with other names; Minton Heath and Sough, Coldshott and Strickland. To residents and pedestrians such divisions are important, but the passing motorist barely notices where one starts and another ends. For the purpose of the survey I defined Minton as the area of unbroken housing stretching in all directions from the village square. This area encompassed forty-three streets, eleven hundred dwellings and a population of about four thousand five hundred people.

I started by saying that Minton is a mining village and before going further we must examine this phrase. So often the vision conjured up by the words 'mining village' is of mountainous spoil heaps, a glowering pit head and rows of dirty, Victorian back-to-back houses. But in Minton, and hundreds of villages like it, some of the housing is post-war, probably most of it post-1920, and neither spoil heap nor pit head are visible from most of the village. A local newsagent sells postcard views of the old village which would not be out of place on the postcard rack in a Peak District beauty spot. Much of the countryside round Minton is very attractive. Minton square is not nine miles, as the arrow flies, from the centre oak of Sherwood Forest. The eastern edge of the Peak District National Park is no more than forty minutes away by car.

In spite of all this the interviewing team, young student teachers from Matlock College of Education, unhesitatingly used words like 'gloomy', 'depressing', 'dead' and 'characterless' to describe their first impressions of the village. My own impressions were similar. What struck me first about Minton was the drabness of the environment and the lack of visual stimulation from any natural or architectural feature. Added to this was the sense of being nowhere in particular; the absence of either the bustle of a town or the visual interest of a country village. In fact it is the lack of features which would lead me to describe Minton as a typical mining village. The area can show villages which are much more stark and dramatic and nearer to the stereotype of the mining village. But really it is these which are the exceptions. There are hundreds of Mintons.

The centre of Minton is a road intersection known as 'the square'. Up the hill is the old village and the church. The houses here are pre-industrial revolution and attractively rural in character. Some open onto the street, others have gardens or are set at interesting angles to the road. To all intents and purposes this is rural Derbyshire with all the gentle warmth of weathered grey stone and slate roofs. If we stand in the square with our backs to the church hill we face a less pleasant prospect. To the left the road curves away into an area of late Victorian red brick terrace housing. Followed to its end this road leads to the worst housing in the village, terraced industrial revolution housing of the worst sort, impregnated with grime and bounded by the cinder tracks which for over a century have been the only roadway. But the worst is uncharacteristic of the whole and most of the houses in this area are more recent terraced houses, sometimes with small gardens at the front and a walled yard at the back. From our point of view two particularly interesting buildings lie in this part of the village. The first is the Civic Centre, a converted Methodist Chapel, which now provides a hall for social activities, a committee room, a surgery and the local branch of the county library. The second building, much nearer to us as we stand in the square, is perhaps the most imposing building in the whole village. It is a large, modern, redbrick building in a mock Elizabethan style. It has a garden, tennis courts and car parking for over a hundred cars. Inside is the largest and most comfortable bar in the village and a concert room to seat hundreds. This is Minton Miners' Welfare.

In front of us the road bends sharply so that we cannot see that it leads to the most modern part of Minton. On the left of this road lies a small modern council estate of pleasant, but uniform houses. This we found one of the liveliest parts of Minton in that even on cold evenings the streets were alive with children until darkness drove them indoors. Even then there always seemed more coming and going than in the rest of the village.

Immediately to our right we can see some of the substantial stone terraced houses of the old village. Again what we cannot see is the road curving away for nearly a mile and providing a link with yet three more quite distinct and separate housing estates. These estates are each a little network of avenues, closes and crescents and two of them were probably the model developments of the thirties. Today they seem cramped, tired and colourless compared with more modern estates, but they are characterized too by the same uniformity of building and absence of amenities which will perhaps damn our housing efforts in the eyes of future generations.

There is just one further aspect of the physical features of Minton to be mentioned. This is the more prosperous private development which is taking place on the perimeter. Because it is an old village Minton has never been the single class community which some of the mining villages have been. Now this is less the case than ever and at several points of the edge of the village there are development areas which include expensive houses for the more well-to-do professional and managerial groups.

As a visitor one comes to grips quite quickly with the scenic aspects of Minton. What is more elusive is the particular character of the place and the extent to which the pit has helped to forge this. The pit no longer dominates Minton as once it must have done, and much of the old mining culture has been eroded by improved living conditions, changing work methods and the incursion of external influences. But what remains is still significant. The analysis of a Yorkshire mining town, *Coal is our Life*,[1] was written in 1956. Much of it could have been written about Minton today even though the physical circumstances are so very different. Ashton, the mining town of *Coal is our Life* was a town with a population of 14,000; Minton is a village of under 5,000. In Ashton 76% of the male working population were employed in the mines. In Minton, in the 18-25 age group with which the survey was concerned, under 30% worked at the pit. In many practical ways the lives of two such contrasting places and periods must be very different, but when I re-read *Coal is our Life* after being in Minton I was continually reminded of phrases and stories and attitudes which I had met only a few days before.

As an outsider it seems to me that three main ingredients compose the culture of a mining community; the danger of the work, the turbulent history of the industry and its present uncertainty, and the imposition of shift work on a large proportion of the community.

The outsider thinking of danger thinks immediately of the pit disaster; the single dramatic episode which for a few days makes headline news and arouses a national wave of pity and concern. Our attention is distracted and we forget. Understandably those working in the mines cannot forget. The daily pithead search for combustibles is a constant reminder of what could happen and sometimes there is a widow in the next street to provide an occasional reminder of what has happened. This is the dramatic side, but at a more mundane level it is a working life made up of personal injury and day-to-day near misses. Outside the pit conversation is studded with joking references to the trepanner which went out of control or the runaway tub which scattered the night shift. A gallery where somebody is buried nearly every day of the week might be grimly dismissed with the words, 'They'll close that bloody gallery when someone gets killed.'

The every-day danger of the job gives rise to attitudes, often complex and conflicting, which permeate the life of the community at all levels. Work is dangerous and hard and uncomfortable and nobody wants to work in the pit. The authors of *Coal is Our Life* illustrate this attitude with a story about shift work. A group of miners were arguing about which was the best shift to work and individuals put forward their personal arguments in favour of each of the three shifts. But the whole group acclaimed the man who clinched the discussions with, 'If you're anything like me, you don't like any bloody shift.' Whether this was an actual incident the authors observed or a conversational story current in Ashton at the time of their study there, is not clear from the text. Interestingly I can match this story with one I found circulating in Derbyshire some twelve years later. A young miner whose absenteeism was such that he was only working three out of the five shifts every week was summoned to the Coal Board Offices at Bolsover to explain himself. 'But why do you only put in three shifts a week?' asked the puzzled manager.

'Because I can't bloody well manage on two!' was the reply. Such stories, and there are dozens of them, are told with enormous glee by the miners themselves. They are an affirmation of the working code. One works in order to be able to enjoy not working. Often the miner is genuinely puzzled over the public attitude towards absenteeism at holiday times. Why on earth should one go to work if there is enough money left to enjoy a holiday?

The danger and toughness of the job give rise to other attitudes also. It is a man's job and there is still pride in it as such. Thus the miner may strongly urge his son not to work in the pit, because of the danger, discomfort and insecurity of the job, and yet at the same time lose sympathy with the boy who 'doesn't know what real work is' and whose different attitudes and habits show his 'cissy' ways. Similarly so gruelling a job is seen as deserving its rewards and great emphasis is placed on this. There is little sympathy for the wife who does not respect her miner husband's right to enjoy his leisure, even though her own leisure life may be severely curtailed. Only slowly are these attitudes breaking down. A wife would still not normally expect her husband to be much concerned with 'woman's work', and other men would tend to look down on any man who knuckled under in this respect.

The history of the mining industry is a history of exploitation, poverty, strikes and unemployment. In Minton Miners' Welfare I heard the phrase 'never had it so good' used to describe the miners' lot today and although in many ways this may be true, it is equally true that the past is not forgotten. Often I have heard people say, 'My old man went to that pit five days a week all his life and most weeks he was damned lucky if he worked two.' Although the younger people largely reject the past as something irrelevant to them and their future they cannot live in a mining community without being aware of it. The legacy of the past is not a specific fear that the thirties will be repeated so much as a generalized attitude towards a 'they' who have shown that they are not to be trusted and relied upon. The present insecurity in the industry heightens this distrust and many miners look cynically upon the assurances of government and coal board. At practical attempts to re-assure him of the future of his pit the miner grows ribald. Improvements to N.C.B. property, putting toilets in the houses or building a new pit head bath for example, he regards as an indication of imminent pit closure. For many perhaps, the future is too frightening to respond to other than with laughter. A planned redundancy may be a bulwark against a repetition of the past rigours of unemployment, but for some the prospect of moving, with all the attendant disruption of long-established friendship and family ties, is every bit as frightening as unemployment. Between pit closure on the one hand and automation on the other, the future looks bleak in many places. Minton itself is a 'long life' colliery, but though the assurances have been made they have only partly allayed the traditional distrust. 'That's what they say now' and 'We've heard all this before' were two of the responses I heard.

Shift work contributes powerfully to the culture of the locality and affects far more people than those directly involved in it. For the young child there is a whole week when 'dad' is not there at all, followed by a week when seemingly he is there all the time. There are times for playing and times for being sent out to play because 'he' must not be woker. Courtship, too, bows to the odd hours of shift work giving the girl a boy friend who cannot be with her on the weekday evenings of one week in the three, and who during another must leave her each night before ten in order to go to work. The total domestic arrangements of marriage, the loving, the sleeping, the eating and the playing, hinge upon the man's hours of work. Even with extra-marital sexual activity it is shift work which has largely determined the form it takes in shift work areas. The club comedian's 'When is your hubby on nights, love?' is only funny because it is also quite realistically the 'fancy man's' opening gambit.

Mining is a shift work occupation and in looking at a mining community we can see the way the shift work routine permeates all aspects of life. Although the majority are not directly involved in it, there may be few whose lives, through their families, their lovers or their friends, remain quite untouched by it. Shift work was one of the subjects touched on by the survey and many of the comments made to the interviewers revealed the extent of its influence on the community.

The survey

The survey itself was designed to find out how the 18-25 year old residents of the village I have just described spend their leisure time. Attempting to reach the total population the team interviewed 76% of the people between 18 and 25 living in Minton in February and March 1968. As a basis for the interviews they used a nine page interview schedule with fifty main questions concerned with work and leisure activities. The questions are almost entirely of a factual nature, but the interviewers were encouraged not to be over-rigid in their use of the schedule, to ask supplementary questions and to note extraneous comment. Some were more able to do this than others, but it is clear that the best of the interviews were conducted as conversations and they produced a picture of the leisure lives of the people interviewed which was both colourful and factually detailed.

The people

The actual 18-25 year old population of Minton was established by visiting each of the eleven hundred dwellings in the village. Of 203 people traced in this way it was possible to interview 157. The remainder are accounted for as follows. The team were unable to contact nineteen people after a succession of house calls spread over four weeks. Three house calls was the minimum made in attempting to secure an interview, but in most cases far more calls were made before the attempt at interview was abandoned. The number of refusals was twenty-seven, and it is possible to break these down into specific and non-specific refusals. The first group of eight was composed of five girls who were pregnant but unmarried and who, understandably, were not anxious to discuss their recent leisure activities; and three men, two of whom had disabilities and one of whom was coping with a recent family bereavement. At reasons for refusal among the second, and larger, group of nineteen one can only guess. Some, doubtless, could just 'not be bothered', but in many instances I suspect that refusal resulted from the fact that we were unfortunate in following into the village a group of high pressure magazine subscription salesmen who apparently gained access to their customers by posing as students on a goodwill mission. What is interesting, in view of the age group with which we were concerned, is that a number of the non-specific refusals were the result of parental intervention. This was something with which student interviewers of the same age as their interviewees were generally unable to cope.

The 157 completed schedules I broke down into six groups which I have used in most of the tables.

Table 1 Classification by marital state

Single women*	34	
Married women	13	
Married women with family	22	
		69 women
Single men	68	
Married men	8	
Married men with family	12	
		88 men
Total interviewed	157	

*The one unmarried mother in the group I have included with the married women with family as her leisure activities showed that she fitted most naturally into this group.

For most purposes this division by marital status proved more useful than division into age groups. The age bracket 18-25 covers a period which for many people encompasses dramatic changes in

Table 2 Details of the ages of the 18-25s interviewed in Minton

Age	Single women	Married women	Married women with family	Single men	Married men	Married men with family	Total	
18	17	2	2	20	0	0	41	⎤
19	7	0	3	18	0	0	28	⎬ 80
20	2	1	0	7	0	1	11	⎦
21	4	2	3	7	2	0	18	⎤
22	1	2	1	6	1	2	13	⎥
23	0	1	7	7	1	3	19	⎬ 77
24	3	5	6	3	4	6	27	⎦
Total number in each category	34	13	22	68	8	12	157	

their way of life. On balance marriage and the arrival of a family of one's own bring greater changes than does the passage of a few years. The unmarried 18-year-old woman may well have more in common with the unmarried 24-year-old than she will with the married woman of her own age with a young baby.

The years within the age bracket 18-25 were by no means evenly represented in the group interviewed. This is illustrated in Table 2.

The total population figures for Minton have shown little variation since 1890 and this suggests some drift from the village. Certainly, we found plenty of evidence of population movement among the age group with which we were concerned. Marriage was a common reason and in Minton the mean age of marriage for girls is about twenty and a half, some two years below the national mean age for women. The men too tend to marry early by national standards. Some of these marriages bring new people into the village, but it seems more move away. Also notably absent from our group were those whose training or further education commitments took them away from the village. In a sense these are still residents of the village, returning for at least part of their long college holidays, but from those I wrote to it seems that few will again live permanently in Minton. A larger group is made up of those who go into the armed services for a period. Many of these certainly return to settle in Minton. We spoke to some who had been through this period and I wrote to others who definitely intended to return.

One interviewee said to his interviewer, 'Eighteen to twenty-fives: you won't find many of those in Minton. They're all getting out.' There is more than a germ of truth in this. It seems that many people in the age group go away, for some reason or other, at least for a time. I had references to thirty-six individuals who had moved within the previous year or so, four more who had moved with their families and two girls of whom their parents had lost all trace. As a part balance to this we found that not all the people we interviewed were born and bred Mintonians though the new-comers all tended to be at the upper end of our age bracket. Generally it was pit closures in other parts of the country which had brought them to Minton.

To establish the social class divisions among the interviewed group I used the Registrar General's classification. As might be expected the majority of the group fell into classes three (skilled workers) and four (semi-skilled workers) with 78 in class three and 33 in class four. A more useful picture emerged when I used the Registrar General's classification into socio-economic groups and this is the table which is reproduced.

Of course, with groups four, five and nine many of the people included were trainees for occupations in these groups rather than

Table 3 Classification of the 18-25s according to socio-economic groups

Registrar General's classification	Single women	Married women	Married women with family	Single men	Married men	Married men with family	Total
Group							
1-3 Employers and Managers. Professional workers, self-employed							
4 Professional workers, employees				1			1
5 Intermediate non-manual workers	5			2	2		9
6 Junior non-manual workers	19	9	1	6		1	36
7 Personal Service workers	3						3
8 Foremen and Supervisors, manual							
9 Skilled manual workers				16	5	7	28
10 Semi-skilled manual workers	3	1	1	21		3	29
11 Unskilled manual workers				10		1	11
12 Own account workers (other than professional)				1	1		2
13 Farmers. Employers and Managers							
14 Farmers. Own account							
15 Agricultural workers				4			4
16 Armed Forces							
17 Occupations inadequately described							
Economically Inactive Groups							
Unemployed	2			3			5
Student	2			4			6
Housewife		3	20				23
Total in each category	34	13	22	68	8	12	157

fully established workers. Some may change their occupations before their training is completed, or, in the case of the four single girls training to be nurses for example, marry before becoming qualified.

An interesting feature of the table is the number of girls in group six; the group for junior non-manual workers. Most of these are girls working in offices. In many cases they work longer hours for less pay than the girls who work in factories. Yet throughout the area as a whole office work for girls seems very highly regarded. Advertisements for office jobs often attract a large number of applicants. At the same time most of the factories employing women always have some vacancies, and casual observation suggests that the average age of the women employed in the factories is considerably higher than in the offices. Certainly it seems that office work is the first choice of many young women and a choice which, with the growth of services in the area, they have been able to exercise.

The men's occupations range more widely and we met lorry drivers and labourers, clerks and farmworkers, plumbers, butchers and greengrocers as well as the skilled and semi-skilled men in the pits or in engineering who made up the majority. A very rough breakdown of the occupations of the employed males in the group appears as Table 4 below.

Table 4   Occupations of employed male workers

Minton colliery	
(underground and pit top workers)	27%
Engineering	
(all types of work)	23%
Building	9%
Retail trades	7%
Clerical work	5%
Agriculture	4%
All other workers	23%
Unemployed	2%

Although only 27% work at the pit Minton Colliery still dominates the employment scene for the eighteen to twenty-fives in Minton. The 23% engaged in some form of engineering work are employed in a mass of different ways in a great number of different places. The smallness of the groups in the other classifications and the size of the 'all other workers' category indicate the diversity of employment among the remainder.

To sum up. The people we interviewed in Minton were all between eighteen and twenty-five. There were more eighteen year olds than any other age year and more under twenty-one than over twenty-one. The eighteen, nineteen and twenty-four year olds were better represented than the twenty to twenty-threes. There were more men than women in the group and more single people than married, though among the women the numbers of married and unmarried were equal. In social class most of the group fell into groups three (skilled workers) and four (semi-skilled workers) with minorities in group two (intermediate) and the group five (unskilled). Most of the men were employed in skilled or semi-skilled jobs in the pit or in what might be very broadly called 'engineering' and most of the women had chosen office work. There were minorities in the intermediate occupations like nursing or teaching and minorities too in the unskilled occupations. The married women without children tended to work unless they were pregnant, but the married women with children did not generally work. Thus within a small age range we met and talked with an enormous diversity of people; a group about whose leisure activities sweeping generalizations might prove dangerously misleading.

Work

My main concern in the survey in Minton was to learn something of the leisure occupations of a particular age group living in a particular sort of community. It will have already been noticed that the team devoted some time to enquiring about the work habits of the group with which we were concerned. It is a truism to note that work and leisure are interrelated. One way of defining leisure is simply to say that it is non-working time and in common speech the word often means just this, but a conversation with someone about their leisure lives would soon reveal a mass of sub-divisions ('working' on the car, 'working' in the garden) to each of which a different, and individual, leisure value might be attributed. Those writing about leisure have explored the relationship between work and leisure in a variety of ways. For example, some have examined the way leisure supplements the working life, others the way leisure might compensate for a working life that was unsatisfactory.

My concern with work in the Minton survey was at a much simpler level. I was interested mainly in finding out how much non-working time people had and into which periods of the day and week it fell. I wanted to know about the incidence of shift work and the timings of the shifts people worked. I wanted to know who worked overtime and when, about the frequency of weekend work and how much time each day was taken with the business of travelling to and from work. I was interested mainly in availability for leisure. Information about this practical aspect of the relationship between work and leisure might, it seemed to me, at least make possible some intelligent guesswork about the reasons for the use or non-use of some forms of leisure provision.

An advertisement in the London Underground reads, 'Two more living hours every day—Live and work out of London'. This sentiment would be endorsed by the people we talked to in Minton who generally seem to spend very little of their lives travelling to and from work. Only eighteen spend more than half an hour getting to work or to their school or college. For the rest, the time spent in this way is under half an hour and for many a matter of a few minutes. The full picture is shown in Table 5

Table 5   Travelling time

Time taken each day travelling to work, school or college. The unemployed gave the time taken to their last place of employment.	Single women	Married women	Married women with family	Single men	Married men	Married men with family	Total
Under ½ hr	27	10	2	56	8	10	113
½ hr - 1 hr	7			6		1	14
1 - 1½ hrs				3		1	4
Varies				3			3
Housewife		3	20				23
Total in category	34	13	22	68	8	12	157

If for only a minority does travel time make incursions into living time one might expect the effects of overtime to be more widespread. In fact, of the 123 in full-time paid employment 71 work some overtime at some periods, but only fourteen work more than five hours overtime regularly each week. Twenty-two work something between one and five hours overtime per week and for the remainder overtime occurs less often than weekly. So although overtime working is common practice it does not necessarily involve the workers in long or inconvenient hours of work. Much of the overtime worked is simply a continuance of an actual working week of forty or forty-two hours of which only thirty-six or thirty-eight hours are paid at the basic rate.

A factor which might be of more importance to a study of leisure is the incidence of weekend work. Of the 123 in full-time paid employment the majority, seventy-eight, are involved in some work at weekends. In some cases this is a regular weekly commitment and in some cases the commitment is a heavy one.

Table 6 Frequency of weekend work

	Single women	Married women	Married women with family	Single men	Married men	Married men with family	Total
No regular weekend work	14	5	0	19	3	2	43
Work every Saturday morning	7	2	1	17	4	5	36
Work all day every Saturday	6	2	1	6	0	1	16
Work every Saturday and Sunday morning	0	0	0	5	0	2	7
Work some part of weekend once a month or more often, but less often than weekly.	1	1	0	10	1	2	15
Work weekends less than once a month	2	0	0	2	0	0	4
Some seasonal weekend work	0	0	0	2	0	0	2
Total in full-time paid employment	30	10	2	61	8	12	123

It is possible to make some definite, if rather limited and negative, statements about weekend work and leisure. We can see from the table that there are twenty-four single men and women whose work precludes them from the Saturday morning shopping expedition. In this area, as in others, this is not a wholly trivial social event for many single people and has a function similar to that of the post-siesta parade in a Spanish village. We can see that a further twelve men and women miss the afternoon edition of the same event. A total of sixteen people can neither play nor watch Saturday afternoon sport. For a small minority, seven men, the joys of Saturday night may be inhibited by the prospect of work on Sunday morning. For the majority any weekend leisure event involving the whole weekend would present difficulties. Probably individuals are able to make special arrangements for special events, but it is the majority, not just a minority, who normally have to work some part of every weekend.

Shift work on the other hand directly affects only a minority, though, as I suggested earlier, its indirect effects may be widespread.

Of the forty-two women in full-time employment only four (9%) were in any way involved in shift work. Of these three were nurses and one worked in a family business. Of the eighty-one men, twenty-seven (32%) worked in jobs involving shift work. Most of these (twenty-one) worked at the colliery. The six others were involved in different occupations: two signalmen, a welder, a quarryman, an iron worker and a steel press operator. With two exceptions, the British Railways signalmen, they all worked the three shift system with the shift changes falling at the weekends. The times of the shifts worked all followed roughly the same pattern; 6.00 a.m.-2.00 p.m., 2.00 p.m.-10.00 p.m. and 10.00 p.m.-6.00 a.m. There would be minor variations of this according to the job done. For example, a common N.C.B. shift arrangement at Minton colliery would be: 6.30 a.m.-1.45 p.m., 1.45 p.m.-9.00 p.m. and 10.00 p.m.-5.15 a.m.

It is easy to imagine the effect of these working hours on the leisure lives of the people involved. Going out on a weekday evening, visiting the cinema in a nearby town for example, is confined to one week in three. Commitment to a weekday evening activity which involves regular weekly attendance is, if not out of the question, certainly very difficult. For example, the shift worker who belonged to a drama group would have to have special rehearsal arrangements made for him. The shift worker who belonged to any activity group where progressions in skill were involved would have to be content to progress less rapidly than the regular weekly attenders. If there were instruction then the instructor would have to be prepared to cope with someone who was always a number of stages behind the rest and so on. These are not insurmountable obstacles and the exceptional individual who is particularly strongly motivated will always find means of carrying on with his class or continuing his group membership. But for the majority there are two obvious alternatives; either to avoid altogether activities involving this sort of commitment or to find a group in which the majority of members are shift workers and where the group organization is geared to their needs.

For the shift worker the odd hours his work involves are not all on the debit side. For example, there is always some weekday leisure time in daylight hours—even in winter. There is the chance to spend time with the young children during their waking hours, a thing many commuters know only at weekends. There is time for the garden, domestic affairs, hobbies. To some these advantages may outweigh the disadvantages. What I want to stress here is simply that the shift worker leads a different life from the non-shift worker. Some of the implications of this difference will be discussed later.

Going out

There are some interestingly divergent popular images of young adults in our society. Some would seem to see them as a brightly and expensively-dressed clan caught up in a vortex of frenetic (and usually immoral) fun making. For others they are a serious lot, the moral conscience of the age, engaged in politics and demonstration, social welfare and community construction, leading us all to a bright new era. The only common ground for these, and some other images, is in the implied suggestion that the young adult group is an active one. If there is disagreement about what it is doing there is at least agreement that it is doing something. The examples I have given may be ludicrous, but they would seem far less ludicrous to many people than the image of the young adult sitting quietly at home watching his telly and reading his paper.

There is some sound statistical support for the idea that as a whole young adults are an active age group; or at least that they are more active than other age groups. In 1965 the B.B.C. Audience Research Department published a work called *The People's Activities*[2] which dealt with the activities of a national sample divided into the age groups 15-24, 25-44, 45-64 and over 65. The 15-24s were more likely to be out of the house at any given time of day than members of the other age groups. As long ago as 1954 a survey in Derby[3] showed that the 16-24 age group were the most frequent users of both the cinemas and the public libraries and the survey hinted at a change in the clientele of public houses. From these and other studies we can see that as a group young adults are out and about more than other age groups. But if this is the general situation what about the specific? Common-sense would suggest certain hypotheses about variations within the age bracket. We would suppose that young marrieds might go out less often than young unmarrieds, that those with young children might go out less than those without and so on. What common-sense ought also to suggest to us is the possibility of wide local variations in the extent of social activity both for the age group and for the community as a whole. All I can try to do is to fill in a little of the detail on a vast and varied canvas.

How frequently do the 18-25 year olds in Minton go out? The group interviewed were asked which evenings of the week they usually spent at home and which evenings they always tried to go out. The combined answers to these two questions give some indication of the frequency of going 'out' and appear as Table 7 below.

The common-sense hypotheses of the difference between the single, married and family groups are supported by the table. It suggests too something of the differences in the leisure lives of married men and married women; of the sort of cultural pattern I

83

Table 7 No. of evenings per week on which 18-25s always try to go 'Out'

No. of evenings	Single women	Married women	Married women with family	Single men	Married men	Married men with family	Total
None	8	2	13	3	2	5	33
One	1	3	5	5	1	0	15
Two	6	2	3	9	2	5	27
Three	8	4	1	8	2	1	24
Four	3	0	0	14	0	1	18
Five	2	0	0	8	0	0	10
Six	1	0	0	9	1	0	11
Seven	2	0	0	12	0	0	14
Varies too much to say	3	2					5
Total number in each category	34	13	22	68	8	12	157

described briefly at the beginning of the chapter. Of course, the table might give only a rough assessment of how often people think they go out. The phrasing of the questions, 'usually at home', 'try to go out', were invitations to guess, and this is what the interviewees did. Few of us, I imagine, run our leisure lives with such clock-work regularity that we can speak of what we 'usually' do on each day of the week with any degree of confidence. We would, however, guess obligingly for an interviewer.

The interviewers pressed their questions, read back the replies to the questions about 'usually at home' and 'try to go out', and then asked the interviewees to say with regard to the remaining evenings whether on these evenings they would be 'more often' at home or out. This whole process does seem to have encouraged people to think harder about their answers and some slightly modified their original responses. Some who originally said they never went out decided that there were some evenings on which they were more often out than not. Conversely others decided that although they sometimes went out on a particular evening they were, on balance, more likely to be at home that evening than out. The total number of people in each category more likely to be out than at home each evening of the week is shown below in Table 8.

Table 8 No. of 18-25s more likely to be out than at home on each evening of the week

Days of the week	Single women	Married women	Married women with family	Single men	Married men	Married men with family	Total
Monday	4	0	0	25	1	3	33
Tuesday	7	1	2	34	1	5	50
Wednesday	6	4	0	21	1	3	35
Thursday	8	2	0	30	1	2	43
Friday	12	0	3	43	2	3	63
Saturday	21	3	2	49	4	5	84
Sunday	15	1	3	40	4	3	66
Never go out	6	3	14	4	2	4	33
Varies too much to say	6	5	2	7	2	0	22
Total number in each category	34	13	22	68	8	12	157

The number of people who said it varied too much to say is really surprisingly small and very few of the people who responded in this way were shift workers. This is probably because the shift work variation is such a commonplace, self-evident variation to the people subject to it, that it is not for them a matter of comment. Where reasons for the variation were mentioned they referred to husband's or boy-friend's shifts or the variable mid-week day off.

To Tables 7 and 8 it is possible to add another factor. At a later point in the interview the people interviewed were asked to say how they had spent their time during the morning, afternoon and evening of the previous seven days. From this we can see how many evenings they spent out during that week. In Table 9 I have compared the information from Table 7 with the number of evenings the interviewees actually went out in the week previous to their being interviewed.

There are some interesting minor variations between the two sets of figures, but over all they follow each other quite closely. Naturally enough the previous week was not 'normal' for everyone. Some were less than normally socially active because of winter colds, others more so because of some special event in their lives. Two of the people we talked to had married during the previous seven days and others had been involved in other important events, like buying houses or losing jobs, which had had particular effects on their lives during that week.

Table 9   No. of evenings 'Out'—Assessed and actual

The top line of figures repeat Table 7. Below are the number of interviewees who actually went out or not on evenings during the week immediately previous to their being interviewed. *No. of evenings*	*Single women*	*Married women*	*Married women with family*	*Single men*	*Married men*	*Married men with family*	*Total*
None	8	2	13	3	2	5	33
	5	6	11	8	1	6	37
One	1	3	5	5	1	0	15
	4	0	7	4	1	0	16
Two	6	2	3	9	2	5	27
	4	3	2	8	1	4	22
Three	8	4	1	8	2	1	24
	9	0	2	10	0	1	22
Four	3	0	0	14	0	1	18
	7	2	0	15	3	0	27
Five	2	0	0	8	0	0	10
	3	0	0	11	1	1	16
Six	1	0	0	9	1	0	11
	1	1	0	4	0	0	6
Seven	2	0	0	12	0	0	14
	1	1	0	8	1	0	11
Varies too much to say	3	2					5
Total number in each category	34	13	22	68	8	12	157

Of course frequency of going out is a very crude measure of leisure activity; but it does tell us some things. For example, so far as the 18-25s in Minton are concerned, we can certainly dismiss the notion of a group of people who are out and about every evening of the week. The majority of the age group go out two, three or four evenings a week with only a minority going out six or seven evenings and a large minority who do not, on a weekly basis, go out on weekday evenings at all. Table 8 echoes the old trad jazz number, 'Everybody loves the Saturday Night' and shows, as we would expect, that Friday, Saturday and Sunday are the most popular nights for going out. I have already mentioned the common-sense differences between the different categories and the table both illustrates this and raises some interesting questions. The unmarried men are the group who go out most often, but we can see that even this group, taken as a whole, are not so very active. There may be only three who would expect not to go out at all and a sizeable minority (twelve) who expect to go out every night, but in the week previous to being interviewed there were in fact as many single males who did not go out at all, as who went out every night of the week. With regard to another group, the married women with children whom the survey shows as going out least frequently, the tables may suggest to us questions like, 'Does this matter?', 'What do they feel about it?' and many others.

Such questions as these were outside the scope of the interview which in any case did not touch on matters of attitude at all. None the less, attitudes were often very apparent during interviews and sometimes made a considerable impression on the interviewers. One striking example of this was the impression made by the interviewers' contact with the married women with young children. The comments of the interviewers when I talked to them about this were as much concerned with the attitudes which had been expressed as with the information they had elicited. It was not simply that some of the young mothers seemed to lead very limited social lives, but also that sometimes they themselves resented this and communicated their resentment to the interviewer. Sometimes it seemed that the interview itself with all its questions detailing the possibilities of a full leisure life exacerbated the situation. I interviewed one young mother-to-be whose expressions of envious resentment of her single friends grew quite alarming as the interview progressed. 'You want to talk to so and so and her lot about that. I don't do nothing like that. Not now', she exclaimed hotly at one point in tones which dripped envy. A number of the interviewers said they felt an acute embarrassment sitting and adding to growing lists of seemingly desirable activities in which their interviewee no longer took part. The cumulative effect of this too, seemed occasionally to act as an irritant. One interviewer, after an interview with a young couple, was shown to the door with the words, 'And I hope to God you do more with your life than we seem to.' Of course far from everyone responded in this way, but the impression of the interviewers was that these were the feelings of a substantial number.

One of the problems for couples with young families everywhere is that of finding baby-sitters. It is sometimes asserted that one of the advantages of the established working class community is that with mother down the street and Aunty Mabel round the corner there is always someone to mind the baby. So far as we could tell this seemed not to be the common situation in Minton. Certainly there were cases where relatives lived close by and were visited during the day, but it was often the same people who specifically mentioned the difficulty of finding anyone to baby-sit in the evenings. Neither did the interviewers find any evidence of the sort of reciprocal baby-sitting arrangements which are sometimes a feature of middle-class communities. Such arrangements do not grow easily in a community with a proud tradition of 'keeping oneself to oneself'.

Perhaps it would be wrong to give much weight to the impressions we received while interviewing. These were not, after all, the matters about which we were making specific enquiries. However, there is the very common assumption that for young mothers the business of home-building and family rearing is so totally absorbing and fulfilling that their leisure needs in all other respects can be disregarded. What all of us who were concerned in interviewing in Minton came to feel was that, at very least, this assumption should be questioned.

6 Young adults, work and leisure in Minton: part II

'He just sleeps here, that's all'—a Minton mother

It is difficult to classify the many activities which come under the general heading of 'going out' and I have attempted little by way of such a classification in this chapter. It is true there are certain sorts of practical distinctions which can be very helpful; like those between activities which cost money and those which do not, between activities based in the locality and those involving travel, between solitary activities and those undertaken in groups. But distinctions like these are likely to occur to all who read this book and to construct a system of classification from them is to run the danger of over-emphasizing factors which may not be of great importance in themselves.

More sophisticated systems of classification, distinctions between degrees of passivity and activity for example, presuppose an analytical purpose which is not central to my theme. It is worth stressing here that my purpose, at this stage, is to describe rather than to analyse and my general comments are intended to be explanatory rather than interpretive. The subject in focus is the leisure activities of a group of young adults in Minton. Clearly some of these activities are 'more important', however that may be defined, than are others and I have commented on certain aspects of 'importance' where it seemed this might be helpful. What I have tried to avoid, however, is any suggestion that the arrangement of material in this chapter implies a value system of its own. There has been no intention on my part to move from the trivial to the profound, from minority interests to popular pursuits or to follow any other significant and judgmental arrangement.

Of course an arrangement of some sort has to be followed. I have started with home visiting because this seemed the most logical next step from the last chapter. I then deal with a number of specific activities, with leisure spending and transport and conclude with educational classes and the membership of clubs and societies.

Visiting in Minton

Visiting provides a very good example of the classification difficulties I have just mentioned. The term 'visiting' covers a complex of activities carried out in a variety of social contexts with such a range of possible motives and degrees of engagement that even the most stringent observation and analysis could hardly unravel all the finer points of the game. Certainly in Minton we came across many different forms of visiting and their treatment here is a very superficial one.

It was interesting that the interviewees themselves did not generally distinguish between friends and relatives and so both are included under the general heading of visiting friends. For this reason it can be taken that much of the visiting by married people is the visiting of relatives, and with this section of the population this is particularly true of the visiting which takes place at weekends. We had many references to this.

Generally the long hours of visiting arose in the case of courting couples where as many as forty hours a week may be spent in this way. One couple spent one weekend with the parents of one of them and the next weekend with the parents of the other and so on throughout the year. Of the thirty-four single women eighteen had a 'steady' boy friend at the time of the interview and of the sixty-eight single men twenty-seven had a steady girl friend. Therefore home visiting, or being visited, for the purpose of courting was a possibility for over half the girls and over a third of the men. It seems helpful to bear this in mind when looking at Table 10 below.

The table tells us that just over a third of the people we interviewed do not visit friends in their homes and that just under two thirds do visit friends for periods varying between one and forty hours per week. This is really as far as the evidence will take us. The gratuitous comments which were received and noted during the course of the interviews suggested the sort of interpretation at which I have already hinted. Much of the visiting by married couples was family visiting either during the day if the family lived close by or at the weekend if they lived further afield. With single people some of the visiting, and particularly the extensive visiting, was in connection with courting. This extensive visiting involved only a minority. Although there were twenty-five people who visited for more than ten hours a week there were only nine of these who visited for more than twelve hours. Some of the visiting was intensive, but irregular. 'When my friends are home on leave I'm round there all the time.' Much of the visiting was casual, 'He comes round and

Table 10 Time spent visiting friends in their homes

No. of hours per week	Single women	Married women	Married women with family	Single men	Married men	Married men with family	Total	% of Total Group	
1-3	6	3	6	17	0	3	35	22%	⎫
4-6	6	3	4	12	2	2	29	18.4%	⎪ 65%
7-9	2	2	0	8	1	0	13	8.2%	⎬
10 or more	7	2	4	10	2	0	25	16%	⎭
No visiting	13	3	8	21	3	7	55		35%
Total number in each category	34	13	22	68	8	12	157		100%

we go for a drink.' Surprisingly, very little of the visiting among the single people seemed to be related to shared participation in any planned activity. One man mentioned spending time with friends working on their cars and one schoolboy played football with a friend at his house after school. No other interviewees made references of this sort.

The other side of the coin to visiting is being visited. The details of this are given in Table 11.

As can be seen more people visit than are visited which suggests that perhaps more people go out of the area the survey covered than come into it. It would not really be surprising if young people who have friends in places which have a much wider social provision than Minton (Worksop or Sheffield for example) visited those friends more frequently than they were visited by them. There were some people who visited but who did not receive visitors and some who were visited but did not visit others, but generally speaking visiting was a reciprocal activity. There was twice as much evening visiting as weekend visiting, but a quarter of the group said that it could be either and many of the married couples pointed out that their visiting was mostly daytime visiting either mid-week or at the weekends.

To sum up what has been said about visiting is difficult. Obviously visiting is an important aspect of life for some people. It probably fulfils specially important, though different, functions for the married and the courting and this is probably true everywhere.

Table 11 Time spent being visited by friends at home

No. of hours per week	Single women	Married women	Married women with family	Single men	Married men	Married men with family	Total	
1-3	6	5	6	16	2	5	40	26%
4-6	7	2	4	6	0	0	19	12%
7-9	0	1	0	5	1	0	7	4%
10 or more	5	0	4	12	0	1	22	14%
No time spent being visited by friends	16	5	8	29	5	6	69	44%
Total number in each category	34	13	22	68	8	12	157	100%

For other groups in Minton it seems that it was far less important. The married and the courting knew when and how often they visited; many of the single unattached people had to think hard to decide whether they ever visited anyone or not, and there was very little indication of a home based social life for this section of the population.

Clubs and public houses

For many of the people we talked to much of the ordinary social life of the village centred on the licensed clubs and public houses. Drink was the item of leisure expenditure mentioned by far the most frequently and visiting public houses was the most frequently mentioned leisure activity. Of the 157 people interviewed only eighteen said that they never went to a public house. Table 12 shows how often people said they usually visited public houses and its bottom line shows the number of people in each group who had visited a public house or licensed club during the previous week.

As with all the other activities into which we enquired the actual attendance during the previous week was rather less than the answers to the question 'How often do you ...?' would suggest. As an explanation I would suggest not deception, but self deception. We are sometimes less socially active than we think we are and we are particularly prone to exaggerate at the extremes. Thus 'very often' becomes 'always' and 'rarely' becomes 'never'. With the

Table 12 Frequency of visits to public houses

Frequency of visits	Single women	Married women	Married women with family	Single men	Married men	Married men with family	Total
Seven times per week or more often	0	1	0	8	1	0	
Six times per week	0	0	0	3	0	0	
Five times per week	1	0	0	7	0	0	
Four times per week	2	0	0	11	1	1	
Three times per week	5	2	0	13	1	2	
Twice per week	4	1	0	5	3	2	
Once per week	6	3	6	10	0	3	
Three times per month	2	0	1	0	0	1	
Twice per month	5	1	2	0	1	1	
Once per month	0	1	3	2	0	0	
Rarely (i.e. less often than once per month)	3	3	5	4	1	1	
Never	6	1	5	5	0	1	
Total in each category	34	13	22	68	8	12	
No. of interviewees who visited a public house in the week before they were interviewed	16	3	3	46	2	4	74

single people we talked to the exaggerations would probably tend to the positive side because for this group particularly it is fashionable to be socially active.

Even if public house visiting is not quite as common as some of those involved imagine it to be, it is still by far and away the most indulged-in social activity into which we enquired. There are several reasons why this should be so and some are worth a brief mention. To begin with of course it must be borne in mind that pub visiting is not an activity which excludes others. In many cases the pub is an adjunct to other things. The session in the pub while the dance warms up or the quick pint after the cinema are simple examples. In cases where an activity is held on pub premises it is hardly possible to make distinction between different sorts of activities. If a pub runs a Bingo session do the people who attend go to Bingo or go to a pub which has a special attraction on that particular night? If there is a discotheque on pub premises do people go to the discotheque or choose that pub in preference to others because it provides a particular sort of setting and attracts a particular sort of clientele? And how does one describe this activity? 'going to Bingo'? or 'I always go up the "Crown" on Tuesdays'? There exist here large areas where distinctions are blurred and many of the people we talked to would, doubtless, interpret what superficially is the same activity, very differently indeed. This, of course, is true of much social, recreational activity. One can go to the cinema to do one's courting, to see the film, or simply because it is wet outside. But there are some respects in which the pub differs from other, specific, social activities; notably its flexibility as a social institution, even the cost of which is in the hands of the user, not the proprietor.

So far as Minton is concerned availability is undoubtedly a factor in the use made of public houses and clubs. This is rather more than a polite way of saying that there is not much else, though this blunter statement may be true enough also. Seven days a week, every lunch time and evening, all through the year, the pub is there. The doors are as open to the man scratting among his small change for the price of a pint on a Thursday night as they are for the big spender at the weekend. There is no question of having to get there in time for the start of the big picture, or of having to stay long enough to get one's money's worth. These are important considerations when work means finishing late or starting early or when the cost of travelling for entertainment makes the difference between going out or staying in.

However, if the pubs attract a reasonable custom it is not solely because the use of other forms of provision is sometimes difficult. They deserve some credit in their own right. The public house can be many different things; it can be a Bingo saloon, dance hall or Athenaeum—all at the same time if it is big enough, and certainly on successive evenings. Perhaps pubs in some areas are never any of these things, but the pubs and clubs of north-east Derbyshire are particularly rich and varied in the provision they afford.

At the time of the survey Minton had seven public houses and three licensed clubs. The most palatial of these is the Miners' Welfare with bar facilities which would credit a first class hotel and an excellent concert room. The others vary from the comfortable and well-appointed to the undeniably third rate. While their relative success depends on a number of factors, geographical situation is, understandably, an important one. As I said earlier the total population of Minton has shown little change since the 1890s, but the same population existed then in considerably less and more compact housing than the present village comprises. Rehousing the village has produced an urban development in miniature, with tiny housing estates some way from the village centre and often as much as a mile away from each other. This means that while the local pubs may be valued just because they are local, it is the pubs at the centre of the village which have a particular function as village meeting places. To hark back to the question of home visiting the distances across the village are such that there must be many cases where it is far more reasonable to meet a friend in a centrally placed public house than it is to call on him.

While the physical provision afforded by the public houses varies a good deal the recreational provision has much in common. All the pubs combine in an indoor games league which goes on throughout the winter months. This more advanced version of the darts league was probably started as a co-operative effort by the publicans to ensure that every pub had a 'good night' once in a while. Whatever its origins it works for the consumer and a few of the people we interviewed took part in the league. Games apart, the pubs provide an easy and relaxed atmosphere into which even an outsider can slip very easily.

So far I have made no distinction between the pubs and the licensed clubs, and this chiefly because this distinction was not always made by the people with whom we talked. The clubs, though, do occupy a special position. The Miners' Welfare is more than a drinking club and it can be the heart of a mining community. In Minton it was one of the most prosperous pieces of recreational provision and therefore at the centre of much that happened in the village. It also seemed to me on my occasional visits to be the political centre where union and local affairs went into the melting pot of discussion.

The other licensed clubs too are usually in the position to operate more adventurously than the normal public house. The weekly programme of one of the clubs in Minton includes a night when a visiting group plays for dancing, a night devoted to Bingo and a weekend floorshow. In addition to these regular events there are special attractions for special occasions. The last night of a bank holiday is commonly either 'a cheap beer night', or even 'a free beer night'; a popular move in a community where holiday spending tends to be lavish.

For those who drink outside Minton the choice of provision is of course much wider. Within striking distance there is a choice of clubs offering casino facilities, a restaurant and a nightly revue. In addition many of the pubs offer free entertainment; usually at the weekends. This may be an up and coming local pop group or 'Ron and Marge on drums and organ' and an invitation to a do-it-

95

yourself concert. Some clubs make a special feature of striptease. Some have a monthly 'Stag' night and at least one club in the area thrives solely on its strippers and its casino. At least two pubs in the area have moved into this field and if the strippers are not up to the standards of Soho they have at least the advantage of being on view to anyone with the price of a pint.

I think it would be wrong to suggest either that many of the Minton group exploit the resources afforded by licensed premises in north-east Derbyshire to the full, or that these resources compare with those available in the heart of northern Clubland. What I have tried to suggest is that pub-going is a complex activity with many facets and possibilities. Besides its value as a meeting place, and generally as one of the best equipped meeting places available in the community, it has in this area particularly, a growing importance in the field of recreational provision. Standards vary enormously, but in terms of involvement and skill satisfaction the pub indoor games league would seem to compare very favourably with, say, the small games activities in youth clubs. The pub pop group would be the same group as that which supports the Big Name group which packs the town cinema for a concert. The club entertainers, if not in the first flight, are at least often people on the fringes of the big time, or recognizably on their way up. The point I would make about the pub and club world is that it is not insignificant and it should not be too quickly dismissed or disregarded. The sort of youth leader who worries about losing his older members to the public house ought at least to console himself with the thought that he has not lost out to a wholly unworthy opponent, nor solely to the demon drink.

The cinema

In most cases pub visiting can be measured in terms of the number of visits made each week. What is clear about the other specific activities we investigated is that they generally take place far less frequently than this. With regard to the cinema, for example, a few devotees (eleven of them) said that they went to the pictures every week and two went more often than this, but for the majority it was more a matter of times per year than times per week. A sizeable number go to the pictures about once a month, but for even more the visits are twice monthly or less frequently.

Minton itself has no cinema. The nearest cinemas are in Worksop which is a two and fourpenny bus ride away and to which there is a half hourly bus service. The times of the last buses from Sheffield, Chesterfield or Mansfield preclude evening visits to cinemas in these towns for those who have to rely on public transport. If the cost of

Table 13 Frequency of cinema attendance

Frequency of attendance	Single women	Married women	Married women with family	Single men	Married men	Married men with family
More often than once per week	1	0	0	0	0	1
Once per week	5	1	0	5	0	0
Three times per month	1	0	0	3	1	0
Twice per month	6	0	0	7	0	0
Once per month	4	3	2	21	3	1
Between six times a year and eleven times per year	1	0	1	1	0	0
Between once a year and five times a year	10	7	10	16	1	5
Never	6	2	9	15	3	5
Total in each category	34	13	22	68	8	12
No. of interviewees who visited the cinema in the week before they were interviewed	6	1	0	7	0	0

transport is included then a night at the cinema for two provides little change from a pound note. The difficulty of access, cost and length of time involved in going to the cinema have all increased over the last few years for people who live in places like Minton. A casual, spur of the moment, 'Let's go to the pictures' is hardly possible any longer, because of the money and organization involved. Going to the cinema is becoming more of a 'night out' and this trend is encouraged by the increasing flow of prestige films for which special admission prices are asked. Compared with other age groups the eighteen to twenty-fives go to the cinema frequently, but for Mintonians in this age group the cinema is no longer casual entertainment.

The discotheque

The only workable definition of a discotheque is that a discotheque is anything which calls itself by that name. In north-east Derbyshire, as in other areas, the name has flourished, but there is an almost ludicrous diversity in the situations to which the name is applied. The basic features of a discotheque are that there is music, the opportunity to dance, and an attempt at a decor which involves the use of lighting effects. At its best this means a twin deck record player and expensive amplification equipment, a suitable room and ultra-violet lighting which picks out the special effects in the elaborate and ingenious murals. At worst it means an old and battered juke box blaring out yesterday's hit tunes in a barn-like pub room which is mercifully cloaked in darkness. Refinements may include a resident disc jockey and a 'live' spot to introduce a group with a 'new' sound. Refreshments may be coffee, minerals or alcohol. The charge of admittance may be as much as six or seven shillings or as little as nothing where the landlord relies on the sale of refreshments to provide his income.

The organization of discotheques varies as much as does their physical provision. Some are public dances held in pub rooms. Others are clubs with a tightly uniform clientele which is constantly

Table 14 Frequency of visits to discotheques

Frequency of visits	Single women	Married women	Married women with family	Single men	Married men	Married men with family
More often than once per week	1	0	0	3	0	0
Once per week	4	0	0	6	0	0
Three times a month	1	0	0	0	0	0
Twice a month	3	0	0	4	0	0
Once a month	3	0	2	4	0	1
Between six times a year and eleven times a year	0	0	0	0	0	1
Between once a year and five times a year	2	2	2	6	2	1
Never	20	11	18	45	6	9
Total number in each category	34	13	22	68	8	12
No. of interviewees who visited a discotheque in the week before they were interviewed	1	0	0	1	0	0

being refined by a resident disc jockey who is likely both to arbitrate on matters of musical taste and to influence on matters of fashion, manners and morality.

In spite of the proliferation of discotheques throughout the area as a whole they seem to have very little effect on the people of Minton. Minton itself has no discotheque and a very clear majority of the people we talked to never went to one anywhere. A handful of people went to one once a week or more often and a few more attended occasionally. Most of the users were single people, but some from every category did go sometimes. The full picture of discotheque use is given as Table 14 above.

Bowling and skating

Another form of recreational provision which has come upon the scene in recent years is ten pin bowling. If this has hardly been the success it has been in the United States it has still been the subject of some of the most massive investment in leisure provision which this country has seen for a long time. That this may have been a mistaken investment is indicated by the cutbacks in development programmes announced by some of the sponsoring companies, the reduction of opening hours of some establishments and public announcements as to the uncertain financial status of some others. What is interesting about this is that bowling sometimes seems to be one of those activities which is more desirable in anticipation than it is in reality. Surveys among young people about what facilities they would like to see in their town have often shown bowling near the top of the list.[1] It seems doubtful whether the actual usage of bowling alleys has ever borne much relation to these hopeful forecasts.

In terms of cost bowling is usually less expensive than going to the cinema. A one-game night would cost about six shillings so that even with refreshment the night out could cost well under ten shillings. But for Mintonians bowling is not easily available. At the time of the survey the nearest ten pin bowling centre was Sheffield and this effectively eliminated bowling as an activity for those who had to rely on public transport.

In view of the transport difficulties it might be thought hardly surprising that only a small, and presumably very keen, minority of four went bowling on a weekly basis. Availability though is probably not the whole of the story in this case. The bowling world subdivides itself into two distinct groups; those for whom bowling is a sporting activity and those for whom bowling is a night out. The various leagues organized by the bowling centre managers appeal to a small number for whom bowling is an important activity. For the majority,

99

however, bowling is a part of the social scene. It is somewhere to go; not every week but now and again. It is precisely because it is not done too often and there is no real expertise developed that the activity retains its fun value. The casual user may value the existence of the bowling alley very highly, but what he values is its availability. From his point of view the important quality is that it should be there when it is wanted.

It is easy to see from Table 15 the sort of use the group in Minton made of the bowling centres. Most of them never went bowling at all, but of the single group about half went bowling between one and five times a year.

Table 15 Frequency of visits to a bowling alley and skating rink

Frequency of visits	Single women	Married women	Married women with family	Single men	Married men	Married men with family	Total
More than once per week	0	0	1	0	0	0	1
Once per week	0	0	0	2	0	1	3
Three times a month	0	0	0	1	0	0	1
Twice a month	2	0	0	1	0	0	3
Once a month	4	0	1	9	0	0	14
Between six times a year and eleven times a year	0	3	1	2	1	0	7
Between once a year and five times a year	11	3	1	21	2	2	40
Never	17	7	18	32	5	9	88
Total numbers in each category	34	13	22	68	8	12	157
No. of interviewees who visited a bowling alley and/or skating rink in the week before they were interviewed	0	0	0	7	0	0	7

A word of explanation is needed about the inclusion of skating in this section. The most accessible facilities for these two activities are under the same roof and so the problems of access are the same for each activity. As none of the people we interviewed mentioned skating among their hobbies it seems unlikely that any serious skaters are included in the above table. However, some of the visits detailed above would be accounted for by organized parties run by one or other of the clubs or societies in Minton and on these occasions either, or both, skating and bowling might be on the agenda for the evening.

The cabaret club

Although I have already mentioned cabaret clubs in the section dealing with public houses they are really a specialized form of provision warranting some attention in their own right. Nationally there has been a considerable expansion and development in the club world in recent years and the development has taken the form of a popularization of what was previously the preserve of a wealthy minority. Part of the attraction of this sort of club life is that it seemingly offers an entry into the glamorous world which the heroes and villains of film and television seem so often to inhabit. The provision itself—the food, the drink, the entertainment—has to

Table 16 Frequency of visits to a cabaret club

Frequency of visits	Single women	Married women	Married women with family	Single men	Married men	Married men with family	Total
More often than once per week	0	0	0	0	0	0	0
Once per week	0	1	0	0	0	0	1
Three times a month	0	0	0	0	0	0	0
Twice a month	0	0	0	1	1	0	2
Once a month	1	1	1	5	0	2	10
Between six times a year and eleven times a year	0	1	1	3	0	0	5
Between once a year and five times a year	6	3	8	6	1	6	30
Never	27	7	12	53	5	4	109
Total number in each category	34	13	22	68	8	12	157
No. of interviewees who visited a cabaret club in the week before they were interviewed	1	0	1	0	0	0	2

prove its worth, but the whole is likely to be enhanced by a borrowed glamour.

Among Mintonians the cabaret club has its devotees; though only three attend more often than monthly. However, its most important use seems to be that it affords provision for a special night out on an occasional basis. Cabaret clubs may not be used very frequently but a comfortable minority, nearly thirty per cent, do make some use of this form of provision and the proportion of married users is high.

Dancing

Today it is much more difficult to determine the frequency with which people go to a dance than it would have been ten or fifteen years ago. It is not simply that the discotheque, the pub and the club all make a provision for dancing, but also that in common speech some of the distinctions have become blurred. The phrase 'going to a dance' has a faintly old-fashioned ring to it, but so far as this area is concerned there are still 'dances' and people still go to them.

Table 17   Frequency of going dancing

Frequency of dancing	Single women	Married women	Married women with family	Single men	Married men	Married men with family
More than once per week	0	0	0	3	0	0
Once per week	5	2	2	7	0	0
Three times a month	0	0	0	1	0	0
Twice a month	2	0	0	8	0	1
Between six times a year and eleven times a year	2	2	0	8	1	1
Between once a year and five times a year	11	7	8	18	4	4
Never	14	2	12	23	3	6
Total number in each category	34	13	22	68	8	12
No. of interviewees who went dancing in the week before they were interviewed	6	3	1	13	0	1

Equally though, they would be quite likely to use this phrase to describe dancing in a pub, club or discotheque. An added complication is that dancing classes are often regarded as dances and it seems clear that a number of those who appear in Table 17 as going dancing every week are doing so by attending a weekly dancing class. Table 17 shows how often the people we interviewed dance, but it is not a table which is exclusive of others.

Transport and expenditure

With the exception of visiting friends the sort of activities which have been discussed so far in this chapter might all come under the broad heading of 'entertainment'. What they have in common is that they demand some sort of financial outlay on the part of the user. Some of the activities I shall look at later in the chapter involve expenditure too, but with club or evening class attendance we are perhaps more inclined to consider whether we get a fair return for the effort we expend than we are to consider simply the financial outlay. With the entertainment activities money is important and so perhaps this is a good point at which to pay some attention to the question of expenditure on leisure activities. Tied in with this is the question of transport. I have pointed out that there are no facilities in Minton for some of the activities I have mentioned and so the cost of transport, public or private, may figure significantly

Table 18 Sum of money spent on entertainment each week

Sum of money	Single women	Married women	Married women with family	Single men	Married men	Married men with family	Total
Ten shillings or less	18	7	15	6	1	2	49
About £1	12	0	4	11	3	2	32
About £2	2	4	3	17	1	4	31
About £3	1	1	0	13	2	1	18
About £4	1	0	0	7	0	2	10
About £5	0	0	0	8	1	1	10
Definitely more than £5	0	1	0	6	0	0	7
Total number in each category	34	13	22	68	8	12	157

in leisure expenditure. First of all though let us take a look at the entertainment expenditure.

The group interviewed were asked to estimate how much money they spent each week on sports, entertainments and 'nights out'. Their answers are given in Table 18 above.

With the single girls the expenditure is generally quite small because in many cases the boy friend pays. Similarly with some of the married women we might guess that the sum they spend on entertainment may be quite different from the sum which is spent on their entertainment each week. Most of the men spend two or three pounds a week on entertainment and the number of really heavy spenders

Table 19 Frequency with which different items of 'entertainment' expenditure were mentioned

Type of entertainment on which money was spent	Single women	Married women	Married women with family	Single men	Married men	Married men with family	Total
Drinking	13	8	6	53	6	9	95
Smoking	6	2	4	28	2	5	47
Dancing and entrance fees to discotheques	3	3	0	11	1	0	18
Entrance fees to entertainments (additional to, or distinct from, those already classified in this table)	7	0	2	7	0	1	17
Skating and bowling	2	1	4	2	0	3	12
Cinema	2	2	0	5	1	0	10
Attendance at football matches	0	0	0	9	1	0	10
Food and refreshment in connection with entertainment	3	0	2	3	0	1	9
Gambling	0	0	0	5	0	3	8
Bingo	2	0	1	1	3	0	7
Club fees and entrances	1	2	0	4	0	0	7
Youth clubs	0	0	0	3	0	0	3
Question not answered	10	1	10	1	1	1	24

is very small. There was one single man who spent ten pounds a week on beer and provoked the interviewer to comment, 'Seeing is believing; and, seeing him, I believe.'

In order to find out how this money was spent the interviewees were asked to say which were the three things on which they spent most money. Twenty-four did not answer this question at all; some, like the single girls, because they had no entertainment expenses in their own right; others because they spent next to nothing on entertainment. Many more provided one or two items of entertainment expenditure, but not three. In collating the information from these two questions, therefore, it would be difficult to comment on the relative importance of the different items of expenditure to each individual, but I think we can draw some conclusions from the number of times particular sorts of expenditure are mentioned.

Some indication of the dominance of drinking can be gained from the fact that in sixty-one cases 'pub' or 'drink' was the first item mentioned and in twenty-two of these cases it was the only item mentioned. Whether or not drink really is the major item of leisure expenditure there is no question that it is seen by Mintonians in this light.

So far as specific entertainment expenditure is concerned there is

Table 20 Frequency with which different items of 'other' expenditure were mentioned

Type of 'other' expenditure	Single women	Married women	Married women with family	Single men	Married men	Married men with family	Total
Clothes	28	9	6	40	5	5	93
Transport (details in following tables)							72
Records	11	1	0	15	2	0	29
'Things for the house'	0	7	6	4	3	5	25
Equipment for sports and hobbies	1	0	0	9	3	1	14
Things for 'new baby' or children	0	2	9	0	1	1	13
Hairdressing and cosmetics	7	1	0				8
Savings	3	1	1	2	0	0	7

only one addition to be made to the table. One unmarried man mentioned snooker. All other activities mentioned by the interviewees appear in the table. I have maintained the distinction between 'gambling' and 'Bingo' which appeared in the answers. The 'gambling' category is made up of the answers 'cards', 'fruit machines' and 'gambling', though whether the term 'gambling' here invariably excludes bingo it would be impossible to say.

Following the question about spending on entertainment was one about other major expenditure.

To the items in the table we must add the following: books (3), girl friends (2), holidays (2), football pools (2), sweets (1). Clothes were mentioned first in forty-five cases and in nineteen of these cases clothes were the only item mentioned. The cost of transport too was a very important item and was mentioned first in a total of fifty-six cases. In Table 20 transport only appears as a total because I have devoted some space below to discussing this item in rather more detail. Categories like 'savings' present some difficulties and it seems likely that not all savers would consider this an item of expenditure.

The special case of expenditure on transport is detailed in Table 21 below.

Table 21 Frequency with which transport costs are mentioned

Type of cost incurred	Place on list			Total no. of mentions
	1st	2nd	3rd	
Cost of running motor car	34	4	2	40
Cost of running motor cycle	8	2	2	12
Cost of running scooter	3	0	0	3
Cost of petrol for vehicles owned by others	2	0	0	2
Cost of public transport	9	3	2	14

It is interesting to see that for two girls a major item of their weekly expenditure is the petrol they pour into their boyfriends' cars; but in whatever strange guise it appeared, transport was a major item for many of the Mintonians.

Some of the heaviest transport costs are likely to fall upon those who run a motor vehicle of their own. However, finding out exactly who these people are is not quite the obvious business it would seem to be, because, for practical purposes, 'having' a motor vehicle includes a great many conditions besides outright ownership. In tabling the responses it seemed sensible to include both reasonable access to a family car and joint ownership. One of the more extreme examples of the latter was a fifth share in a van.

Table 22 The number of single people aged 18-25 who 'have' motor vehicles

Type of vehicle	Single women	Single men	Total
Car	2	20	22
Motor cycle	0	10	10
Scooter	2	1	3
None	30	37	67
Total in each category	34	68	102

With the married men and women the position is much more difficult. My assumption would be that the married women answering this question would refer to cars which were joint family possessions and therefore there would be some overlap between some of the married women and their husbands who also answered the same question. But, as this point was not satisfactorily clarified, except in a minority of cases, the interpretation of the responses from the married men and women needs to be a very cautious one.

Table 23 The number of married people aged 18-25 who 'have' motor vehicles

Type of vehicle	Married women	Married women with family	Married men	Married men with family	Total
Car	12	10	6	8	36
Motor cycle	1	1	1	1	4
Scooter	0	0	0	0	0
None	0	11	1	3	15
Total in each category	13	22	8	12	55

In spite of the difficulty mentioned above the table is worth reproducing, because of the interesting difference between married people with and without families in the ownership of motor vehicles. Whatever the various causes may be, it is those couples whose lives are restricted by the need to care for small children who also lack the family mobility afforded by a car.

It is perhaps useful to try to sum up what the tables tell us about leisure and transport expenditure. Under the heading 'entertainment' drink is by far the most frequently mentioned item, not only for the young single men, which we might expect, but for every other category too. While it is not necessarily the item on which most money is spent, there is some ground for supposing that this is so in many cases. Smoking too constitutes an important item of expenditure for all groups, but after this the numbers mentioning the different expenditure items decline dramatically and the overall total of different sorts of entertainment expenditure mentioned is not high.

With other expenditure it is clothes and transport which predominate so far as the single people are concerned and which are very important for all groups though for those with families it is the children or the house which usually take priority.

Just under half the single men have reasonable access to some sort of motor vehicle and cars are twice as popular as motor cycles. Only four of the thirty-four single girls have vehicles of their own, though many have access to transport through their boy friends and occasionally contribute considerably to the cost involved. With one exception, all the married people without children have some sort of vehicle shared between them and their partners. Those with young children fare less well. Taking all the categories together it would seem that about half have some form of motor vehicle of their own, or at least reasonable access to one, and about half do not, though some of these will go out with friends who have cars.

Some picture of the use to which all these vehicles are put will already have emerged. They take their owners to visit friends and relations, to public houses and to take part in all the other various activities which have already been mentioned. However, it is hardly enough to see motor vehicles simply as means to other ends. Indeed it might be useful to stand this proposition on its head and ask whether, in some cases, what is presented as being the 'end' is not really the means: the activity being the excuse for the drive rather than the drive being the means to undertaking the activity? Leaving such questions on one side it is still important to accord to cars, motor bikes and scooters their due position as the most important toys of the age, and certainly toys which can consume enormous quantities of leisure time. With the young this may be especially true, partly because, for them, possessing this sort of toy is a novel experience and partly because, with this group, a serious interest in either the appearance or performance of motor vehicles is commonly accorded high prestige. With the younger age groups particularly, concern with the appearance of vehicles has a good deal more to do with individual self expression than it has with maintaining a good second hand price and the pursuit and practice of skill in maintenance and tuning is frequently more of a hobby than a necessity. The possession of a motor vehicle may extend the scope of possible leisure activities, but, because it is a consuming leisure activity in itself, it may equally have the effect of making other leisure activities less necessary.

In addition to considering motor vehicles as elaborate and potentially satisfying toys, they are also the means to a variety of activities far less specific than any we have so far mentioned. For many groups motoring is still an activity in its own right. The family go out in the car at weekends, the courting couple go for a drive, the unattached go for a burn up, or set out on some freebooting and nebulously hopeful expedition. That these activities defy classification does not mean that they are unimportant. For some they may be the most highly-prized parts of the leisure timetable, though not the parts which emerge most clearly in a mainly quantitative survey of the kind conducted in Minton.

To return to what is firmer ground for the Minton survey there remain two more formal uses of leisure time still to be considered in this chapter. These are attendance at classes and membership of clubs and societies.

Vocational education

Some of the people we talked to were involved in part-time vocational education, usually because they were engaged in an apprenticeship scheme or undertaking secretarial training. Mostly these were people released by their employers to spend a day at a technical college. Sometimes this was the extent of their commitment; in other cases they were expected to attend evening classes as well, and five were engaged in vocational studies by evening class alone.

In general the commitment to vocational evening class attendance was not heavy. Two attended one night per week, eight two nights per week and one on three nights. For those on day release, evening class often takes the form of an extended day, the evening class falling in the early evening of the day at college. Similarly, for the majority, home study appeared to be neither a time consuming nor a burdensome business. Only two put in more than two hours per week, three studied for about two hours and seven disposed of whatever needed doing in about an hour per week.

It seems from the above that with the eighteen to twenty-fives in this sort of community the demands of vocational education impinge little on other leisure activities.

Table 24   Frequency of vocational study

Type of Study	Single women	Married women	Married women with family	Single men	Married men	Married men with family	Total
Day release	5	0	0	20	2	0	27
Evening class study only	2	0	0	3	0	0	5
Extent of evening class commitment (both groups)							
1 night per week	1	0	0	0	1	0	2
2 nights per week	2	0	0	6	0	0	8
3 or more nights per week	0	0	0	1	0	0	1
Extent of vocational study at home							
1 hour per week	1	0	0	5	1	0	7
2 hours per week	0	0	0	3	0	0	3
More than 2 hours per week	0	0	0	2	0	0	2

Non-vocational education

Non-vocational education is a very wide category and one which presents very considerable difficulties of definition. The group interviewed were asked about 'classes not related to your job' and their response included reference to many different sorts of class activities. It seems likely that many of the things they included, and which, therefore, I have included also, are classes which strictly are of a vocational nature, though they may not have been related directly to the work the interviewee was doing at the time the class was taken. Typing and teaching are two examples. Some of the exam subjects taken, if not vocational, were probably taken with a particular job, or job preferment, in mind. Not all the classes mentioned are necessarily run under the auspices of the local education authority. It seems likely that the singing class and some of the dancing classes are not.

In looking at the information about non-vocational education I was interested in both those who were attending a class at the time of the interview and in the number of people who had this sort of experience in the past.

Table 25 Past and present numbers attending non-vocational education classes

	Single women	Married women	Married women with family	Single men	Married men	Married men with family	Total	Total as %
Number in each category attending a class at the time of interview	6	3	1	6	1	0	17	11%
Number in each category who have at some time attended a class or classes	10	5	11	17	2	0	45	29%
Number in each category who have never attended any class	18	5	10	45	5	12	95	60%

It is interesting to see that the percentage of eighteen to twenty-five year olds who were attending some form of class at the time they were interviewed is roughly the same as the percentage usually claimed for non-vocational class attendance in the community as a whole. While not wishing to draw any over-optimistic conclusions from this, it does suggest that the possibility of this age group wishing to involve themselves in formal classes is not as remote as is sometimes suggested.

The twenty-nine per cent who referred to classes they had at some time attended in the past were in many cases delving back a very long way. Remarks like 'just after I had left school' were quite common and certainly one interviewee referred to a class attended as long ago as 1958.

Of the sixty-two (40%) who had some experience of class attendance, a number had attended more than one class. Forty-five mentioned one class only, but eleven mentioned two classes, four mentioned three classes and two mentioned four classes.

A breakdown of the subjects of all the classes mentioned (past as well as present) is given below.

Table 26 Type of class attended (past and present attendances combined)

	No. of times mentioned
Physical activity classes	
Keep fit	4
Judo	1
Football training	3
Physical education	2
Total	10
Domestic science classes	
Sewing and dressmaking	16
Cookery	10
Total	26
Examination subjects	
English	6
Mathematics	2
Accountancy	1
Business studies	1
Physics	1
Book keeping	1
Total	12
Arts and crafts	
Pottery	1
Painting and sketching	2
Drama	2
Total	5
Useful arts	
Metalwork and woodwork	4
Motor mechanics	3
Total	7

No. of times mentioned

All others	
Dancing	10
Nursing	3
Conversational French	2
Typing and shorthand	7
Singing	1
Teaching	1
Total	24

Total No. of classes mentioned	= 84

Details of the classes taken by present attenders are given in Table 27.

Table 27 Breakdown of the 17 respondents taking part in some form of non-vocational educational activity

3 of the 17 attended 2 classes each
14 of the 17 attended 1 class each
therefore total class/attendances = 20

Of these 20 classes
   10 take place in Minton
    4 ,,   ,, ,, a neighbouring village
    3 ,,   ,, ,, Chesterfield
    3 ,,   ,, ,, Worksop

Subjects taken

Dancing	7 respondents (different classes in Minton, a neighbouring village, Worksop and Chesterfield)
Dressmaking	4 respondents (the same class in Minton)
Conversational French	1
Typing	1
Singing	1
Teaching	1
St John's Ambulance Brigade	1
Painting and sketching	2
Motor mechanics	2

The sixty-two who had some experience of classes had attended classes in a wide variety of different venues some of which involved travel. So far as local authority provision is concerned, the venues mentioned were:

Table 28   Venues for classes (past and present)

Venue	No. of times mentioned	
Local evening institute	23	
Other evening institutes	4	
Local youth club	11	
Ambulance brigade headquarters	2	
Worksop technical college	16	
Chesterfield technical college	4	25
Clowne technical college	4	
Mansfield technical college	1	

In the context of Table 28, 'local evening institute' means one either situated in Minton itself or in a neighbouring village. The 'other evening institutes' were very much further afield and were generally associated with having lived in another locality. For example, one referred to was in Scotland. The local youth club may be the same physical premises as the local evening institute, and this category is included to distinguish between separate evening institute classes and those held as part of the youth club programme, though it may be that the interviewees did not always distinguish between them.

Generally it would be the classes held in technical colleges which would involve the expense and inconvenience of travel and in view of this it is interesting to see that, collectively, classes held at technical colleges account for a sizeable proportion of the class attendances. Of course, some of the subjects mentioned would normally be beyond the scope of a local evening institute and in many other cases the facilities available at a technical college would be superior. In addition I would suspect social motivation plays some part. Even where the technical college offers no social facilities to its evening class attenders, it still affords a very favourable opportunity for meeting people of the same age and the opposite sex.

Membership of clubs and organizations

Another fairly formal aspect of leisure is club membership. In asking questions about this aspect of leisure the team encouraged a very wide interpretation of what constituted a club and in collating the information I have included all these responses except, 'Co-op' and 'Book Club', both of which were either facetiously or seriously offered. Table 29 shows the number of people who belonged to some sort of organization and the number of organizations to which they belonged.

Table 29 Extent of membership and multiple membership of clubs and organizations

Number of clubs, societies or organizations	Single women	Married women	Married women with family	Single men	Married men	Married men with family	Total
One	9	3	3	29	3	0	47
Two	1	0	1	11	1	3	17
Three	0	0	0	3	0	0	3
Four	0	0	0	1	0	0	1
None	24	10	18	24	4	9	85
Total number in each category	34	13	22	68	8	12	157

Before attempting any conclusions about this information, it is as well to look also at Table 30 to see the range of possibilities which was covered by the terms 'club or organization'.

Some explanatory notes are necessary with both these tables. Membership of school and college societies is excluded from Table 29 on the grounds that these are something of a special case and for 'joiners' it is the rule rather than the exception to belong to a number of clubs. This exclusion only affects four people and these appear under the appropriate heading in Table 30.

The youth club predominates as the organization to which the greatest number of people belonged. Minton Over Eighteens Club is an extension of a neighbouring youth club with which its membership overlaps.

The category 'other sports clubs' includes clubs concerned with cricket, cycling, swimming and tennis.

A wide range of activities is included under the heading, 'All other clubs and societies'. These were:

Public house darts team	1
Pigeon racing club	1
Clay pigeon shooting club	1
Pathfinders (a lay preaching group)	1
Political organization	1

Astronomy society	1
Oddfellows	1
Royal observer corps	2
Youth hostels association	1
Bingo club	1

Put together, Tables 29 and 30 present a fascinating picture. At first glance the picture suggests a section of the community with a high level of involvement in a variety of clubs and organizations. Closer examination makes this a more questionable proposition.

Table 30   Membership of different clubs, societies and organizations

Type of club	Single women	Married women	Married women with family	Single men	Married men	Married men with family	Total
Youth clubs ⎫ membership	1	0	0	21	0	0	22 ⎫
Minton Over ⎬ overlaps							⎬ 32
Eighteens club ⎭	0	0	0	10	0	0	10 ⎭
Commercial Clubs	0	0	4	2	2	3	11
Sports clubs (excluding football)	4	0	1	2	2	0	9
Football clubs	0	0	0	5	0	2	7
Miners' Welfare	2	0	0	3	0	1	6
St John's Ambulance Brigade	1	0	0	5	0	0	6
Fishing clubs	0	0	0	5	1	0	6
Motoring clubs	0	1	0	3	0	0	4
Student clubs and societies (school or college)	0	0	0	3	1	0	4
All other clubs, societies and affiliations (listed below)	2	1	0	8	0	0	11

Numerically dominating the club scene are the youth clubs and in this category one must include Minton Over Eighteens Club which, though it has some special features, is still basically a youth club run as an off-shoot of the main L.E.A. youth club in the district Jointly the youth club membership represents 44% of all club memberships and organizational affiliations, and, bearing in mind that the age group with which this survey was concerned is not that normally associated with youth club membership, this is an impressive percentage. Minton is unusual in having a youth club which makes a special provision for those over eighteen and the neighbouring youth club itself has a tradition of provision for its older members. Fourteen of those we talked to were members of the over eighteen club in Minton and the others were for the most part members of the youth club in the neighbouring village, though this distinction is in itself a little misleading as the effective situation is one of joint membership.

The most immediately obvious characteristic of this membership is that it is single and male. Of the group interviewed only one single girl said that she was a member of a youth club. Other questions revealed other interesting features of this group. For example, five of the thirty-two youth club members made it clear that they were 'seasonal' members only. The 'season' in this instance being the football season. However, it was obvious that the majority of the youth club members were a committed and frequently attending membership. Fifty-three per cent of the youth club members went to their clubs more than once a week and most of the others attended at least once a week. Equally it was among the youth club members that the majority of the multiple membership were to be found. An extreme example of organizational commitment was the young man who went to two different youth clubs on four nights every week, to St John's Ambulance Brigade meetings once a week, and to Minton football club at least more often than monthly. There were several others who approached this. A high level of commitment to a variety of organizations is normally something which is presented in a favourable light, but in discussion I sometimes felt that some of those in many organizations were more timid, less robust, less adventurous and less socially aware than those outside them.

The other clubs and societies encompassed a considerable range of activities and wide variations of commitment and involvement. While I have no doubt that some people were very involved either in club life or in the activities which those clubs fostered, I think it is often true that commitments of this sort tend to appear over-important when listed in print. For example, of the nine sports club members, eight attended on a seasonal basis only and for sports like tennis, cricket and swimming not only is the season a very short one, but also it is only the serious club and the serious players who take part for the whole season. With drama the activity may well be intensive for a short period, but, even allowing for the amateur's love of a protracted rehearsal period, it is usually only a matter of a few weeks with rarely more than two productions a year.

With considerations such as these in mind it seems possible that membership of even half a dozen clubs or societies is not necessarily very demanding in terms of time or of absorbing interest. Of course, for many people, commitment to an organization is fully absorbing and of tremendous personal value. The danger is in assuming that this is invariably the case.

The survey in Minton was a very simple head counting operation and, as I have already hinted, some sorts of heads are very much more countable than others. It is much easier to give a seeming precision to facts and figures about going to the cinema, attending an evening class, or belonging to a club than it is to deal adequately with activities like 'shopping', visiting or going for a drive. The particular danger of this is that we pay too much attention to the aspects of leisure with which it is easiest to come to grips, and allow ourselves to be bamboozled into believing that those leisure activities which, superficially, we can most easily recognize, are also those which are most 'valuable'.

7 Young adults, work and leisure in Minton: some conclusions

'They ought to have more for young people to do'—letter from an ex-Mintonian

Most of the people in this country live within the conurbations of the big towns and cities, but those who don't certainly do not all live 'in the country' in thatched cottages with roses round the door, nor even in rural villages. The mining zone of Nottinghamshire and Derbyshire stretches southward from the mining towns and villages of north-east Derbyshire, which lie to the north-east of Chesterfield, down to the fringes of Derby and Nottingham. The population of this area is around one and a half million and is expected to rise to two and a quarter million by the year 2000.[1] Yet there are few towns in the area with a population of more than 15,000 and no major centre of population.

The preceding two chapters described the leisure life of young adults in one small community in the area. The object of this study is to provide what might be called the 'consumers' perspective' and the chapters are not about 'leisure provision', but about people and how they spend their leisure time. It might well be argued that this information is local, specialized and already out of date, has no relevance outside Minton, and because of the passage of time very little relevance there. In some respects this is fair argument. All localities and all points in time are special circumstances producing special responses which are not the responses of other people in other places at other times. However, there are also some general considerations which arise from the detailed examination of Minton. For example, there are difficulties relating to leisure provision for small towns and villages wherever these are situated and the problem of the relationship of leisure services to the shift worker is relevant wherever there are services and shift workers.

The consumer view of leisure in Minton is a view which is probably very different from that which might come from those responsible for leisure provision in the village. Much of the provision which exists in Minton was not mentioned by the young adults featured in the survey and it would be difficult to say to what extent they are aware of the existence of this provision or to what extent, in real terms, it exists for them. There is a tendency, explicable on many grounds, for 'official' accounts of leisure provision to give an over favourable impression of the level of involvement in community activity. No 'official' account of the leisure opportunities available in Minton in fact exists, but if it did it might well look like this:

Leisure provision in Minton

Commercial provision
Public houses and licensed clubs; all of which make some kind of recreational as well as social provision. The Miners' Welfare sponsors a drama group and clubs for badminton, tennis, bowls, archery and chess. The clubs also sponsor bingo, dancing and cabaret entertainment.

Sports facilities
Good football pitches and tennis courts and clubs for both these activities.

Adult groups and organizations
The Women's Institute
Mothers' Union
Young Mothers' Guild
St John's Ambulance Brigade
Salvation Army
The British Legion
Royal Navy Association
The Minton Band
Labour party
Church Organizations
Oddfellows and similar organizations.

Youth organizations
St John's Ambulance Brigade
Small youth groups attached to the churches
Scouts and Guides
An over eighteen club which is a branch of a youth club in a neighbouring village.

The evening institute
An evening institute is held at Minton junior school and non-vocational classes on subjects such as dressmaking, flower arrange-

ments, millinery, sketching and photography are available.

For a village with a population of about five thousand this is a not unimposing list, yet, as has already been said, it perhaps suggests a far greater community activity than really exists. The age group we talked with in Minton were very little involved with any of the above provisions except the pubs and perhaps the list includes comparatively little that one supposes would be attractive to them.

In other towns and villages in the area, the social and recreational provision is really very similar to that available in Minton. Even places with three times the population do not necessarily afford much more in the way of leisure opportunities, nor do smaller communities necessarily provide much less. The chief difference which size makes is in the statutory provisions of adult education and youth service. With adult education the large communities can support a greater range of classes and where there is a modern secondary school the classes have the opportunity of meeting in circumstances which for adults are more pleasant and more workmanlike than those afforded by a primary school. With youth service there is more likelihood of full-time staff and purpose built or converted premises being available in the areas of greater population but even here any differences may not be readily measurable. For example, the school based, part-time leader club which served the Minton area would compare favourably so far as membership and range of activities was concerned with many full-time leader clubs occupying their own premises in other towns and villages in the area. One would hope that the quality of work carried out by the full-time workers would be higher, but from the limited point of view of the numbers involved in different activities a distinction between full-time and part-time leader clubs would not always be evident.

Superficially some of the towns and villages differ with regard to the commercial leisure provision available, but what is interesting is that so often these *are* superficial. Two of the small towns in the area each boast three discotheques, a form of provision absent from Minton, but these discotheques could not in any real sense be regarded as attractions. They are part of nobody's 'swinging scene' and are viewed entirely realistically by the customers. Nobody dances, except the occasional couple of girls who would probably do the same in a pub room with a juke box when a record came up which they particularly liked. These discotheques are not valueless because they provide a different kind of room in which to drink and a meeting place for some young people who would not go into other pub rooms[2] but as social provision they are not highly regarded. To say that those towns and villages which have discotheques are 'better provided' than those which do not would therefore be a questionable statement.

121

The successful provisions in the area from the point of view of their attractiveness to young people are not necessarily those situated in the larger places.3 Dotted about here and there throughout the whole area of north-east Derbyshire are particular pieces of provision which work. There are some public houses where on certain nights of the week a special social atmosphere arises from the expectation of the customers. At some fish and chip shops attendance is a ritual accompanied by the assurance of lively gossip and fireworks of wit. Thus some towns and villages which seemingly have no social provision have sometimes forms of provision which are highly valued and probably very satisfying. However, it would be nonsensical to sentimentalize about these and I would stress my impression that this is 'some' and not 'all' and that the deserts of non-provision are frighteningly vast.

One of the main characteristics of the area as a whole is the absence of many forms of commercial and public leisure provision. Understandably the area cannot support restaurants, art galleries or theatres, but equally it supports very little by way of swimming baths, cinemas or dance halls. Nor are any of these facilities very easily accessible to many of the people who live in the area. Thus certain kinds of 'going out' have to be concentrated at the weekends while weekday leisure is more often spent locally.

Nearly all the sixteen ex-residents of Minton who wrote to me about their impressions of the village mentioned the lack of things to do. The general comments were very mixed. Some found the village 'fairly clean' others described it as 'filthy, worse than the city'. On the credit side most made some reference to the friendliness of the people and to the relaxed atmosphere, 'not the ceaseless need to be on one's guard for dishonesty, crime etc. that one finds in a city' and 'the people are friendly and the whole atmosphere is much different from that of ...'. But, also, there were some reservations about industrial village life 'the local council are a self perpetuating, narrow minded load of ...', 'the people of the village are content to let everything flow over their heads without doing anything ...', 'the gossip and curiosity of the people ...' 'if one attempts anything in the least ambitious, half the village eagerly awaits one's failure'.

However, the point which united fourteen out of the sixteen correspondents was the absence of social and recreational facilities for young people. Under the general heading of likes and dislikes this was the subject to which most comment was devoted, and the general impression can best be summed up by the phrase 'no entertainment except Bingo and public houses'. But it is worth stressing that most of the people who wrote in found a good deal that they liked about Minton. There was criticism that for entertainment there was 'only the pubs' but the pubs themselves came in for praise, particularly from those living in southern cities. That there should be regard for the people was natural from people who had been brought up in the village, but the students who did the interviewing and who were strangers and outsiders, also commented on the friendliness with which they were often received. Some of the comments from the ex-residents were highly critical, but more often than not criticism of some feature of the village was balanced by praise for some other aspect. They agreed that what spoilt Minton as a place to live was the absence of things to do and the difficulty and expense of reaching centres with better amenities.

The problem of leisure for Minton, and all under-provided areas, is a highly complex one. What people do in their leisure time depends very largely upon what there is available for them to do, and whatever it is that is 'done' rapidly becomes a matter of habit. Leisure very quickly becomes non-exploratory and unadventurous, unless the environment in some way stimulates and rewards exploratory attitudes. One of the problems for Minton and hundreds of places like it is the absence of any such stimulation. For many young adults in the village leisure seemed dull and routine, lacking in excitement and involvement and often, seemingly, in enjoyment. Value judgments about other people's leisure are highly suspect, but an expressed lack of enthusiasm for the life they were leading was one of the main characteristics of many of the interviews.

What is difficult about this is that dissatisfaction with leisure does not of itself breed the will to change. The habits of leisure which the Minton environment engendered absorbed the resources and energy which might have gone into doing something different. The habit of a certain kind of leisure was often deeply ingrained even upon the young people of the village.

The reasons for this are not hard to see. In some respects, Minton is a community which has established traditions about the way leisure is spent. Minton is by no means extreme in this respect and many other mining villages are, by their traditions, much more controlling and much less tolerant of individuals who deviate from the pattern of accepted behaviour. It is not impossible to be different in Minton, but it requires some determination and some particular stimulus and support. The young man who does not put in a regular appearance at one or other of the pubs or clubs is likely to be thought a little odd and anyone who did anything very unusual with their leisure would not escape a certain amount of leg pulling. The community is small and close enough to resent anyone who 'gets too big for his boots', and the correspondent who wrote 'if one attempts anything in the least ambitious, half the village eagerly awaits one's failure' illustrates only too clearly what the pressures towards conformity can feel like to those on the receiving end.

123

Also, there is little in the village to provoke anyone to different leisure pursuits. Unlike the city there are no leisure amenities which prompt curiosity by their very existence and there are no shop windows crammed with holiday clothes and leisure equipment. Unlike the resort or many 'rural' villages there are no tourists whose odd behaviour may provoke ridicule, but which is none the less a reminder of a different kind of existence and a different style of life. Most importantly, there are comparatively few new and provoking human contacts. In Minton, one may well work and take one's leisure with one's neighbours, and in many mining villages even holidays are spent away together as the whole village community moves to one of the east coast holiday camps for a week or a fortnight.

The habits of leisure are habits of mind as well as habits of behaviour. How far one travels to visit friends, or to undertake a particular activity or how much money one considers it appropriate to spend on a meal, on drinks or on a particular entertainment all reflect habits of thinking which are not easily changed or broken, so long as one continues to live in a community which provides support for the habits in question.

To some extent these habits of thinking relate to social class divisions. The middle class acceptance of 'the principle of deferred gratification'; the postponement of immediate satisfaction in order to reap the benefit of greater satisfactions at a later date, is as noticeable with leisure pursuits as it is with any other aspect of life. Much of the leisure in Minton and in the area as a whole tends to be concerned with immediate satisfactions and this is often a source of frustration and irritation to those workers in the leisure services who apply other standards and in some cases work mainly with those who fundamentally share their attitudes. To many youth workers in the area, their members seemed 'apathetic' and uninterested in many of the pursuits they tried to foster and in some cases perhaps the seeming lack of interest was due mainly to the terms in which the activity was presented. Not all workers were sympathetic to the difficulties members experienced in coming to grips with the, for them, new concept of long term planning.

Another kind of difficulty arises for those seeking to foster leisure opportunities for young adults in Minton because many young adults in the area have an ambivalent attitude to city entertainments of all kinds. They want them, but are often not prepared to expend the time, money and effort which would be necessary for them to gain access to them. Here they are doubly disadvantaged both because it would require more time, money and effort for them to reach city entertainments than is the case for their town cousins and also because their leisure habits incline them to less effort and expense than that which many town dwellers of similar income and background might find acceptable. The people who go away from the village for a time jolt into new habits easily enough and certainly many of the present inhabitants use a wider range of leisure facilities than was the case twenty or thirty years ago, but even so the leisure lives of many eighteen to twenty-five year olds seemed, to the Minton interviewing team, narrow and uninspiring.

In this connection it is worth comparing some of the information from Minton with surveys from other areas. Direct comparison is not very easy because there are few, if any, surveys of the eighteen to twenty-five age group. None the less it is possible to gain some rough and ready idea of the comparative use of two kinds of commercial provision from the following table.

Table 31 Frequency of visiting cinema and going dancing compared with other areas

Cinema	% of sample of 18 year olds in Bury, Lancs., attending cinema weekly	% of 15-19 year* olds in sample from Scottish survey having visited cinema in 7 days prior to interview		% of Minton 18 to 25 year olds (single men and women only) attending cinema weekly
		Male	Female	
	25.5%	49%	46%	10%
Dancing	% of sample of 18 year olds in Bury, Lancs., going dancing weekly	% of 15-19 year olds in sample from Scottish Survey having been dancing in 7 days prior to interview		% of Minton 18 to 25 year olds (single men and women only) going dancing weekly
		Male	Female	
	37.2%	33%	40%	10%

*Pearl Jephcott writes 'As many as 81% of the sample went regularly to the cinema, 69% to dancing and 51% to a cafe. Neither sex, age nor educational situation made any marked difference.' *Time of One's Own*, page 115.

What I have done here is to take some figures from two recent surveys[4] of the leisure activities of young people and compare them with similar information obtained from Minton. Because of the difference in the age groups covered by the surveys, the comparison is a very crude one, but the difference in cinema attendance and dancing between the young people from the urban areas and the Mintonians shows up in a very striking way. The Mintonians in the table are only the single people of both sexes because it is precisely this group which one would expect to be frequent users of commercial provision of all kinds and yet very obviously so far as cinemas and dance halls are concerned this is not the case.

All this prompts some very difficult questions and for the purpose of this book perhaps the foremost is: 'What is the function of the voluntary and statutory leisure-providing services in a situation, far from uncommon, like that I have described in Minton?' At this stage it might be helpful to point to some of the factors in this very considerable problem.

1 There is a lack of diversity in the leisure occupations of the 18-25 year age range in the area which I have described.
2 There is a lack of opportunity for people in the area to undertake many normal leisure activities.
3 There is little evidence of the existence of a compensating home based leisure life. There has been a marked, and comparatively recent, decline in the traditional home-based leisure interests of the area such as pigeon racing, whippet breeding and racing, and cage birds. This decline may be due to changing interests brought about by greater prosperity and the influence of external stimuli such as television, but the process has perhaps been accelerated by the regulations relating to the keeping of animals which affect most of the new houses, local council and coal board alike, in mining areas.
4 There has been a comparatively recent decrease in some forms of leisure provision which were in the past available locally. Many small towns and villages had their own cinemas, but these have now closed in most places or have been converted into Bingo Halls. Similarly local dances have undergone changes with regard to style, frequency and patronage. While these changes may properly reflect general changes in the interests of the majority it is possible that they have been disadvantageous to the leisure lives of some age groups within the community.
5 There has been a general decline in public transport facilities during the past few decades. Again this reduction in services affects particular groups in the community.
6 Under normal circumstances individual small towns and villages cannot support very much by way of commercial leisure amenities.

Given these factors it may be that it is necessary for the adult education and youth services to perform a different function in under-provided areas from that which they perform in areas where commercial leisure provision and environmental leisure amenities are more readily accessible. The obvious answer here is that the services should simply provide more, and in the sense that 'community need' rather than sheer density of population should be a factor in the consideration of the over-all allocation of resources, this argument has some strength in it. But it is surely unrealistic to suppose that high levels of provision can be easily made in low population density areas and the evidence from Minton does not suggest that simply a more lavish provision of what is already being provided would, by itself, be attractive to the age group with which this book is concerned.

However, to this conundrum there may still be some answers for the services concerned. Basically there are two things which it seems worth trying to do. One is to increase the leisure amenities of the immediate locality, and the other is to facilitate the accessibility of the amenities of the nearby cities. On the face of it both seemed impossible because of the cost involved and indeed if the services can only see themselves as 'providers' in the sense that they 'give', 'maintain' and 'control' then this is almost certainly the case. But if the services are to be truly helping services, rather than providers in this narrowest sense, some other alternatives are open. Here the 'discontent' which those involved in the Minton survey so often noted may provide the key. If there is a genuine wish for something different to what extent might it not be the proper role for those involved in the leisure provision services to be the facilitators of change? The traditional role of such services is to stimulate and to provide, but in areas where what can be provided falls so far short of the aspirations of some of the community is there not a case for the services themselves adopting a more positive role in attempting to help groups within the community achieve some of their objectives by the deployment of their own resources?

8 The project in Moortown

'It's given us a responsibility. If we decide something is going to happen it generally happens. It were never like that before.'—group member

Although there is nothing new in the idea of helping young people other than through institutions the idea itself still presents a number of difficulties. A fundamental one is simply that some of the conventions of such work are different from the conventions of institution-based work which in general we accept uncritically as the 'proper' way of going about things. In particular we tend to take for granted the extent to which institutions define the relationship that is to exist between worker and client, patron and customer and we find it difficult to come to terms with other sorts of working relationship. The institutional relationship may not remain confined within the four walls of the institution, but it is there that it starts, surrounded, for good or ill, by a structure of expectations which has to be further built upon, modified or broken down completely. Whatever happens subsequently the institution is where it all begins. Need this be so? While technically it is not difficult to begin in other ways it is something which seems to involve for many people an imaginative leap of some magnitude.

During the past decade the youth service in Great Britain has conducted a number of projects involving working with young people outside institutions. This kind of work has been practised for a longer period in the United States and is now not uncommon in other European countries either in connection with youth or social work. The first British projects tended to be short-term and experimental and to be sponsored by voluntary organizations or trusts. More recently some Local Education Authorities have begun to appoint youth workers to 'detached' youth work projects. This chapter is an account of one very simple, very unsophisticated project conducted in a town in north-east Derbyshire.

Moortown is a mining town with a population of under twelve thousand. It stands on a steep and windy ridge overlooking the

M.1. and some of the houses in the town have an uninterrupted view across the valley to the hills of the Derbyshire Peak District. It is an old town once famed for its production of spurs and buckles, the durability of which were proved under the iron wheels of carts in the market square. Today the town has spread itself into a variety of housing estates which cover the hillside and most of their male occupants go to work in one or other of the local pits or at the coalite works which dominate the valley below the town.

The basic idea of the project in Moortown was that it might be possible for a part-time youth worker to contact and to make his skills available to groups of young people in the town, who appeared not to be served by the existing provision.

Initially there was no reliable information upon which a project could be based, but rather a number of tentative suppositions which suggested that a basis for work might exist. For example, a glance at the attendance figures for the youth clubs in the town showed that these clubs, although well attended, catered for only a minority of the teenage population of the town. Of course this is true almost everywhere and is certainly no reflection on the clubs concerned. In Moortown, however, there seemed little alternative provision of any kind. A number of people testified to there always being young people on the streets who seemingly had nothing to do and who seemed not to be very happy about the situation. Testimony like this is common and is often misleading, but at least one youth leader felt that this situation was more apparent in Moortown than in some other towns in the area, and Moortown is different from some other towns in north-east Derbyshire in that it has a central town square with a thriving fish and chip shop which acts as a meeting place for young people. Collectively, these factors suggested that a basis for work might exist.

The literature about detached youth work in this country suggests that it is a job demanding expertise in a variety of social work skills and that the worker is frequently subject to very considerable stress. It is normally regarded as a job for a full-time worker already professionally qualified in one of the social sciences, education or youth work and some form of on the job training is often built in to the structure of the job. With this in mind, I had some reservations about the project in Moortown.

There seemed to be two main dangers. Firstly, it could be that the worker would fail to make contact with any young people at all. Information from other detached work projects shows that while establishing contact with young people on the streets or in commercial provision is not necessarily technically difficult, it does take a long time and demands a disciplined approach. With the Moortown project it was impossible to say what would happen.

Was two nights a week in the town sufficient time in which to make an initial contact with completely unknown groups of young people? If, as might well have been the case, the groups of young people using the town centre were different groups on different nights of the week then the answer would almost certainly be 'no'. Failure to make any contact at all was certainly a possibility which had to be considered. The question in my mind at this point was, that if this happened what would be the effect on the worker? The particular danger was that he would emerge from this situation with his enthusiasm destroyed and with a sense of personal failure. Morally, it seemed indefensible to put anyone in a working situation of this sort. It is not the employing agency's responsibility to ensure success or to pretend success where there is none, but it is reasonable to suppose they have some responsibility to their employees not to put them in working situations which are likely to be personally damaging. With the Moortown project it seemed to me crucial that the worker should have some protection against the worst effects of failure. It seemed that this protection might be best afforded by providing someone who would give the worker support and who would help him maintain his objectivity.

Secondly, there was the danger that the worker, having successfully contacted a group of people, would find himself embroiled in a situation which he had neither the time nor the expertise to handle and that his 'interference' would be detrimental rather than beneficial to the young people involved. Some detached youth work projects have set out deliberately to work with young people who are deprived, maladjusted or delinquent. Clearly this is not a job for a two nights per week part-time worker. What was envisaged in Moortown was a project involving a different sort of approach to 'ordinary' young people. There was no question of an attempt to work with the maladjusted or the delinquent. However, the detached worker does not have a door he can close to shut out those with whom he does not want to work. He can be selective in that he tries to involve himself with some groups and individuals rather than with others and the more skilled the worker, the more selective he is able to be, but the limits within which this selectivity operates are totally different from those possible in a structured working situation.

With the Moortown project, it seemed to me likely that the worker might need help in deciding what demands he could and could not meet and support in coming to terms with the idea that there would be much that would have to be left undone.

All this pointed to the need for supervision. Of course, the provision of supervision would not remove the dangers inherent in the situation, but it could provide the worker some degree of protection. If the project collapsed around him, then it might at least be possible to ensure that he emerged from the wreckage unscathed. In this specific instance, I saw supervision as something which could tip the balance and make the project a justifiable experiment. Without it I would have preferred the experiment not to go forward.

I shared this view with colleagues and superiors in the Derbyshire youth service and approval for the experiment was made conditional on my acting as supervisor for the worker. I was happy enough with this decision though I knew that there would be some special difficulties in trying to evaluate a project where I had acted as the supervisor for the worker concerned. It was not an ideal arrangement, but it was probably the only practical one in the circumstances. There did not seem to be anyone else in the locality who could have undertaken this role. My qualifications for the job were that I was interested enough in it to devote the time to it that was needed, I had had experience of detached youth work and, most important of all, I had had a satisfactory and helpful experience of being supervised. I knew the sort of relationship at which I was aiming and the ways in which such a relationship might be helpful.

Work started in Moortown on Monday, 15 May 1967, when Gordon Wainman, the appointed part-time worker, went into the town to begin the exploratory phase of the project. The first four visits produced some varied and perhaps inaccurate impressions. On fine evenings there were several groups of young people in the square. These were mainly 'Rockers' and Gordon suspected that they came from out of town. The fish and chip shop did not seem to be attracting large numbers of young people and neither, surprisingly, did the public houses, though there were one or two self-styled discotheques of the 'juke box and dark room' variety. Visits to the youth clubs in the town showed the absence of people over eighteen, although the largest club in the area had recently made an attempt to cater for people of this age. This attempt had produced an initial recruitment of older members, but one which had fallen away very rapidly. The youth leader commented that the club was unable to provide the sort of adult activities required. This was interesting in that the initial recruitment success suggested that there was a group of people in the town who were consciously seeking some form of provision.

The most successful piece of social provision which Gordon found was a discotheque which operated on Monday nights in a pub which bordered the market square. This was clearly a cut above its competitors and on a good night attracted some eighty or so young people many of whom could be seen queuing to go in twenty minutes before opening time. Gordon chatted to the landlord and gained the impression that this was a well organized provision which presented the landlord with few problems. It was run by a group of people who hired the room from the landlord and moved in with their equipment on one night a week. The same group operated a similar system in other pubs in other areas.

Visits to Moortown continued throughout May and into June. Hours were spent in the square watching the comings and goings, and hours too were spent tramping the streets, in an attempt to find out everything about the social life of the town. Visits were made on every different night of the week and at weekends, something which in itself demanded a very considerable commitment of a part-time worker. Every visitable form of provision was visited at least once and most were visited many times over. Gordon's own terse notes record these visits; pub A 'deserted', Pub B 'a depressing place— most of the customers older adults', and more promisingly Pub C 'packed with teenagers, a few dancing, many under age. Most seem to sit the night with one drink only.' The local cabaret club had 'a hefty doorman' but 'no teenagers'.

Sometimes, there was incident, 'Returned to the fish and chip shop and had a short conversation with a boy about eighteen called John. The talk was trivial and I sensed his suspicion of me.' Sometimes, conversations with adults helped to fill in parts of the jigsaw if only in bringing to light a floral art group or some other social activity of which we were previously ignorant.

At the end of May, Gordon had written, 'It seems that I shall have to make contacts through the casual groups which meet in the square.' In fact, this never proved possible and the unapproachability of these groups in this situation became increasingly apparent. In other settings, too, Gordon began to feel uncomfortable. He had a long and varied experience of youth work. He had met a wide range of young people in a variety of places besides youth clubs. He did not expect meeting people to be easy in this new situation, but at this stage he was not even trying to meet people and yet he felt the barriers were going up. He had the new and unpleasant experience of realizing that his very presence was often resented. Some places indeed seemed absolutely unbroachable. The popular Monday night discotheque, for example, seemed the sort of place that it would be useful to visit, but more than ten years separated Gordon from the oldest of the clientele. He could hardly wander casually into a place with a formal charge for admittance, nor could he hang around the door when the door was at the top of a flight of stairs.

There is considerable strain attached to being an object of suspicion and there is strain, too, in doing nothing, in hanging about, in not having a clear identity. The two are interrelated and it is easy for the worker to come to feel that because he is doing nothing, he is justifiably an object of suspicion. By 24 June, Gordon was writing, 'I am feeling out of place and less confident than when I started. I would like to have some reason for being here.'

This was a difficult period for the worker and one when support was particularly important. This support entailed understanding the feelings of the worker and making it clear that these feelings were understood and helping him to come to terms with them as one of the difficulties of the job. In part, this was not too difficult to achieve. It was useful to be able to point to the experience of other detached workers who had had similar feelings. 'In the cafes, where they (the toughest type) meet, I must confess I feel very conspicuous and somehow very remote ...'[1] Helping the worker to understand the way people respond to him and his own response to his new working situation does not remove the uncomfortable emotions associated with this stage of work, but it does help reduce them to manageable proportions and later in June, Gordon wrote, 'I am too anxious to make acquaintances and am thereby creating some of my own problems.' Having perceived his own anxiety and the causes of it he was able to a large measure to control it.

A thornier problem was that of identity and this was never satis-factorily resolved during the early stages of the work. Gordon was a detached youth worker and there was never any pretence that he was anything other than this. This is how he would describe himself to anyone who asked and the further explanation was that he was a youth worker, not attached to (i.e. 'detached' from) any institutional provision, who was prepared to help any of the young people in the town who wanted his help. Once work with groups of young people actually started, it was possible to affirm this identity and it became an acceptable, and surprisingly respectable one.

In the early stages, however, Gordon could not be identified by the community in which he was trying to work. He was not someone who could be labelled because they were known in the locality, nor was he a stranger who could be labelled because he was carrying on some clearly recognizable occupation. Much of the suspicion to which he was subject arose not because he 'hung about', but because no one knew why he was hanging about. After all, communities accept a large number of people who hang about providing their activities are in some way explicable. We are not unduly disturbed by those who wander round the town killing time waiting for a bus or train or those who sit alone in pubs waiting for friends, *providing* we have some reason to suppose that this is what they are doing. In Gordon's case, there was no obvious reason for his being there and no way he could allay the suspicion this aroused.

This lack of an externally accepted identity is particularly difficult for the solitary worker. If there is a team structure, then belonging to a team can help to reinforce the workers' sense of their identity. The workers can meet and say to each other, in a variety of sophisticated ways, 'We are detached youth workers.' If there has been training[2] one of its functions will have been to establish for the worker a strong sense of professional identity. A trained worker who is a member of an adequately supervised team is still likely to experience stress in establishing his identity in a community, but the stress element is much greater for the solitary worker who has had no previous training and supervision is likely to be particularly important in providing a relationship (probably the only one) in which the detached worker is recognized as being a detached worker.

One of the ways in which the stress which arises from having no clearly recognizable identity can be radically reduced is by the worker embarking on a secondary occupation which provides him with a satisfactory identity. From the worker's point of view this is often an attractive proposition. It seemingly solves the identity problem and taking another job can be rationalized as providing new opportunities for contacting people. Mary Morse writes, 'It was only when the Seagate worker became a part-time teacher and was able to use this identity that he really felt comfortable 'hanging around' in a coffee bar; similarly with the Midford worker, when he took a job as a swimming instructor and began inquiries about school teaching. It seems that the "hanging around" approach only presents difficulties if the worker is unable or unwilling to give his reason for doing so, or, if he lacks a recognizable identity in the local community.'[3] The project of which she writes had particular difficulties because the workers operated anonymously—that is they did not reveal their identities as detached youth workers to those with whom they worked. But the sting of what I have quoted lies in the tail. Detached youth workers cannot have a 'recognisable identity in the local community'. They have to establish one—and this takes time.

The Y.W.C.A. project[4] to some extent side-stepped the identity problem by starting operations from a coffee stall which was at once both the contact point and the supportive secondary occupation for the workers. This seems to have worked out very well, though presumably some of the early misconceptions about the coffee stall, that it was a police cover or, later, a tax dodge, cannot always have been helpful to the work in hand. The workers still had to establish their identity, to make it clear what they were really trying to do.

There is no easy answer to this problem. The worker feels stress because he lacks an identity in the community. He can relieve this stress by taking on an occupation which has a clearly recognizable identity, but the identity he then takes on is not that which ultimately he seeks to establish and may in fact postpone the realization of this objective.

With Gordon in Moortown, I was anxious to support him in his role as a detached youth worker and although I sympathized with his expressed desire to have 'some reason for being here' (i.e. a secondary occupation) there seemed grounds for reservation about the long term usefulness of this. I have said that we never resolved this difficulty and this was because a series of events resulting from a mixture of good management and good luck provided a satisfactory resolution for us. What remains debatable is how long the demoralizing business of 'hanging about' could have continued. Because the stress factor was recognized and openly discussed, it was considerably reduced and I have little doubt that Gordon could have continued on this basis for months if necessary. What it seems important to stress is that this could well be necessary. We were fortunate in being able to terminate the hanging about stage fairly rapidly, but with other projects it might well be necessary, or desirable, to prolong this stage for several months.

I have devoted some space to this because it is a matter of crucial importance for any similar projects attempted elsewhere. The lesson learned is the importance of support for the worker during the initial period of the project. So far as the Moortown project is concerned the worker has no reservations about saying that support at this stage was essential and its absence could have resulted in disaster for the project and for him personally. Certainly, it seemed to me during the early weeks that my insistence on some form of supportive supervision had been justified.

Finally, it is important to put the subject matter of this lengthy digression into perspective. The early discussion sessions I had with Gordon were not exclusively devoted to discussing the strain to which he was being subjected. In fact nothing could be more misleading than to give this impression. It was rather an important, and in the long term, potentially dangerous, factor in the working situation to which we gave some serious attention. Understanding the stress element was part of the total business of understanding the nature of the job in hand. I have spent a disproportionate amount of space on it here only because it is an aspect of the work which is not always adequately appreciated by those who have no experience of working in this way.

One of the things which we had discussed since the beginning of the project was access to the Monday night discotheque which Gordon had observed to be so popular on one of his first visits to Moortown. As I have already mentioned this was not the sort of place to which it was easy to gain a casual, uncommitted access. Gordon had found out a good deal about the organization of the discotheque by chatting to the couple who held the licence for the public house in which it was held. In the course of this he had also been able to form some impression of them and of their possible response to his next course of action.

One Monday, at the end of June, he suggested to the landlord that he ran a bar for him in the discotheque. The position here was that this had been tried, but that the sales of bottled beer and soft drinks did not justify the employment of the barman. Most of the customers either did not drink at all, or preferred to buy the cheaper draught beer downstairs and take it up to the discotheque room. Gordon explained exactly why he wanted to do this and told the landlord about the job he was trying to do. Before taking this step he had come to the conclusion that such a proposition would be an acceptable one. That is, that whether or not his offer were accepted, the making of the offer was not in itself something that would damage his relationship with the landlord. In fact, the landlord and his wife were delighted by the offer and extremely interested in the whole project.

This immediate interest was typical of the response Gordon met in negotiating with adults in the town. Not everyone immediately understood what he was trying to do, but there was generally a willingness to try to understand and with understanding a willingness to try to help that was exciting to discover. Partly this arose because of Gordon himself. His own enthusiasm and unaffected concern for the young people in the town evoked this response. Also, there were many adults who were concerned at seemingly inexplicable eruptions of anti-social behaviour among young people in the town and who were beginning to suspect that perhaps Moortown was not the best place in the world in which to be young. To some extent the size of the community helped to breed this response. The young people *in* Moortown were the young people *of* Moortown and what they did mattered. If a broken bus shelter could be laid at the door of marauding young savages from Sheffield, then this was all right. It was disgraceful, but explicable. There were also the home grown tearaways of whom one could expect no better. But when it was young Bob or young Jennifer or 'our Margaret's boy' who was involved, it became a matter of genuine local concern.

At the beginning of July, Gordon began working in the discotheque and as a way of meeting people this proved immediately successful. The set up was ideal. The discotheque room was illuminated at two points only; a light over the disc jockey and a light over the small bar at which Gordon presided. For an hour and a half no one came near the bar, but eventually someone took the plunge and after this there was a steady flow of people who came up to buy something or to chat. Most came to talk rather than to buy and bar sales were very low. At the end of the first evening Gordon wrote, 'I feel that once I am accepted in here relationships will develop rapidly due to the intimate nature of the place and the fairly obvious need for somebody to talk to.'

At the beginning of the second evening, some of those who had talked on the first occasion made a bee line for the bar and settled themselves down for the evening. Others came and went. Business at the bar improved, but not to the point where it ever made extended conversations impossible. Subsequent evenings followed the same pattern and slowly it became possible to form some impression of the clientele. The bar hangers were of two kinds. First were those who simply wanted an adult to talk to, perhaps because adult contacts elsewhere were not very sympathetic, perhaps because the discotheque environment was not one in which they felt entirely at home and secure. Typical of this section were two young girls who had been among the first to latch on to Gordon and who chatted unreservedly about their work, their leisure and their whippet racing activities. Second was an older male group in their late teens who, after exploratory conversation, quickly saw Gordon as someone who might help them achieve their immediate ends. This group played pop music together and for the immediate future wanted somewhere to rehearse and in the long term were interested in anything which might further their progress as a pop group. Through this group it became possible to know something of the sixty or seventy regular attenders and this key group's acceptance of Gordon made for an easy relationship with the mass of the membership.

The establishment of Gordon's identity as a detached youth worker came slowly and it was of course now obscured by his occupation as barman. He was happy to answer whatever questions came, but often they came very slowly or very obliquely. It was nearly a month before one of the two girls I have already mentioned worked round to asking Gordon if he worked as a barman anywhere else. When he replied that he did not, both girls accused him of not being a proper barman at all. He was, they said, 'a religion'. For Gordon the opportunity to explain that he was not 'a religion' and to explain exactly what he was was a very welcome one, but it had been a long time coming and the incident illustrates one of the difficulties of detached work.

Not everyone thought Gordon was 'a religion'. Some imagined him to be something more dangerous than this and others had fears a good deal less specific. In November 1968, I conducted some confidential, open ended interviews with some of the people who first met Gordon at the discotheque. Some of them could remember quite clearly their initial suspicion of him and were quite happy to recount it. One of the most likely things for any unaccountable adult to be is a policeman. This is what one eighteen year old had to say:

'Well, I didn't know who he were really. At first I thought he were somebody on t'police side like. You know, under age drinking and that. Well, I were under age then so I didn't have a deal to do with him.'

Others had less specific suspicions:

'I thought Gordon was a very funny fellow, because there was a coloured youth who did this discotheque over here and I got talking to him one night and I'd seen Gordon coming and doing the pots and I said, "Is he your manager like? Does he go round with you?" "No," he says, "He's nothing to do with us." So then I thought to myself, "He's nothing to do with pub here because it's the only night he comes." But I never asked him what he was doing. I just talked to him and got quite friendly with him, and I never asked him. I wondered what he was doing, but it never occurred to me to ask him.' It was in fact several weeks before this particular individual found out what Gordon was really doing in Moortown.

A girl who subsequently became one of the key members of the group thought he was a bit cheeky:

'He came up to us ... he came up to me and M– and asked us to carry on dancing because we were holding things up or something. I thought it was a bit of a cheek. Then we got talking ...'

The early growth of relationships was a complicated business. The most suspicious held off and quite deliberately let their mates conduct the initial investigation. Only when it was said that 'he seemed all right' did they draw closer. A relationship pattern became established which presented diagramatically would be a series of concentric circles. At the bulls eye were those who knew Gordon as Gordon the detached youth worker. Next came those who knew Gordon as Gordon, someone it was all right to know. Next came those who knew him as "Im that washes glasses at the pub', and again the connotation was favourable. Finally, would be the group who knew of him, but to whom he was an object of suspicion.

All this led to a very wide acquaintanceship. Soon everyone who used the discotheque was known at a superficial level and this led to a widening acquaintance with people in the town as a whole. At this stage Gordon probably 'knew', in the sense of there being some sort of mutual recognition, well over a hundred young people in Moortown. The question now became not, 'How can I get to know people?' but 'Which people is it important to know better?'

To this question there were some ready-made answers. It seemed reasonable to suppose that the pop group which had first approached him had practical needs which they themselves recognized and which it was desirable he should try and satisfy. They had selected him, not he them. Similarly with the two girls I mentioned, he was being helpful simply by being there. But beyond this the problem of selection was a difficult one. Some of the people in the discotheque displayed behaviour problems with which Gordon felt he would be unable to cope with the limited time and resources at his disposal. He had to work with those he could help and in his position this was not necessarily the section of the community in greatest need. At the other end of the scale were those, like the one or two in full-time further education, to whom specific help would not have been refused, but whom it would have seemed wrong to have made the focus of the project. Between these extremes lay the mass of young people who gave the impression of wanting something without knowing what that something was.

Some of my interviews eighteen months later suggested that this early impression was a very accurate one. It is the rule rather than the exception for young people, talking about leisure life in their home town, to complain that there is 'nothing to do'. Many of this group explained exactly what they meant by this. Most had tried the youth club and either grown out of it or rapidly had found that it was not what they wanted. This left them with the resources of the town, which had very little to offer young people. For the girls the choice was between staying in and watching 'telly' or going out to 'hang about the streets', and this was the phrase which many of them used. In practice this meant the chip shop, the square and the occasional pub visit. Some of the girls were squeamish about visiting some of the pubs and as these were the pubs the lads used they had to hang about until the boys came out if they really wanted to meet them. Usually all this 'hanging about' cost money and one girl put her nightly expenses at about half a crown. In a sense this was money spent in order to survive the process of doing nothing. It was a resented expenditure.

In recent years in Moortown, the number of places where it was possible to hang about with some protection from the elements had decreased. One night two girls took Gordon round the town to show him the number of shops which had railings across the shop door-ways. Many of these had appeared since the closure of the town cinema and while it is easy to see why the shopkeepers took this step it was taken by the girls as a deliberate attempt on the part of a malevolent authority to keep them out in the cold.

For the boys, 'hanging about' meant the square, the chip shop, and the pubs whenever there was any money. All those I spoke to like a drink and an occasional 'blinder' on a special occasion, but looking back on their 'hanging about' days many felt that they spent all their money on beer simply because there was nothing else to do. Sometimes they did not even like their drinking companions very much.

'I used to go around with ... Do you know the estate down here?
... the ... estate? I used to be one of that lot. Christ, they're hard on
there you know. But they weren't mates. You couldn't turn round.
If you were one of them you couldn't turn your back. No chance.
You had to keep your eyes on all of them. Although they were your
mates, you know. I used to come up here drinking most nights.'

One or two had been in trouble, one seriously. Trouble meant
theft or vandalism or a 'violence' charge. With the two I talked
to it was vandalism and theft and both of them quite independently
attributed their patches of trouble to boredom. There is nothing
unusual in this. There are various conversational scapegoats for
delinquent behaviour such as ,'I was drunk', or 'I don't know what
came over me', or, perhaps most commonly of all, 'I got into bad
company'. They are all gross over-simplifications and sometimes
rationalization of something which otherwise would not be acceptable. The two lads I spoke with chose 'boredom' and stuck to this.
They had got into trouble because they were bored and they were
not going to get into trouble again because they had learned how not
to be bored. Certainly this was a misleading over-simplification, but
not, perhaps a complete misrepresentation.

The difficult job Gordon had to try to do during the summer of
1967 was to select a group with whom to work. He was trying to
work with 'ordinary' young people, like those I have quoted above,
who had some need which it would be realistic for someone in his
situation to try to answer. 'Selection' in this context meant that he
had to choose to which groups to make himself most easily available.
This left the final choice in the hands of the young people, who would
have their own criteria for choosing or not choosing Gordon. This
is really the only basis on which detached work can operate and
those who see it as an unjustifiable intrusion into the lives of other
people must be singularly unaware of the enormous capacity we all
have for resisting such intrusions. Very possibly there were some
young people whom Gordon could have helped who rejected him.
These we cannot know about. Certainly there were some who
latched on at various stages of the project who Gordon decided he
could not help; usually either because they had needs beyond his
resources or because their requirements ran contrary to those of
other groups or individuals. One of Gordon's particular strengths
in all this was the way in which he was able to maintain friendly and
helpful relations with people with whom he had no intention of
working on an intensive basis and so to avoid any suggestion of
rejection. Most of these more casual relationships were still extant
eighteen months later.

The selection process did not take place at a particular stage in
the project and then cease. In a different form, complicated by the

selectivity of established groups, it continued throughout the project. It was particularly important during the initial stages because what happened then would determine how the project developed. It demanded assessment, reflection and action from the worker and the whole process went on as a background to other events, over some of which he had little or no control.

Some practical help for the pop group was possible immediately and Gordon was able to help them negotiate for a practice room at the pub at a rent they could afford. Contact with this group led to introductions to other groups working in the town and to their customers and all this contributed to Gordon's understanding of the community in which he was working.

An incident in mid-July was important in establishing the character of the working relationship Gordon was to have with the young people in the town. One or two people in the discotheque, including a key member of the pop group, suggested organizing a trip from the discotheque to the Cavern Club at Liverpool. Gordon was asked if he would run this. He said that he was not prepared to do this, but added that he was prepared to help them in any way he could with the organization of the outing.

This was an important step and one which a less capable man would have been unable to take at this early stage. In practical terms 'helping' to organize this outing involved much more work than would have been necessary had he agreed to undertake the whole of the organization for them. But from the outset it did mean that an important principle was clearly established. Gordon was not prepared to 'run' anything. What he was prepared to do, and what he demonstrated he was prepared to go to considerable lengths to do, was to help groups of young people to run things for themselves. This was the key to the whole project. The project was set up to help young people and this was how the word 'help' was to be interpreted.

The arrangements for the trip to Liverpool were protracted and complicated. Liverpool became London and the Cavern was ousted by the Pink Flamingo. An enormous number of people were involved at various stages, though only a handful eventually took part. As an enterprise aimed at providing a night out in London for a large number of people it failed miserably.

While the arrangements were being made for the trip to London, a whole complex of other events were taking place. Some of these were to have far reaching results.

One of the local councillors who was also a Justice of the Peace sometimes used the public house in which the discotheque was situated. He heard of Gordon's work through the landlord and arranged to meet Gordon in the bar one night. Gordon found this

141

councillor extremely sympathetic and the meeting gave Gordon the chance to express his personal conviction that the local community had some responsibility towards helping their own young people. He explained what he was trying to do and the way in which this differed from the work of the youth clubs. All this was received with understanding and there were laid the foundations of a relationship which was to play an important part in subsequent events.

Concurrent with this was the final stage of another development which has not yet been mentioned. At the beginning of the project it was decided that Gordon should have a base in Moortown. There was some confusion as to the exact purpose this base was to serve and I think the three people who were involved in planning the project, the Area Youth Officer, the Senior Youth Leader for the area and myself, had rather different ideas about this, though the matter was never clarified to the point where disagreement would have been possible. Where we clearly agreed was in thinking that one of the facilities which a detached worker might well need would be a place of his own where he could meet people. What was less clear was whether the people he took there were 'all' people or 'some' people and whether this provision was of primary or secondary importance in relation to the project as a whole. My feeling was that work should start without such a provision being available and it should in any case be something the worker should feel free to use in whatever way circumstances suggested were most appropriate. I think my colleagues saw the 'meeting room' occupying a rather more central place in the scheme of things and in each case saw its function rather differently.

It is difficult to judge what effect all this had on the project. Delays over negotiations about the room meant that the project had started before the room was ready and when at last it was ready it came to the worker with certain built in assumptions about its use. It had been called a 'meeting room' and this terminology probably influenced the way the worker regarded it; at least in so far as it did not help him to consider the full range of possibilities for the room's use. There is a difference between providing a detached worker with a room in which he can meet people, if and when he wants to, and providing him with a 'meeting room', a phrase which has a suggestion of the club room about it. Whether in the event this was detrimental to the project it is impossible to say, but looking back I think it would have been a healthier situation if the room had been available to the worker on a very much more 'take it or leave it' basis. Whether the various committees of a local education authority could have been persuaded to make such a provision, even on a rent as low as three pounds per week, without a more specific case being made for its use is another matter.

142

The Senior Youth Leader for the area had been responsible for finding and negotiating for a suitable room and he had devoted a lot of time and effort to this. The room he eventually found was in many aspects ideal. It was a small room which had been part of an attic flat above the fish and chip shop in the market square. The ceiling sloped interestingly and there were two small floor level windows. The bathroom next door was not in use and had a lavatory. The approach was direct from the fish and chip shop, past the restaurant on the first floor and up the attic stairs.

The room was ready for use at the end of August and Gordon mentioned its existence at the discotheque one evening early in September. His approach was deliberately off hand. The room was there, unfurnished ... it might be possible to do something with it ... It would probably need a lot of work doing on it ... This news spread rapidly and the same evening enquiries and offers of help came from people Gordon had never even spoken to before. He said he was going to look at it the following evening and if anyone wanted to come with him he would meet them outside the chip shop at about eight o'clock. When he arrived the following evening he was met by thirty people and a large crossbred alsatian dog. The project had moved into a new phase.

It is easy to understand why the room should arouse some initial interest. It was new and different and something about which to be curious in a town which provided few opportunities for the exercise of this emotion. It is perhaps harder to see why this interest should be maintained once the initial curiosity had been satisfied. Logically, a bare room, no more than fourteen feet square does not seem to afford much by way of an attractive provision. Although the town was socially under-provided it could at least offer the chip shop, a range of pubs and at least four youth clubs all of which had considerably more facilities at their disposal. The answer can probably be summed up in the phrase, 'A place of our own'. To say 'what sort of place?' one would have to enter into the imaginative lives of all those who at some time or other ever went there and it seems unlikely that these individual visions could be reconciled or were ever fully realized. What the behaviour of the people who went to the room would lead me to guess at is that one of their major satisfactions arose from pride of possession and control of a tiny fragment of their environment.

This was shown by the behaviour of the first group into the room who quickly set about the business of making it their place. Decoration was outside the terms of the lease, but a profusion of murals and invocations rapidly covered the walls. There was no room for furniture, but it was a good floor for sitting on. A record player was borrowed and a whip round provided the money for some coloured lighting and spot light. There were those who did, those who suggested, and those who silently and uncommittedly watched. Gordon helped with materials and kept the peace. Sometimes he went away altogether and strolled across the market place to chat with the pop group in their newly acquired practice room. This manoeuvre, particularly, helped establish his non-proprietorial role in relation to the premises.

Very soon indeed the room at the top became an established part of the social scene and attracted about fifty visitors a night. As it was physically impossible to cram more than about thirty people into it at any one time there was a good deal of coming and going. There emerged a hard core group of about a dozen, most of whom were there most of the time. The others displayed varying degrees of interest and there were usually some new faces. Here is how one lad described his first meeting with Gordon:

'It were upstairs in that little room and there were me and two others...(remembering)...No, I used to see him in here wash pots... and you know he got that room going, that little room and there were a few of us downstairs in the cafe... I don't know where we'd been. We'd been in the — (name of pub) or somewhere. And we saw these people coming up and down stairs, so I said, "What's going off upstairs then?" And they said, "It's that feller who washes pots at —. He's here. He's upstairs. Decorating." I said, "What the bloody hell is he decorating a little room at the top of the cafe for?" Anyway, I said a most stupid thing, I said, "Let's go upstairs and boycott it." And the chap who I were with said, "If we want to boycott it we want to walk outside." But anyway we were interested and so we went up. Lot of folks. But he gets on with anybody Gordon does you know.'

J.L. 'What did you think when you first went in there?'

'I thought, "well it's different". I can't remember really...I thought it were a bit of a dive. He made everybody welcome, you know. Cos you know he stressed that he weren't no more important than him like.'

However, if Gordon seemed welcoming and egalitarian this was not true of the group as a whole. Despite all the coming and going and the apparent open access of the room there were some people whose faces did not fit and to whom the room was as prohibited as if there had been an iron gate at the bottom of the stairs. This situation posed some immediate practical problems for Gordon who wanted to maintain a contact with some of those who were excluded. It also suggested that one of the educational aims for the project should be to try to increase the tolerance of some of the people involved.

Concurrent with the move to the room were some changes at the discotheque. Gordon found that he no longer had to bother very much about the practical side of running the bar. A number of people had been helping with this for some time and gradually Gordon found that there was no shortage of people to look after it for a short time if he wanted to go and do something else. This meant that he was no longer tied to one corner of the room and could take the initiative in contacting people when this seemed appropriate instead of always having to wait until people came to him.

It was at this period too that the long laid plans for the trip to London came to fruition. As I have already mentioned it was not, in the event, a very rich harvest. Over thirty people had indicated their intention to go and a forty-one seater coach had been booked to ensure that any hangers on were not disappointed. At the appointed time only five people turned up. This group rapidly adjourned to the nearest public house to lick their wounds and to decide what to do. Some of the group were disappointed, others frankly angry with their friends for letting them down.

The immediate question which faced Gordon was what to do next. His answer was to take the five people who had come, to London in his car and to do his best to see to it that the experience was an enjoyable one for them. This was an important decision. Naturally, Gordon was concerned that a group with which he was associated was disappointed and he wanted to help alleviate that disappointment. But what was even more important, both for those who took part and those who did not, was that things which it was said were going to happen actually happened—and happened even when the odds seemed strong against their doing so. Partly this was important at a personal level. The worker was seen to be a person of integrity. Partly it was important as a demonstration of the possibility of social organization. A very ambitious project which had been initiated and organized by a group of young people had been carried through into action. True it had not worked out as planned and would have been a complete failure had it not been for Gordon's intervention, but the fact that it happened at all demonstrated the possibility of its happening more successfully.

Probably there were two main reasons why those who had expressed an interest in the London trip did not turn up for it. With some the expression of interest had probably never been very closely related to reality. It was a great idea and one with which they wanted to be associated and so they expressed a sincere enthusiasm for it. But they knew they would never actually go. Others, I think, had really intended to go, but had not had the necessary money when the time came. Without help they were quite unable to save for special events in the future and this trip was outside normal weekly expenditure for the majority. To some extent, Gordon misread the situation both with regard to interpreting the true nature of the enthusiasm which the trip aroused and in not taking into account the difficulty some people might have in saving for future events. But his situation was a very difficult one. He was not organizing the trip, but advising on its organization. The young organizers desperately wanted the event to take place and were, therefore, predisposed to place the most favourable interpretation they could on what they were told and the assurances they were given. It was difficult for Gordon both to encourage and support the organizers and at the same time urge caution.

On the Monday following the Saturday of the London trip, there was considerable discussion about it at the discotheque. Many of those who had not gone felt it necessary to make some sort of excuse for their non-attendance. Those who had gone felt satisfyingly superior and were therefore much less inclined to be recriminatory towards those who had 'let them down' than would have been the case had they had no such satisfactory experience to draw upon.

On the Tuesday there was an excursion of another kind which was important for future developments. This was a late evening to be spent at the L.E.A. Arts Centre at Stainsby.

I had suggested Stainsby to Gordon as one of the local facilities which he might find useful and I had arranged for him to meet Peter Ellis, the warden, so that he could make arrangements with him if this seemed useful. I was able to do this because I knew the people involved and the way in which they worked. This led me to suppose that the young people with whom Gordon was involved would be acceptable at Stainsby and would themselves accept the sort of reception they received. The fact that Stainsby was an 'Arts' centre was, at this stage, irrelevant. For present purposes, it was just somewhere else to go. Like driving down the motorway to the nearest motorway cafe, it provided a break in the evening routine and provided a miniature adventure.

Twenty-three people went on the first visit to Stainsby in a caravan of scooters, cars and vans. They looked round the centre, drank coffee in the canteen, beat on the piano and looked at some film extracts. The warden came from stoking the boiler to show the films and the offhand informality of his dress and manner destroyed any unease which strangeness had created. Many of the group were intrigued by Stainsby. It was strange without being threatening. On the way home they joked about 'this place out in the wilds where a bloke showed us films in the middle of the bloody night'.

This first visit to Stainsby led on to a chain of events which stretches up to the present and which are probably best dealt with here. There was soon a demand for other visits to Stainsby and the next one or two of these were mass excursions, the chief benefit of which was probably that they satisfied the curiosity which had been aroused. Some minority groups, however, wanted to explore the possibilities of Stainsby further. By January 1968 twenty-one people were regularly involved in film making, folk singing, painting, photography and pottery. Not all these people managed to go to Stainsby every week and probably not all would have wanted to. One of the difficulties was transport. The three girls who became interested in pottery probably attended most frequently because the voluntary art tutor at the centre could take them in his car as he travelled through Moortown on his way to the centre. For others, it was much more difficult and if they had no transport of their own they had to rely on Gordon or on friends in order to make the five mile journey. Sometimes, Gordon ran a shuttle service, but such arrangements were always very complicated and time consuming.

The film which the group made as a result of their contact with Stainsby was an interesting piece of work. It set out to show the group's view of Moortown. It showed Moortown's industrial setting with the coalite works belching enormous clouds of steam and smoke over the surrounding landscape. It showed the centre of the town and the barred shop doorways. It showed the worst of the town's housing with a telling shot of the half open door of one of the outside lavatories. It showed the leisure life of the community; the adults in the bright lights of the bingo hall, the young talking and drinking and engaged in an explicit sexual maul at a party. The film will not win prizes at Cannes, but it is technically competent and the average home movie would look pale by comparison. It has something to say and it says it with guts. When some members of the town council saw it, it made them angry. It was, as they rightly pointed out, biased and unfair, but it is a film with a point of view and it is not insignificant and dismissable.

The film, the pottery, the opportunity for small group activities were all positive gains from the contact with Stainsby. Equally valuable, though much less obvious was the simple fact that Stainsby was there and a body of people in Moortown knew about it and felt they could use it if they wanted to. When the group moved to new premises it was to Stainsby that they looked for advice and help with decoration. When they wanted to make posters they knew who would be able to help them. Most important of all they knew that the sort of advice and help they would receive would be concerned with helping them achieve what they wanted to achieve and not with telling them what they ought to want.

The fact of Stainsby made the arts both more accessible and more acceptable. It is difficult to evaluate its influence, but so far as the Moortown group is concerned it seems to have influenced attitudes at a variety of levels. It seems to have helped foster the attitude that participation in some arts activities is fun, that not all art is characterized by solemnity. It seems to have aroused a curiosity about the arts, and made them realize that aspects of the subject were worth talking about. At a practical level, it seems to have influenced attitudes to design, not in the sense of distinguishing 'good' design, but in drawing attention to the importance of the way things look. The chip shop premises the group occupied were decorated as a mark of occupation, and the decorations were individual and haphazard. Later, the lay-out and decoration of the new premises were the subject of frequent, fierce and intelligent argument. Partly this was because the group had become a cohesive unit which was trying to create an integrated environment, but partly also, because they had become more conscious of design and lay-out.

This brief account of the relation of Stainsby to the Moortown Project has taken us a long way from the events of September 1967 and it is now necessary to return to the historical context and to examine some other developments which were taking place.

What had happened up to September was that Gordon had become involved with a large number of people whom he had been able to help in a variety of ways. The practical help to the pop group was one sort of help, the provision of the meeting room was another and the introduction to Stainsby yet another. In order for these forms of help to be possible there had to be a relationship between Gordon and the people concerned, but at this stage most of these relationships were of a very superficial kind. For some of the things which it was useful to do, a superficial relationship was all that was necessary, but there were indications that some people looked for a deeper relationship and Gordon came to recognize the need to organize his work so that he worked with different groups of people at different levels of intensity.

Slowly, there emerged a group with which there were deeper relationships and which became the hard core of the project. At the end of September Gordon wrote, 'The meetings are popular and attract between fifty and seventy people per night. However, it is possible to work in depth with a small nucleus within the larger group and so the project is controlled through the strong relationships with about fifteen young people.' At the time this was written, there was probably an element of projection about this statement. The relationships were hardly long-lived enough to be 'strong' and were certainly destined to become very much stronger but the passage illustrates the view the worker had of the situation and the way in which he thought it was going to develop. It is interesting to note that the seven or eight key members I talked with more than a year later were all people who had become more closely involved with Gordon at this time.

There was no systematic study of the groups of people with whom Gordon worked, but it might be useful to make some broad, general comments about this central group by way of description. In September 1967, they were all seventeen or eighteen years of age except for one or two older members who were in their twenties. With one exception, they had not enjoyed school, usually because they resented some aspect of the discipline, though some of them had done quite well. One boy had gone to a selective secondary modern school and had gained a number of passes at 'O' level G.C.E. Others had been in the G.C.E. stream and passed in one or two subjects. Altogether, about half of the group had stayed on at school beyond the age of fifteen. Most of the girls worked in shops or in factories and most of the boys were skilled or semi-skilled workers at the pit. Most had had some experience of youth club membership, but the majority of these seemed not to have been very active members and with some 'membership' had only lasted a matter of weeks. Two of the group had appeared before the courts and yet another subsequently became a police cadet.

What I am trying to stress here is the ordinariness of the group, and its lack of easily labelled characteristics. It was not an 'intellectual' group nor one characterized by the low academic achievement of its members. Many of the group changed their jobs after leaving school, but they were neither feckless nor noticeably low on job satisfaction. Probably most were employed in occupations that under-used their abilities, but this, too, I would regard as a characteristic of ordinariness. Their uncommitted youth club membership is normal enough in an area where many clubs lose as much as two-thirds of their membership every year. Probably all the group had committed offences like under age drinking or minor infringements of the traffic laws and in this too they were probably well within the statistical norm. They were all natives of Moortown and some had known each other since their schooldays. However, at this stage, their real link with each other was through Gordon.

The only purpose in presenting these sorts of generalizations about the group is to make it quite clear that they were neither a well integrated, high ability group who could effortlessly overcome the obstacles which came their way, nor were they a set of tearaways and delinquents whom it was Gordon's object to reform.

In addition, there seemed to me to be one or two rather tenuous characteristics which all the members of the group possessed to some extent. At the time Gordon met them, most of the group were finding their leisure lives boring. Many spoke about this at length. The boys spent a lot of time and money in public houses and while this was felt to be better than staying at home they were not finding it very satisfying. The girls used the pubs less frequently, but tended

149

to hang about the town centre an as alternative to staying home every night. There were highlights in the leisure time table, the pub dance or the occasional party, but for the most part, leisure was routine and dull. So although different individuals had been involved with different groups of friends, there were some points of similarity about the sort of leisure lives they had all been leading. The important common characteristic was a recent experience of boredom.

There had been some efforts by small groups of friends to relieve the boredom by some sort of group organization, though it is difficult to give examples of this because usually these attempts never progressed beyond the stage of being 'ideas'. One small group had met for a time in a disused air raid shelter in the town and these meetings had some sense of 'club' about them, but the meetings rapidly degenerated into sexual mauling sessions and the group dispersed. Some of the pop group had ideas, never very clearly expressed, of forming some sort of club to be centred on their activities. Others had ideas for forming a club or for trips or excursions, none of which ever came to anything.

One of the chief reasons for failure was a lack of faith in the possibility of social organization. When Gordon first met this group, this was still very apparent in the way they tended to scorn any ideas for action which any group member put forward. Often the terms in which new ideas were ridiculed was extremely cruel and the whole process destructive. There was a similar streak in the attitude towards some forms of provision. For example, it was always held that the commercial discotheque at the public house 'wouldn't last'. To take this attitude was, of course, a kind of insurance policy against the eventual disappointment of closure, but it meant, too, that participation tended to be geared for a full exploitation of the present rather than a participation which included any hopeful vision of the future.

Associated with the above, was a general lack of self-confidence which displayed itself in a variety of ways; often very difficult to describe. There is a manner of speaking, for example, which suggests that one does not expect to be listened to and this was a characteristic of many of this group when Gordon first met them. More strikingly, they had a series of expectations about the way they would be treated in certain social settings and the group which went to London with Gordon expected, quite groundlessly, to be asked to leave one rather 'posh' bar which they visited. They undervalued their own abilities both individually and as a group and it was only considerable first hand experience of success that brought individual self-respect.

Finally, many of the group displayed a characteristic I can best describe as low intellectual curiosity. I mean curiosity of a speculative kind, like the mental activity which is involved in wondering 'what lies at the end of that street', or, 'behind those doors' or 'what that man does for a living'. There seemed to be enormous areas of life about which many of this group expressed no curiosity at all and in the place of a potentially useful inquisitiveness there often stood a mixture of unquestioning acceptance and unthinking prejudice.

I have already described these characteristics as 'tenuous' and it must be admitted that to provide evidence of their existence would be very difficult. All that one can safely say is that it seemed to the worker and to me that in many cases there had been a recent leisure experience characterized by boredom, that there was a lack of faith in the possibility of social organization, a lack of self-confidence and a lack of this quality of intellectual curiosity.

To return to the autumn of 1967, what was now happening was that the work was beginning to settle down into a recognizable pattern. There was a fixed place of meeting and regular meeting nights and though there were special meetings for special occasions, these regular meeting nights were usually adhered to. People who wanted to find Gordon for any reason knew when and where to find him. The different sorts of work with which Gordon was involved were beginning to present themselves more clearly. It was possible to begin to distinguish between groups and individuals on the basis of their needs and to think of how best to approach each particular group or individual. Some needed a lot of attention, some very little. Some, at a particular crisis point, needed the worker's concentrated attention for a short period, others, like the central group which I have just described, presented a situation which could only be 'helped' by long term measures. To an outside visitor all this would have appeared indistinguishable and chaotic, but to Gordon it was beginning to make sense.

At the end of October came a difficulty which had long term effects. The meeting room was attracting large numbers of people. On some evenings between fifty and seventy people might visit for a short period. While this was far more than Gordon could hope to work with in a room which was full when it held thirty, it in fact presented no practical problems. In spite of the stream of comings and goings, Gordon spent time with the groups which needed it and, as far as one could tell, remained accessible to the people who needed him. Despite this considerable traffic, behaviour was exemplary, and this seemed the case whether Gordon were there or ot. However, it became clear from snatches of conversation that some of the visitors to the room were also youth club members.

The question here was, did this matter? Obviously any new provision in Moortown was likely to be investigated by the young people in the town and indeed if anything started up about which they were not curious, there would be ground for serious concern as to their mental welfare. On the other hand if they were becoming involved in the happenings at the meeting room to the point where they were leaving their other club commitments, then something was happening which warranted further investigation.

I wrote to the youth leaders in charge of the three main clubs in the town saying that I would be interested to have any comments they could let me have about the project. The letter varied slightly according to how well I knew each leader, but I asked whether they had heard of the project and if it had been commented on in their clubs, approvingly or disapprovingly, and whether it had had any effect on club membership or attendance. I also asked that there should be no special enquiries made as I did not want to arouse a curiosity where none had previously existed. All three leaders responded to my enquiry and in two cases the existence of the meeting room had gone virtually unnoticed. Certainly the leaders were not bothered about it. Some of the members were aware of the existence of something, but did not seem to be either very well informed nor very interested. The third response was very different. In this case, the youth leader provided a list of just under a hundred of his club members who, he said, were also regular attenders at the meeting room. He also pointed out that the existence of the meeting room was having an adverse effect on his club by distracting members on two of the clubs programmed nights so that they left the club early and did not stay to clear away. He said this affected the table tennis teams, one of which had had to be withdrawn from the local league and it also affected the club coffee bar which was taking much less money and which the leader was finding it impossible to staff.

This was a development which I had not foreseen. That youth club members should want to investigate something which was happening in the middle of their town was understandable, that they should, in large numbers, desert a long established and well equipped youth club to sit on the floor of a draughty attic room seemed rather unlikely. None the less, it was clear that this was what was happening in some cases. It was not happening on the scale which the youth leader supposed, but it was disturbing that it was happening at all and it created a new set of problems for Gordon at a stage in his work when he could well have concentrated all his attention on the groups with which he was immediately concerned.

Had it been possible to do nothing, this situation might well have resolved itself. The youth club members were not the main focus of Gordon's attention and given a few months they would probably have made their own choice between a peripheral position at the meeting room and the possibility of a much more established position at their youth club. A few might have wished to maintain a foot in both camps and it is difficult to see that this would have been in any way harmful. The real difficulty was that the project was alleged to be having a detrimental effect on one of the existing youth clubs in the town and this situation was complicated by the attitude of the leader concerned, who both disapproved of the way Gordon worked and, understandably, saw this new provision as a threat to his own position and the ideals for which he had worked.

It was difficult to assess the facts of the situation. The number of youth club members who used the meeting room on a regular basis was probably in the region of ten or fifteen though presumably many more visited at some time or other. Bearing in mind that the meeting room was packed to capacity with thirty people in it, it seems clear that whatever happened in the room itself could hardly have provided a counter attraction for very many from the youth club. If, simply by existing, it created an indirect attraction it is difficult to see how and why this was. It seemed to me more likely that the youth leader misconstrued the situation in attributing his club problems to the work Gordon was doing in the town. A far more probable counter attraction was perhaps the chip shop itself, the ground floor of which had been recently enlarged and fitted out as a coffee bar. What was irrefutable, however, was that the leader saw Gordon's work as damaging to his club and was upset about it.

Gordon visited the leader at his club and spent the evening talking with him and his assistants. He came away feeling that the meeting had not been constructive, but that it had perhaps 'cleared the air'. He undertook to try to keep people under seventeen or eighteen out of the meeting room altogether so as to remove any apparent threat to the youth club. What he felt he had been unable to convey was any sense of the complexity of such an undertaking for someone working as he was. He was rather dismayed by the aggression he had met from the youth club staff and his own inability to communicate with them about the job he was trying to do. It was plain that one of the difficulties here was not simply that there were misunderstandings about what was happening but that at a fundamental level there was a clash of ideas about the way adults ought to work with young people.

There was nothing new about what happened in Moortown and probably most detached work projects have met criticism of some sort from established agencies. Some of the points which the Moortown youth leader made to Gordon were very similar to the comments made about the Y.W.C.A. project in London. For example: 'The following comments that had been made to us and/or about us were noted:

1 We gave things away to the young people, which made them expect the same from clubs—this was not good for the young people, and even if it had been, the clubs did not have the same resources as the project.

2 We were not working with the 'unattached'. Many of the young people with whom we worked were known to several leaders, but they came to us because we were 'soft' with them.

3 It would have been better to put the project money into the clubs so that they could do a better job. It is always easier to get money for fancy research than for the ordinary work of established clubs.

4 Recording everything that people say and do is not ethical. In any case, the youth leaders wouldn't have time to do it, and this 'social group work' was not new. Everyone had been doing it for years in the youth service.

5 The lack of discipline in the project made it more difficult for the youth clubs, and would not help people to face life realistically.

6 The club leaders would like to work with the young people we knew but if they did the clubs would be in a shambles'.[5]

In particular, the first three of these comments and to a lesser extent the fifth are very close to what some of the youth club staff in Moortown said about the project there.

An added difficulty in Moortown was that both the youth club experiencing difficulty and the project were sponsored by the L.E.A. and a conflict of ideas within the same agency is always particularly threatening. This is especially the case with an L.E.A. where it is seen as desirable to present all educational enterprises as unified and interrelated, and although there may be some brisk in-fighting between, say, a school and a youth club, the top administrative staff will always see to it that such squabbles are kept within domestic bounds and do not bring public criticsm. The L.E.A. aim is to make a provision which is varied but united and so there are strong internal pressures toward the reduction of conflict. The danger here is that useful lessons which might be learnt from the juxtaposition of conflicting ways of working may be lost in an unseemly scramble for peace at all costs.

The particular tea-cup storm in Moortown was buried rather than resolved and it re-erupted again later in the project. I would like to have seen a situation where it was possible to clear up the misunderstanding between the youth leaders and the project worker, but in practical terms it is difficult to see how they could have met frequently enough to have achieved this. As it seemed they often perceived the same events very differently, it would be rash to suppose that an easy resolution was ever near at hand. But with

154

the misunderstandings out of the way, there would still have existed a healthy state of conflict. Had each seen the others' point of view clearly, he would still have seen that it was a very different one from his own. It seems to me foolishly idealistic to suggest that they had similar aims or that their working methods were, in any strict sense, complementary. If there were grounds for co-operation, and this is by no means certain, these could only be achieved through a full recognition of the basic differences. This was a stage we never reached.

While some of Gordon's attention was going into sorting out the difficulties with the local youth club, the group with which he was mainly concerned was beginning to settle down into a recognizable and integrated group of people. This was the period of the developments at Stainsby which I have already described and because many of the group were involved in exploring new activities they had both the bond of common experience to gossip about and new experiences to share with their friends. The meeting room hummed with talk of past, present and future activities.

At the discotheque, however, the scene was a less happy one. Attendance had dropped by about twenty and this was enough to enable people to see their surroundings all too clearly. It was the sort of room which served the purpose well enough so long as it was packed to capacity. Half empty it looked dreary. The organizers seemed to have lost interest in the enterprise, or were perhaps more fully occupied elsewhere. They no longer turned up in force and in fact passed on the job of looking after the door to one of the local lads with whom Gordon was involved. After continuing for a month or two like this, they announced their intention of withdrawing altogether. Gordon's group discussed this and decided that they should take over the running of the discotheque.

This was a big step. Running even a tiny discotheque is still a business enterprise. The group had no resources and no equipment. Initially at least there could be no question of running at a loss. From the first night the takings would have to cover the rent and obviously the original organizers had withdrawn at a point where the profit margin was negligible, and 'goodwill' was a doubtful asset.

By working through the weekend the group managed to set out the room in a way which was more to their liking. It was difficult to do much because the room was let out for a variety of purposes and all the discotheque fittings had to be movable, but a good clean out, some decorations and a change of layout did bring about an improvement.

It would be misleading to say that the discotheque thrived under the new management. It did not. However, attendances improved and it continued as a going concern comfortably above the financial survival line. The group learned how to manage and in fact deployed their forces so that they managed extremely efficiently. One of the group who worked in the accounts department at the local pit kept the books and, as other members of the group grimly commented, he was even more tight-fisted with the discotheque money than he was with his own. The premises were always well staffed and more orderly than they had been previously. Relations with the landlord were excellent. All the decisions which day to day management necessitated were made informally by the group. Who was consulted depended on who was present at the time the decision was made and those who were not grumbled, but abided by the rule. What was being achieved was being achieved by group unity and although there were squabbles no one was inclined to behave in such a way as to put the success of the group enterprise in jeopardy.

This business enterprise had a tremendous effect on the self-confidence of the individuals involved in it as well as on their sense of what they were capable of achieving collectively. For the first time in their lives they were taking decisions and playing a part in running something which, if it was not a roaring success, was unquestionably a going concern.

It seemed to me that this growing self-confidence changed the nature of their relation to the other activities with which the group was involved. The group were beginning to meet more people and more situations, but qualitatively they were meeting them in a new way. Their attitude was more exploratory, more curious, more questioning. They were less inclined to scoff at what they did not understand because it no longer constituted such a strong personal threat. With a piece of their environment firmly under control they could be more relaxed with the unknown and untried. This is of course a speculative projection, but some of the activities of the group support it as a possible interpretation. For example some of the group took part in an archaeological dig conducted by one of the Sheffield societies and talked interestedly with much older people from very different academic backgrounds. A small group went with Gordon to a youth leader training weekend and talked to an audience of seventy youth leaders many of whom later commented that this was the highlight of the course. On another occasion, others talked to research workers from the Government Social Survey who were interested in talking to a group of people who were not in a youth club. Some months later the Diocesan Youth Chaplain took the Bishop of Kansas, who was in England for the Lambeth Conference, to visit the group. About twenty of the group turned out on Saturday night to meet the Bishop and after showing him round, one of the group opened the batting with 'Now tell me, Bishop, honestly, what are you doing here?—I mean what's the Bishop of Kansas doing in Moortown on a Saturday night?'

In each case it was an unusual combination of circumstances which put the group in the way of these disparate experiences, but the point is that they had become the sort of group which could avail themselves of the opportunity when it arose. They looked at the possibility of new experience with critical interest and in this respect, it seemed to me, they had changed dramatically from the attitude they would have adopted a year earlier.

The next major event in the project was the closing of the meeting room. This followed an inspection by the local fire officer who said that without adequate fire escapes it was not suitable for the purpose for which it was being used. This was an inconvenience rather than a serious set back, because the project was now rooted in the community and although the room was useful it certainly was not central to the project. Besides the discotheque, there were a host of places where different groups could and did meet, and where Gordon was known and accepted. However, the main group decided to look for new premises where they hoped it might be possible to combine the functions of the meeting room and the discotheque.

For a long time it seemed as though the search would be a fruitless one. Between them the group had a very wide knowledge of Moortown and they followed up every possibility which occurred to any of them. They took to touring the streets and enquiring about any building which seemed as though it might serve. To hire a pub room or a hall was easy, but to find a place where they could really take possession, have freedom to decorate and reasonable access was a very much more difficult matter. After several weeks, they were lucky enough to find what they wanted and surprisingly it lay under their noses. This was a stable which was in the yard of the pub where the discotheque was held. It was accessible through a double gate at the side and had no direct link with the pub. The stable was still divided by wooden stall partitions and was used for storing coal. Upstairs was a loft accessible by ladder.

Negotiations with the landlord were swift and straightforward. Then came the enormous job of converting the property. This fell on the small main group and although fringe members dropped by and helped from time to time the whole undertaking was so unquestionably a job of work that few stayed the pace. Tons of coal and coal dust and the accumulated dust of ages were carried out in bins and the stalls ripped out. The council provided a lorry to remove the debris. Then came the cleaning out and decorating and repairing and rewiring. Altogether this work took several weeks with gangs working every evening and through the weekends. By the beginning of July, the work was completed and on the third, there was the official opening.

It was some time later before the discotheque at the stable had

157

its opening night. Before this was possible, there was still some work to be completed on the premises and some attention had to be given to the timing of the opening, to publicity and to obtaining a singing and dancing licence. By the time these final touches were complete a great deal of work had gone into the whole enterprise.

The opening night was a roaring success with over a hundred young people present—until ten past ten. At ten past ten, the local fire officer and police sergeant arrived on the scene, and, after a cursory examination of the premises, ordered its immediate closure. Again the problem was the fire regulations which for a building used for this sort of purpose are particularly stringent. This was a severe blow and discussion with the fire officer revealed that a tremendous amount of costly alterations would have to be made before the building would comply with the necessary regulations. Had the group been completely dispirited by this, it would not have been surprising, but in fact it had the reverse effect of consolidating the group in a determination to complete the job they had started. In this they were helped by the publicans who asked the brewery for some financial support and by the fire officer who made compliance with the regulations as simple as possible.

Soon the discotheque re-opened and by mid-autumn was a thriving concern. Improvements to the premises went on all the time and materials for decoration or construction came from a variety of sources. Many of the group had 'business' contacts of one sort or another and the generosity of many individuals and firms was considerable. One member acquired bamboo runners from carpet salesmen, the local pit supplied some pit props and the proprietor of the local fish and chip shop loaned a mass of expensive lighting equipment.

I visited the discotheque one evening and talked to some of the customers. They were united in their praise of the venture and said it was 'terrific', 'fantastic' and 'the best thing that has ever happened in Moortown'. Asked to be more specific about what it was that they liked about it, they particularly mentioned the friendliness of the people, the atmosphere and various physical characteristics of the building itself. I followed up the comments about friendliness and several people described how it was more friendly than other forms of provision of which they had experience and they gave accounts of how they had made new friends. Even though the talks were individual and confidential, I found it impossible to elicit much by way of criticism. About the most damning comment that was made was, 'Well, it gets a bit cold in there some nights.' For the handful with whom I talked there were perhaps many who had come to the discotheque, considered it a dismal failure and gone away again, but from those I did talk with the praise was unstinted. This seemed to me unusual. More often in talking to people who are using some particular form of provision I have found many who though using the provision regularly are none the less highly critical of it. Often so much so that one wonders why, if it is so poor, they bother to keep on going. This group of customers were different and perhaps their difference lay in the fact that although they were customers, they also felt themselves to be participants. They refer to the central group as 'they' and thought 'they' had done a good job, but at the same time they felt themselves associated with the enterprise either because they had made some practical contribution like decorating or serving coffee, or because they felt that the 'they' to whom they referred were also their friends. While there was no doubt about who ran the show, it was clear that the paying customers found nothing unusual in being asked to help out with a variety of odd jobs and felt themselves part of the whole concern.

The discotheque venture occupied most of the group's energies during the autumn of 1968. They did, however, take time out for other activities and one of these is worth a brief mention. At the end of September, they went away together for a weekend at Derbyshire Education Committee's Residential Centre at Lea Green, near Matlock. The group had often talked about going away together and the suggestion of Lea Green came from Gordon who knew the centre from his club work days. The group organized their own course and Gordon made the necessary arrangements with the centre. One of the items which was much discussed and which demanded considerable long term planning was a mock trial to be held on the Sunday morning. The accused was the chairman of Moortown Urban District Council and the charge was that the council had conspired to neglect the needs of young people in Moortown. The councillor and J.P. who had earlier befriended the group agreed to act for the defence and the chairman agreed to stand trial. One of the older members of the group who was a shop assistant in Chesterfield prosecuted and prepared his case in conjunction with others in the group, many of whom he called as witnesses.

The event itself was very interesting because although there was a jocularity about the way the proceedings were conducted, there was no mistaking the serious intent below the surface. In many respects it was an unfair battle because what was an off the cuff exercise for busy councillors had been the subject of meticulous preparation on the part of the group. The outcome, a face saving conditional discharge, was the least important part of the proceedings and what was useful was the voicing of two quite different views of the same town. It was an interesting and useful exercise, but of course one which was only possible because of the sympathies

159

of the councillors concerned. Those less sympathetic to the needs of young people would never lend themselves to such an encounter. As one of the group said to me later, 'It were alright, but we'd got the wrong folk in the dock.'

Towards the end of 1968, the group faced two problems. The first of these was a re-erruption of the clash with some of the youth leaders in the town. The trouble here was that the discotheque provided a rival attraction to the youth club and operated on some of the same nights. The youth leaders felt that they should not have to compete with another L.E.A. sponsored provision. The situation became very trying and some very bitter public statements were made which added fuel to the fire. For example, one youth leader announced that he would see to it that the discotheque was closed and this statement, not unnaturally, angered the young people concerned. One of the difficulties was that there was considerable misinformation about the number of youth club members who went to the discotheque and as the youth leaders declined invitations to visit and see for themselves this was never satisfactorily resolved. Eventually, there was a meeting which, after much recrimination, laid the basis for an uneasy co-existence. However, it would be irrational to be hopeful about a long term resolution because, as I suggested earlier, the immediate practical disagreement masked a more fundamental disagreement about aims and methods. The youth leaders concerned believed that the activities they provided were, of themselves, good and 'wholesome' experiences and that discotheques were either directly bad influences or at least only justifiable as a means of raising money to provide more valuable activities. They disapproved of the degree of responsibility carried by the young people in Gordon's group and felt that he was 'putting old heads on young shoulders'. They had reservations about the personal qualities, honesty, integrity, truthfulness, of some of the young people with whom Gordon was involved and thought Gordon foolish to trust them. These attitudes imply a very different approach to work with young people to that which Gordon employed, and while expediency demands that both the youth club and Gordon's group should peacefully co-exist, perhaps the healthiest co-existence would be that which helped clarify the essential differences between the two work methods.

The second problem was much more mundane and was simply that of providing adequate heating for the discotheque in midwinter. The group invested in some wall heaters which made an appreciable difference, but did not create anything approaching a comfortable temperature unless the room was crowded. This meant that in winter the building was only useful as a discotheque and its intended dual usage was lost.

As the winter progressed the popularity of the discotheque also declined. Once numbers fell the cold took further toll and discotheque evenings became occasional rather than weekly events. This removed the activity which had for months been central to the life of the group and there was during this period a decline in total group activity.

There was also during this period evidence of the beginnings of the break up of the group. This was not, I think, in anyway casually related to the temporary failure of the discotheque. Over the months Gordon had been drawn into many conversations about jobs and had of necessity engaged in a certain amount of vocational counselling. In this he had help from a school counsellor who unstintingly gave his time in order to give tests and conduct interviews with one or two people needing special help. At this time, for a number of reasons, change was in the air. However, I would stress that it was a period of change and not of depression. It was at this time that one of the boys said to me, 'If you had told me a year ago this lot would have done all this, I wouldn't have believed you. I was prepared to give a hand because I hoped it would work, but I didn't really believe it would. Never.'

For many months Gordon had been planning his withdrawal from the group. Initially he had intended to withdraw in order to work with other groups in the town, keeping peripheral contact with the core group who seemed now to be a long way on the road to independence. Changes in his personal circumstances led him to decide to withdraw completely and the fact that the discotheque activity was in abeyance made this easier to achieve.

The actual withdrawal period took just over six months though in fact contact continued beyond this and still continues on an occasional basis. There was a good deal of discussion about what to do about the discotheque. There was little enthusiasm for continuing it in premises which proved untenable for at least four months of the year, but a number of other plans were thrashed out. In particular one of the public houses in the town came up with what seemed to be a very attractive proposition about the use of their premises and resources. This would have solved all the financial problems as well as the practical ones and discussion of what to do about this occupied several weeks. In the event the group eventually decided not to go ahead with this and this I think for no more complicated reason than that they were tired of discotheques and had other things which they wanted to do more.

At Christmas there was a party and almost immediately after Christmas plans began for a continental holiday in the summer. Gordon advised on this, but it was not something in which he was taking part. It was a big step for members of the group to go abroad together without any adult leadership. For most it was their first experience of foreign travel and for some even the first experience of being away from their families for a protracted period.

During the spring Gordon introduced some of the group to sea fishing and talk about this in one of the pubs in the town led to the formation of a local sea fishing group. A Festival was planned in the town for the summer and the group were active in this and had in fact been the originators of the idea. They collected material for and organized a photographic and art exhibition which they staged in their premises. The collection of the material led the members to many new contacts.

In all this Gordon deliberately played a less and less active part. He went to Moortown less frequently and by late summer stopped going altogether. There were no farewells and no need for any. Although he lived ten or twelve miles away from Moortown all the group had been to his home and knew how to contact him if they wanted to. Gordon's departure was preceded by the departure of other group members who had moved to new jobs. Subsequent meetings with some group members suggested that what they saw was simply a process of natural change. There was no evidence of any sense that something had ended, no nostalgia for the past and no particular fears for the future.

I should emphasize that not all the problems were solved at the end of the project nor were some of the major problems remaining at the end of the project substantially different from those which had existed at the beginning. During the two years there had been a shift in degree; no more than that. A fundamental difficulty identified near the beginning of the work with the group was their seeming inability to work co-operatively to achieve their own ends. Despite the evidence I have given of group achievements the difficulty substantially remained. Verbal ability within the group varied and with some was not very great. The lack of verbal ability made non-violent disagreement difficult for some and for others more able there was still the strongly ingrained habit to fall back on abuse rather than reason. The presence of Gordon allowed the group to keep the necessary group conflict within bounds. At points of crisis he could help the less verbal, modify the more violent outbursts and provide a match for the glib. Slowly members of the group became aware that they used Gordon to contain group conflicts and through their awareness of this process many gained insight into the nature of their difficulties. But knowing these things is very different from being able always to do something about them. Even at the end group life remained precarious.

Similarly I wrote earlier of the apparent lack of tolerance among the users of the first meeting room. As members of the core group became more confident they came to accept strangers and newcomers. It is perhaps significant, however, that they did not recruit to their own numbers though there were points during the project when it seemed as though it might have been advantageous for them to do so and when such recruitment seemed a practical possibility. Their development in tolerance has to be seen in the context of how far there was to go.

The positive gains for the project were perhaps strongest in relation to the personal development of the relatively small number of people who had been worked with most intensively. Particularly noticeable were the gains in confidence and self-respect. Inevitably in two years young people change a good deal, but I do not think that the changes in many members of the core group could easily be attributed to the normal process of development. Certainly the young people themselves felt that what had happened was valuable to them.

9 Providing for the leisure of young adults

This final chapter does not contain conclusions in the sense that this is sometimes meant and any one who has turned to the end of the book in search of the easy answers will therefore be disappointed. I cannot provide conclusions about provision for young adults because to do so is to give support to presuppositions I do not support. My argument is that 'it is not quite like that'. We cannot look at leisure provision for young adults without considering their leisure experience as school children and their leisure opportunities as adults. If we want to achieve change we are unlikely to do much by tinkering about with only part of the machine.

Almost everything which is said or written about the young stresses the need for their involvement and participation and for the desirability of their playing 'a full part in every aspect of our national life'.[1] But in spite of the growing frequency with which such sentiments are expressed, movement towards greater participation in public and social life is, in many fields, barely discernable. Participation and involvement are easy words to use but difficult conditions to achieve. In this chapter I try to show some of the ways schools and youth and adult education services might foster fuller participation in some forms of leisure activity.

For the sake of convenience I have divided the chapter into three sections for the main topics with which I deal. These are 'young adults and the youth service', 'resources for leisure' and 'non-institutional approaches'. I have also used sub-headings where these seem helpful.

Young adults and the youth service

With youth club provision I would draw attention particularly to the special social needs of the under eighteen age group. This is the group which needs a youth club provision and although it has been no part of my brief to look at the needs of still younger people I would hazard a guess that much would be achieved also by making new kinds of provision available to the under fourteens. The argument against youth clubs for those at school is that it duplicates provision and one implication of the Newsom Report[2] is that social provision for those up to sixteen should be made by the schools.[3] But much of the argument about duplication of provision is very hard to swallow. It reflects a provider's view rather than the point of view of a consumer and it would be difficult to find many situations where young people are really faced with an embarrassingly wide choice of social provision. Duplication arises when the same opportunities are offered to the same people in the same way, and where this happens the most likely cause is often a lack of co-operation between providing agencies rather than an overall superfluity of provision.

However, for youth clubs and organizations my clear priority is for a service for those young people under eighteen years of age. It is to this age group that one can ascribe special needs in the field of social provision and it is about this group that it is possible, to this extent, to generalize.[4]

When one moves from the general to the specific the argument becomes very much more complicated. It is clear that there are many young adults who gain personal satisfaction and benefit from a continued association with a youth club provision long after the age of eighteen, just as it is clear that with the youth service as a whole the effective terminal age of youth club membership is a good deal nearer to eighteen than it is to twenty-one.[5] The argument about how youth clubs can provide for young adults is relatively simple, but the argument about whether they should make such a provision is a good deal more complex.

The basic fact about social provision is that it must be what people want; and thus it is no more difficult to provide for young adults than it is for any other adult age group if the terms are right. There is a sense in which we all have our price and it is in no way cynical to suggest that we all jump through some social hoops when the cost is not too high and the rewards are great enough. Providing we are not asked to behave in a way which is an affront to our most cherished conceptions of ourselves we remain socially very malleable creatures. The difficulty about 'holding' senior members in youth clubs is simply that where counter-attractions exist it is likely to cost more.

So long as a youth club offers to young adults better provision than is available elsewhere then they will make use of it. There are considerable variants in what constitutes 'better', but there are no special or mysterious features about this. If belonging to a youth club provides the easiest and cheapest way of playing football then many young adults will use that provision. If the social provision of the club is better than that available elsewhere commercially then it will be used in preference to the commercial provision. Provision which is not very good, but cheap, will be favoured for its cheapness and used when money is short. If membership is conditional and there are restraints upon behaviour then these factors will be weighed, against other factors, like what is offered, availability and cheapness. Some will continue club membership because the protective environment of the club is what they want, whilst others will maintain membership because it offers personal leadership opportunities which do not exist for them elsewhere. In some cases a male senior membership will thrive because it provides the best opportunity of affordable girl friends and in other cases because it provides the only local opportunity to follow some esoteric pursuit like parachuting.

The use young adults make of youth club provision is explicable in very ordinary, common-sense terms. Naturally the use they make is conditioned by all the other alternatives open to them and the cost of youth clubs making a wide appeal to young adults is the cost of competing with these alternatives. But this is not simply a question of providing comparable or superior facilities, which in many socially underprovided localities it is not difficult to do. It is also very much a question of the conditions under which whatever is provided is available. There are therefore two factors with which to juggle; the actual standard of the provision and the conditions under which it is made available. Within limits, the higher the standard of provision the more conditional can be its availability. However, this is no more than the law of supply and demand which applies to all of us every bit as much as it does to young adults.

It is difficult to imagine a general provision on non-adult terms because the cost of such provision would be so very high. None the less, this is something which in youth service circles is talked about and in particular areas there has been a large investment in pieces of glamorous provision designed to attract young adults into attendance. Certainly such provision provides in the short term the opportunity for social control and in the long term the opportunity for 'adult' influence. In addition it may be an excellent shop window for a whole range of educational and social services, but it is an immensely costly means to such ends, and with regard to the ends themselves, one must still ask, what 'social control', what 'influence' and why special services for this age group?

To all these questions I can provide no answer which has any general application. I would not dispute for a moment that young adults would benefit from there being more and better social, recreational and educational provision available as we all would, nor would I dispute that there are many thousands of young adults in urgent need of particular forms of help from the welfare and social services. There is, however, an enormous difference between saying these things and suggesting a specific development such as that of youth clubs for young adults.

I have already suggested that there are a variety of ways in which youth clubs are used by young adults and it might be useful to try to distinguish between them, but it is necessary to remember that in talking about young adults in youth clubs one is talking about a small minority of the youth club population.

Some young adults welcome the protection which continued youth club membership affords and in some cases it may be advisable that such protection be continued. Some people grow up more slowly than others and need elements of a protective environment for longer. But what has to be borne in mind is the ultimate aim, which is surely concerned with growing up and induction into adult society, and if some people take longer over it, it may mean that what they need is not simply a longer period of protection, but also more positive help in eventually managing without it. I have some reservations about the willingness of many staff in the youth service to provide this sort of help and I would feel a good deal happier if the service as a whole could be persuaded to take a hard, critical look at the implications of 'holding senior members' and the approbation which surrounds success in this field. The phrase itself is a significant piece of current youth service jargon and can be put alongside less respectable but equally common phrases about 'giving in to the pubs', or 'handing them over to the commercial boys'. The desire of many people in youth service that young people should have the opportunity to grow up in a 'better' society than that which exists is understandable and laudable, but it can easily lead to over protective attitudes which are unrealistic and may well be individually damaging.

Some young adults continue youth club membership because it offers special opportunities and special services and about both these aspects of club life there are also questions which need to be asked and answered. A common opportunity offered by clubs to senior members is some form of leadership opportunity. This may well be admirable and just as one can see those who seek the continued protection of the club as being people who have failed to grow up as rapidly as their peers, one might see those who transfer to some sort of leadership role as people whose growing up has been particularly successful. Instead of exploring the possibilities of commercial entertainment with their fellows who have left the club, they elect a particularly demanding adult role and, perhaps a more intensive association with a wider range of other adults. However, the situation is not necessarily one which contains these ingredients and the employment of young adults in this way is something which should receive always the critical attention of the employing agency. They have here some responsibility to see that what is offered is an opportunity for adult responsibility rather than a retreat from it and this latter is always a possibility where leadership situations are in some way contrived, instead of arising from the real needs of the situation. With a statutory upper age limit of twenty-one it is very difficult for the statutory services to offer realistic leadership opportunities to people below this age, although with voluntary organizations it is not uncommon to find well-run clubs the sole responsibility of young people in their late teens, and scout leadership is almost entirely in the hands of ex-members.

With the provision of special services, even something as simple as a senior football team, the moral question which youth club staff have to ask themselves is whether a genuinely useful experience is being provided which will contribute to the maturity of those concerned or whether the attendance of senior members is being bought. Rationalizations of the answers to this question are all too easy and it is possible to feel that to make any social provision is always justified. Also, work with young adults may not be easy, but it is an aspect of youth work which offers the worker the possibility of finding his own social satisfactions, and for this reason may be dangerously seductive. The genuinely useful experience is that which leads the members towards the independence which inevitably they must achieve one day if they are 'to live the life of mature, creative and responsible members of a free society'.[6] Yet perhaps highly subsidized soccer, with 'old Bob' to book the coaches and the referee, and to undertake the dozens of other tasks which are necessary to the survival of a football club, is not one of the experiences which come into this category. What is difficult is that 'old Bob' may well be a youth leader or at least is someone who is there with the full knowledge and approval of people who are. For him the role of football club manager is an immensely satisfying one and no one would doubt that he works very hard at it, possibly to the point where what happens to the team is more important to him than it is to the players, but in this enthusiasm the long-term youth work aims may become completely submerged.

However, there are more factors in the 'old Bob' situation than these. It is quite likely that what he does works; that his devoted hard work provides for the team the very best of footballing experience and an experience superior, perhaps, to that which could be provided on other terms. What he does is also very human. It is natural that those who have played sports and games should want

168

to maintain an active interest when actual playing is no longer possible for them and because part of the enjoyment of a game is tied up with its traditions and rituals, as well as with simply playing the game according to the rules, what such people have to communicate is very important. What old Bob does is also realistic. He is not a special feature of youth club life, but of amateur sport life as a whole. Many amateur teams have someone like old Bob and are the richer for it.

It seems there is conflict here between educational ideals and normal community pressures. What the educator wants for the football team is their growth and their independence. What the team wants on the other hand is simply the opportunity to play football on the easiest possible terms. My imaginary figure 'old Bob' is part of the easy terms. He may have a great deal of valuable experience to offer, but he certainly doesn't want the team to be independent of him because they are as valuable to him as he is to them. What the educationalist has to reconcile in this situation are his educational objectives, and the reality of old Bob as a valuable part of the community into which his senior members are emerging. If people like my imaginary old Bob are taken on as youth leaders then in all probability educational objectives like independence go onto the scrap heap, but on the other hand to ignore their potential contribution in a context wider than the club is to be unrealistic.

What I suggest here is that youth clubs offer an experience which has a conclusion. Their object is to help people to grow up and do without them and perhaps concern over young adults in clubs ought for the most part to be concern over the fact that they are still there. Of course there is a difference between youth clubs and other kinds of opportunities and services which statutory and voluntary organizations might make available with young adults particularly in mind, but it might be helpful to spell out this difference by having a ceiling age for youth club membership which is more realistic than the present upper age limit of twenty-one. This would not mean a withdrawal of services, but it would mean a much closer definition of that kind of service which is provided by youth clubs.[7]

Youth clubs are there to provide for young people who are not adult and all the terms of their existence are related to this fact. They can be made more adult and in a great many cases should be more adult in their provision and the approach of their staff, but they cannot be an adult provision. This is not to say, of course, that even all adult provision is necessarily conducted in a very 'adult' way, but at least the potential of its being so conducted always exists. Those provided for in adult organizations and services have the same independence and the same political and legal rights as do the providers. This is clearly not the case with youth clubs, nor indeed can it ever be so.

There will always be a good deal of argument about where adulthood begins and by what criteria it is established, but the argument here is not concerned with the conferring of adult status, but with the length of time for which specifically non-adult provision is made.

My argument is that youth clubs are the wrong sort of provision for young adults; that sooner or later the special conditions which arise from there being provision for 'the young' blocks further progress towards adulthood. They cannot be adult enough until they allow for the possibility of being wholly adult and yet this they cannot do. I am not suggesting that all young people over the age of eighteen are adult, for obviously by some definitions many are not, but what I am suggesting is that they are not helped by associations which do not allow for this possibility, and which do not allow them to be as adult as they are capable of being. Thus it is necessary to distinguish between youth clubs and forms of adult provision, educational, social or recreational, which are geared to the needs of young adults. I hold no brief for the creation of a special service for young adults, nor for any upward extension of the kind of youth service which exists at present and I would happily see the present youth service age limit reduced to eighteen. On the other hand I would certainly want to see a variety of services much more readily available to the young adult section of the population than is the case at present and there is nothing irreconcilable in these points of view. Having made this point I want to go on to look at the sorts of services which young adults may need and the ways in which these services may be provided.

Resources for leisure

To begin with it would be helpful if we were able to escape from the idea that the school, the youth club or the adult centre is something which necessarily exists in a state of glorious isolation completely removed from other forms of provision in the community. It is true that it very often does, but it need not. At their best the village college and the community school show that there are other possibilities and these possibilities need not relate only to those situations where a variety of provisions is gathered together on one campus.

What is different about the best of the village colleges and community schools, is not simply the geographical proximity of school, adult and youth services, but also the ideas about the management of provision. It is assumed that the different services are capable of a high degree of co-operation and it is assumed that they are all there to serve the community. There is at least in some degree an openness to community pressures and a deliberate attempt to involve large numbers of people in creating a richer social life. For example, the school or college may provide the focal point for some form of community action, like the building of a swimming pool. I am not saying community schools or village colleges provide an 'answer', but in practice they do sometimes illustrate the possibility of co-operation between services and a different kind of use of resources.

Physical resources in the shape of buildings, equipment and playing fields are one of the factors which has a bearing on leisure provision for any age group and it is important at this point to look at the use which is made of the resources which already exist. In this country local education authorities hold the keys to resources which have a tremendous leisure provision potential. What use is made of these resources? Obviously the answers to this question vary enormously,[8] but in a great many cases there is a drastic under use of what in industry would be regarded as very expensive plant, and there is room for examination of the use to which this plant is put, and in many cases a drastic re-organization of the terms on which it might be made available for leisure time use. A full leisure life includes the exploration of the possibilities afforded by the immediate locality and yet many of those professionally involved in both education and youth service behave as though it were their duty to protect premises and to actively discourage their use.

The problem here is one of priorities. For example, to whatever use a school is put, it must remain in a condition which enables it to provide adequately for the school children for whom it was intended. But it may be possible to satisfy this priority and still make extensive use of the building. Adult classes and youth clubs use school buildings in the evenings and while this sometimes creates friction between headmasters and the staff of the other services there are comparatively few problems here which better caretaking, more frequent decoration and more frequent meetings between all the staff concerned would not resolve.

What needs to be extended is not simply the educational service use of school, youth club, and adult centre provision, but also the community use of such provision in leisure time. Why shouldn't the school hall be let out for dances on Saturday night? Why shouldn't the workshop facilities be available to those who want to use them? Why is the adult centre pottery only available to those attending classes? Why isn't there a film club in the locality when perfectly satisfactory 16 mm. equipment exists at the local school? Why are the excellent social facilities of the £60,000 youth club only in use fourteen hours a week in areas where young married mothers have nowhere to meet during the day? Why are rare and valuable pieces of provision like playing fields, gymnasia and even swimming baths locked up for as much as a hundred and sixty days every year?

There are difficulties in making more widely available the leisure provision over which statutory bodies have control, but we cannot go on for ever as though it were sacrilege even to suggest such a thing. Increased use would cost money in repairs, maintenance and caretaking; and certainly a few sacred cows would have to go to the slaughter. The deep wax polish of the school hall will not survive Saturday dances and usage will take some of the spring from the Wembley-like turf of the school playing field, but these are small prices for the increase in community provision which would result. The school education of children would not suffer and in the long run their leisure lives might benefit immeasurably.

The public use of public provision is no panacea, but there are many areas where it could be a substantial beginning to tackling the problem of leisure provision and indeed until full use is made of the provision which exists it is really impossible to know what further provision is needed. Although there are areas where flinging open the door of the local school or youth club would be rather like opening Mother Hubbard's cupboard, there are certainly many other areas where a major contribution could be made in this way.

What I mean by the public use of public provision has very little to do with anything which I have seen happening at present. What I mean is this: the priority use of the provision goes to those for whom the provision is intended, but once this priority is satisfied the provision is available, twenty-four hours a day, three hundred and sixty-five days a year if need be, as leisure provision for the people who live in the locality in which it is situated. The local authority manage and maintain the provision, but there is no reason why they should have sole control of it or that such control should be centralized. I would visualize a controlling management committee with a very large measure of power over the uses to which the provision is put, and a situation where the main representation on this committee is composed of the users of the provision.

The use of the provision would be conditional on its being properly treated, but it would be the users who decided what constituted proper treatment. There is no reason to suppose that such a body would be any less capable of taking, or ignoring professional advice than the bodies which at present control the same provision or that they would behave any more democratically or autocratically, wisely or foolishly than do the existing bodies. The important difference would be that the users would have a large say in determining the conditions of availability of the provision they use.

The economics of such a scheme would need skilled attention, because the balance between the uneconomic under use of provision, which is the situation which we have at the present, and its equally uneconomic over use, is a narrow one. The rationalization of existing resources still constitutes a development and this development would cost money, at least initially. However, the full use of some of the more lavish school, club or adult centre provisions would yield a very considerable income from even a small per capita charge for use, and I do not think it is unrealistic to visualize a situation where massive extra provision becomes available at relatively little extra cost, and in some cases where development of the provision is made possible, by the profit which accrues by virtue of this wider usage.

The role of the education service staff in all this is to encourage diverse and adventurous use of the facilities which exist in their locality. There cannot be a tailor-made demand for opportunities which have not previously existed, and the more depressed and culturally deprived the community the less demands there will be and the fewer the number of people able to avail themselves of new opportunities. The educator's job is to stimulate and influence demand, to help people sort out what it is they want, and to help them present their wants realistically and in the best possible way. I see no confusion here between the role of the educator and that of the community worker, though it is true that the community worker might operate in this way in this area of work. But what is being discussed here is not housing, or racial integration or loneliness, but quite specifically that section of leisure provision which is under the control of local education authorities, and it seems fair to suggest that the use and misuse of this provision is properly the concern of all those professionally involved in education.

This proper concern must include some reckoning of the existing under use of provision and the current peculiar 'educational' practice of leading people into activities which they lack the facilities to pursue. With those education services which relate to leisure it is the proper business of the educator to concern himself not only with the creation of wants, but also with the possibility of their satisfaction. Further than this, in dealings with the adult community, the educator cannot start work from the assumption that he is dealing with only those wants which the education services have themselves created, but by aiding the satisfaction of all legitimate leisure needs the educator puts himself in a position which enables him to influence on educational matters, and it is this influence, and not control or manipulation, which is his business. But far beyond this the very process of helping people to do what they want to do is one of the most vital pieces of education which it is possible to undertake in any state which aspires towards democracy.

Any change in the use which is made of publicly owned facilities depends very largely on the work of teachers, youth workers and adult education staff. Administrative staff can influence their committees towards some relinquishing of control, but any real degree of local participation in the management of local provision depends in the long run upon the existence of strong local demand that this should be so, and it is difficult to see how such demand can come into being unless education staff seek deliberately to foster it. The mass of people unquestioningly accept that the control of their local provision is in the hands of some remote body far beyond their influence and so many educators have for so long behaved as if it were their brief to civilize the savage rather than to ply their trade among equals that the establishment of any real degree of community participation demands from the educator conscious and protracted effort. Student bodies in adult centres are unlikely to suggest that the centre should stay open half an hour longer or that the art room should be open on Sunday morning so long as they believe that such matters are not their concern. Even if they have the temerity to make such suggestions they are all too likely to take 'no' as a final answer simply because they are accustomed to the idea that the management of the centre is not something about which they can make decisions nor towards which they can contribute.

There are some rays of hope of course. Some youth clubs do also provide a local community service, some student bodies at adult centres do influence what happens at the centre and the community school is based on the idea of the wider availability of its provision. But such developments are all too rare and in many cases these still duck the central issue about who makes the rules. So long as the terms of availability remain the same, a cost-conscious rationalization of leisure resources is only a very partial answer to leisure provision. What is really needed is that degree of community involvement which can only arise from a measure of local community control and to achieve this I believe it is necessary for teachers, youth workers and adult education staff both to seek maximum community contact and to deliberately foster demands for the use of the provision which they manage. In many cases this constitutes so much a reversal of present practice that it would be unrealistic to hope for rapid progress along these lines, but such progress could be helped by more statements from the Department of Education and Science and from local authority education officers encouraging the wider use of existing provision. At very least this would be a positive encouragement to those in the education services who would like to develop their work in this way.

All this is relevant to work with young adults. Young adults are one of the groups in society to whom extended leisure provision is likely to be particularly attractive, and there are a number of ways in which such provision might be made available to them. The two most obvious ways are the letting of premises to established groups and the letting of premises to groups which the youth service has created. There is nothing new in either of these ideas but the practice of both is much less common than it might be.

Just as questions about adult education tend to be focused upon what happens at 'the centre' and not on what happens in the locality as a result of the existence of the centre, so questions about youth service tend to relate to the club rather than to the effect of the service on the lives of young people. While I am sure that most youth officers and youth leaders would be very pleased to try to help any-body in their area who presented a specific request for help, I think that many have little idea just how unapproachable they and their offices may seem and just how unaware the general public may be of their existence. Unwillingness to approach youth service staff may arise either because the staff seem too remote and official or, and I think this far more common, because the youth service so often projects an image of being something one is 'drawn into' and many young people would sooner do without help rather than risk an over involvement they do not want.

A healthier situation would be one where it is an established part of youth service practice for youth workers to make personal contact with all or some of the established groups in their areas with a view to making their existence known, offering whatever help they can and particularly offering the use of their premises and equipment wherever this is possible. Local authorities and voluntary associations could give positive encouragement to such work, not by making it an extra chore for youth officers and youth leaders but by making it a central and accountable part of their work.

All this is very much in accord with the recommendations of the Albemarle Committee which laid great stress on working with self-programming groups. But youth workers cannot offer to help groups which do not exist and I would not suppose the incidence of independent self-programming groups, and particularly of groups with an appeal to young people, to be very high in many areas. There is also something else which needs to be considered here. The brilliant performer can perhaps win acceptance in any sports group he chooses to join, but for most of us a two-way social acceptance is a very important factor in determining what we choose to do. We may want to play tennis, but we would have to want it very much to join a tennis club composed of people we did not like or who did not like us, or who were very much older, or richer or more clever or with whom we were at odds in any respect which was important to either side. Often it is all too easy to fall into the trap of assuming that the existence of formal groups concerned, say, with badminton, tennis and cricket is the same thing as a wide availability of opportunity to play these games. The stratification of society and social groupings mitigates against this.

For these reasons it may be very necessary for youth clubs to attempt to create self-programming groups as well as to serve those which already exist in the area. I have no illusions as to just how difficult this would be, but consider the rewards in terms of community leisure development sufficient to warrant making this the long-term aim of youth service. It is faintly ridiculous that most of the aims attributed to youth service both voluntary and statutory, have laid emphasis on the individual and his development, and have avoided reference to the relationship between the club and the community and the part it should play. Now that it is becoming common to talk of youth and community work it is important that aims should make some reference to the function of the youth club in its community. I have already suggested that its short-term aim is to make leisure provision for the under eighteens and I would suggest here that its long-term aim is to equip people with the ability both to make full use of existing leisure provisions and to create new provisions of their own.

Many people would argue that this is what the youth service is already doing, but my observation of youth clubs would lead me to suppose that very few youth club groups ever achieve an adult independent status and there are a number of reasons why this may be so. One is the unrealistically high 'official' terminal age of youth club membership and the unwillingness of many bodies to enter into serious adult negotiations with people below the age of twenty-one.

Also there is the seeming unwillingness of some youth leaders ever to let go the controlling reins. I have mentioned some of the attitudes which are associated with this, the protectiveness of the service, the common idea that it is in competition with commercial social provision, and of course the idea that it is the job of youth leaders to work with young people up to the age of twenty-one is a powerful encouragement to maintain a strong element of patronage in the relationship.

In addition to this an important factor is the common idea of what constitutes independent adult behaviour, and if this is taken to mean the behaviour of the middle aged and middle class then there are likely to be wildly unrealistic expectations about the way adult groups of other ages and other social classes may behave. Part of the unwillingness to surrender direct influence and control may come from a sincere concern for the welfare of the group involved, but this concern may not be related to whether the group can cope with independence, so much as whether they can cope with independence in the terms it is seen by the youth leader. Too narrow a concept of what constitutes 'adult' behaviour can be a serious limiting factor, and perhaps from the point of view of encouraging people to make an independent use of provision all that really matters is that a particular group should express a willingness to pay their way and should behave in a manner which can be endured by other users. The job of the youth leader in this context is to extend the borders of tolerance of all the users of provision and in practice if he fails to operate in this way the provision with which he is involved is likely to fall under the effective control of particular groups and cliques with the resultant narrowing of its possible educational usefulness.

Not unassociated with the narrow concept of adult behaviour is that voluntary and statutory bodies want groups they initiate to be permanent. Very often wholesale failure is attributed to clubs, organizations and groups simply on the grounds that 'they did not last'. Yet unless a massive and continuing recruitment is possible, self programming local groups for those under middle age are always likely to be of a temporary nature. The smaller the group is and the more dependent the members are on each other for either the pursuance of their activity or their social satisfactions, the more likely the group is to disband when some members leave because of marriage, children, moves from the area or simply a change of interest. This is one reason why earlier, I placed so much emphasis on social organizational skills and I see the experience of taking part in an independent self-programming group as an important part of learning such skills. That the groups themselves may not last very long seems a poor criterion of their worth and my argument would be that what matters is that the young should have an experience of independent group life which they can draw on to help them create other groups in other circumstance should they choose to do so.

Youth club sponsoring agencies often seem mesmerized by the dubious virtues of permanence, while what may be really important is the fostering of the ability among the young to create, destroy and re-create whatever groups and organizations they need to achieve their ends. The need to foster such ability can hardly be doubted by anyone concerned for community development and in passing it is perhaps worth noting that some firms engaged in selling cosmetics and kitchenware on housing estates make the formation of simple social groups for housewives a key part of their selling programme. Yet surely this technique is only possible because of the urgent social needs of the women involved and their own inability to initiate their own groups to satisfy these social needs. It is for such reasons that I would see one of the community aims of youth clubs as being the fostering of independent self-programming groups

177

and I would see this as being a continuous process as I would assume that the changing individual circumstances of the young would mean that many such groups would necessarily be short lived.

I want to move now from a consideration of direct provision for leisure and the use of existing resources to look at some of the non-institutional approaches which might be adopted. Before doing this let me summarize some of the main points which have been made so far.

1   Varied social and recreational provision needs to be made for young people under the age of eighteen because this group has special social and recreational needs.

2   The management of provision for under eighteens should be conducted in such a way that besides making an immediate and needed social and recreational provision it also leads users towards independent, self-controlling use of existing leisure provision and in such a way that it helps users to form, organize and participate in groups, clubs and organizations.

3   It is the job of youth workers to foster self-programming social and activity groups and to take positive steps to help create the circumstances under which such groups can function independently.

4   It is the job of all those concerned with the management of premises which might in any way be used during leisure time to encourage demands for the use of premises and equipment, to seek ways of making existing provision more widely available and of bringing users into partnership in the control of the leisure-time use of premises and equipment.

A general summary

My discussion of the youth service has concentrated on leisure provision and in doing this I have ignored some of the most cherished dreams with which the service indulges itself. There is no disrespect intended here to those many men and women of truly formidable ability who through the medium of the service undertake educational, social or reformative work which by virtue of its imaginative inspiration and skilled execution stands to be judged with the best work in its field taking place anywhere. But what I have been writing about is the youth service as it mostly exists; a service where comparatively few adults, capable, hard working part-time workers, try to work out ways of making a leisure provision for very considerable numbers of young people, and who do this often in physical circumstances which are ludicrously distant from the ideal. In most clubs to talk about counselling, case work or intensive group work is so much academic hot air, and yet the jargon of the service and a very great deal which is written about it would suggest that the practice of these skills is the normal stuff of day to day youth work. What I have tried to suggest so far in this chapter is that less sophisticated objectives might be more appropriate, that the need is for leisure provision for the under eighteens and for a provision which is geared towards community development through group action.

However, I hope that I have suggested other things too. I have tried to give the impression that to provide for the leisure of the young is a demanding and worthwhile job in its own right and that it might be rather a different job from much current youth work where the emphasis is often on certain kinds of moral and social training and where the provision is regarded simply as the means to this end. Certainly I have tried to convey the idea of a youth work which demands a very high level of skill, but of skill which, given more thoughtful selection and intensive on-the-job training, might not be impossibly unattainable for the part-time workers who remain the mainstay of the service. One of the present difficulties about part-time training is that it tends to be a reflection of all the diverse aspects of a diverse service. Bits of psychology, educational theory and group work mingle with talks on club organization and club accounts and with discussions on drug addiction, coloured immigrants and counselling, and while all this may be of considerable educational interest and benefit it is doubtful how much of it really contributes towards the average youth worker doing a more effective job of work.

Finally, I have tried to suggest that to see youth service in neighbourhood community terms does provide a view of the service which might be helpful. It is at least a view of the service which is related to what actually happens, to those 'providing' functions of the service which are most observable, and which are most readily comprehensible. It provides the opportunity to formulate general aims which have practical and local application and which to many workers might make more sense than the global aims of educationalists which are often so wide in scope as to be almost meaningless.

So far in this chapter I have dealt with physical provisions and the use which is made of resources. This is important and deserves the space which it has been allotted, but it is not the whole story and I want to turn attention now to what I have called non-institutional approaches.

Non-institutional approaches

The first thing here is to point out that development of the leisure services has been an institutional development. This is the basket into which the financial eggs have been dropped, and this for so long that in a general way very little consideration is given to the alternatives. Youth clubs and adult centres are places to which people go. A youth worker is a man who runs a youth club and an adult education worker is someone who teaches adults in a building set aside for that purpose. Youth and adult workers are appointed to work in clubs and centres or, if on an area basis, to organize the work of clubs and centres. Youth service communication is, in the main, not communication with the young people of a locality but communication with those who belong to a network of clubs. The mass of youth service is a service to clubs; not simply because these are the people who are organizationally most easily served, which of course may be the case, but also because it is generally assumed that these are the only people who want the service. In adult education there is general talk of bringing people into 'an educational environment' which means bringing people within the physical boundaries of an adult centre, and this is a highly approved achievement.

The intensity of this institutionalism is often quite remarkable. Buildings and equipment are not simply regarded as the tools of the trade, but are often spoken of as though they had personalities and independent existences of their own. The legendary possessiveness of headmasters who speak always in terms of 'my school' is very closely paralleled by many others who have the control of premises in their hands. Such close identification may be very touching to observe, but whether it always leads to practices of educational or social value is highly questionable. We have reached a situation where too often the only developments which are seen as being valuable are those which occur in institutions. It is highly significant that over the past few years there has been quite a lot of discussion about bringing bars into youth clubs while concurrently there has been comparatively little support for the idea of putting youth workers into bars.

The danger of a protracted institutional development such as we have experienced in this country is that it grows skills which can only be practised within the narrow confines of what is institutionally possible. If youth clubs are the only things that there are then we will train youth workers to work in youth clubs. If adult education means adult centres then we are likely to produce a crop of adult educators who can only function in a particular kind of 'educational environment' and who are disinclined to recognize that other possibilities exist.

The alternatives to solely institutional development are numerous and I can only deal with some of the possibilities here. I want first to look at the way in which established services might make use of non-institutional approaches and then go on to look at the need for new services, or at least the need for new developments from existing services.

Adult education I can deal with quite briefly because I have already given some idea of possible developments here in Chapter 3. The obvious extension here is that services can be made more widely available. Work with groups away from the centre means the appointment of staff to do the job and while, for their own salvation, I would like to see a situation where all full-time adult education staff spent some time away from their centres, I would recognize the need to appoint some staff who worked mostly in this way. These staff would need to be education workers with some training in group work and I would see them functioning in three main ways.

1   They would aid the development of independent groups arising out of classes held at the centre. Here they might work either through the class instructor or by direct contact. They would perform the same function for the evening institute work which is carried on in youth clubs where this was appropriate.

2   They would contact, and provide a service for, all the clubs and societies in the area. They would arrange lectures, courses and demonstrations where these were needed, but they would concentrate on making adult education services available rather than on recruiting people for classes.

3   They would attempt the formation of new groups by wide community contact. They would, for example, examine the educational needs of people using working men's clubs, ex-servicemen's associations and other local bodies of a primarily social nature. They would seek means of co-operating with local industry and in some cases of making use of *their* social and recreational provision. They would examine the educational needs of shift workers and the feasibility of making special arrangements to meets these needs. They would look at the situation of the housebound and the practicability of making educational provision available to young mothers.

The service needs broadening and strengthening in this way if it is to become a service with the general appeal and availability which many people would wish it to have. Education hunger has perhaps never been so pronounced as it is at the moment and is continually stimulated by media like television, but services to satisfy the hunger cannot rely on crude formulae which ignore the physical circumstances, prejudices and habits of mind of so many people. The local authority service seems usually to have developed within particularly narrow terms of its own creation and what is needed to fulfil the leisure provisional role of the service is not simply more development of the same kind but what an American might describe as 'a whole new ball game'. I would see new developments like those I have described as having considerable relevance to the leisure needs of many young adults.

It is much harder to write about non-institutional developments in the youth service because of the diversity of the service. I have probably irritated many readers by concentrating on youth service as a service of leisure provision and by writing about it as an education service and though I am unrepentant about this, a word of explanation might help. The leisure provision tag I would justify simply on the grounds that this is the function which youth service most obviously performs. The education label is much harder to defend and I have used it simply because whether or not youth clubs are concerned with 'education', the major resources of the service are drawn from bodies which have to do with education and which are staffed and influenced by people who have educational interests at heart. It has seemed helpful to bear this in mind.

However, though I have found it useful to regard youth clubs mainly as social provision they are certainly also places which allow for the possibility of social work being carried out. Much social work is already carried out in youth clubs and some youth workers devote most of their energies to this. But the difficulties about this are obvious. Intensive case work or group work does not easily go hand in hand with the business of running a youth club and problem groups need a concentrated attention which does not fit in with youth club hours.

I do not at this stage wish to become embroiled in a complex discussion of social work among young people, but because I cannot duck the subject entirely I make some brief comments to indicate a possible approach.

I have already ascribed to the youth service the role of making social provision for the under eighteens which leads outwards to a community provision. This I would expect to be a difficult and demanding job and it seems to me to devalue this job to suppose that it can go hand in hand with intensive social work, besides making nonsense of the complexity and intensity of some of the problems which have to be resolved. This does not mean that youth workers have not a social work job to do, but I would like to set this job within rational limits by saying that they help young people so far as they are able and that they make far greater efforts than are common at the present to help other workers to help young people.

The missing ingredient is of course the 'other workers' and what is needed is the accelerated development of special services to help young people in difficulty and distress. The youth service has already made a striking contribution to the development of such services through its experimental work and the development of the best of these ideas needs the positive encouragement of government and local authority investment.

However, much work with young people in difficulty must necessarily be work which does not directly involve the use of special premises. Even if premises are used for some of the time the workers must have the freedom to spend working time away from them. In the main, however, it seems likely that the best approach to young people in difficulty is that indicated by the various detached work projects and recruitment and training of people for this work should be a matter of priority.

Counselling

The development of counselling services is something I would include under the broad heading of non-institutional services but it would perhaps be fairer to say that counselling services should not be conceived in solely institutional terms. Counselling depends upon the availability of the counsellor and to tie him to an institution confines him to the service of those who are willing or able to visit the institution with which he is associated.

An example of this occurred in connection with the Moortown project which I described in Chapter 8. Two of the young adults involved in the project needed vocational counselling and it was possible to arrange for the school and youth service counsellor attached to a large comprehensive school some six miles away to come to see them. A pub room was borrowed from the helpful landlord and on this and subsequent occasions a series of interviews totalling several hours duration were conducted. The willingness of the counsellor to make himself available on these terms was an important factor in the success of the whole operation and whether it would have worked at all on other terms is doubtful.

The general success of counselling services would indicate that there are many young people who will go to considerable lengths in some circumstances to avail themselves of services which are situated a long way from their homes or places of work. In some cases the added anonymity of going to a distant service would seem to be a positive advantage. But for normal counselling where the client is not himself conscious of particular urgency or stress the case may often be quite different. The two young adults in Moortown needed some persuasion before they would consider seeing anyone; not because they did not want help but because their past experiences of 'seeing' people had not been satisfactory. They needed the worker's reassurance that this would be different and indeed the whole process depended to some extent upon his being able to give this assurance from the knowledge that whether or not the interviews were 'helpful' they would at least be conducted in a civilized manner. Besides this, for the two people concerned to travel to see the counsellor would have been difficult enough to constitute an additional reason for not going at all, and although the worker would certainly have taken them had this been necessary, this could not have been arranged easily.

This flexibility in counselling is important and though it may be possible for some counsellors to conduct one kind of service from behind the desk it is difficult to say how much of a service can be provided in this way. Static counselling services work for some people, but it might be very dangerous to assume that they could ever work for all the people who need counselling help even if they were more widely available. At least until the point is reached where counselling is a normal and accepted part of most people's lives it seems likely that counselling services may be used mainly by those who are able to verbalize about their difficulties and by crisis cases.

In many areas the provision of normal counselling services is totally inadequate. A school counsellor makes the following points about the services available to young people in one north-east Derbyshire town.[9]

The only statutory service widely used by young people is the youth employment service which has a branch office which is open two afternoons and early evenings in the week. The head office for the area is ten miles away. No family planning advice is readily available in the town, nor is there any advertisement as to where such a service is available. The nearest family planning clinic is six miles away. The nearest marriage guidance service is twenty miles away. It is true the probation officer has a statutory responsibility here, but his current juvenile case load is over seventy.

There is no citizens' advice bureau in the town and the nearest service of this kind is again six miles away. The service is not advertised even in the town where it is situated and clients are referred via the public library and the town hall. On its present basis the service could not cope with more work than it at present deals with. The R.D.C. offices are located six miles away and so a difficult journey faces any resident who wishes to see the clerk to the council. Certain types of problems can be discussed with the public health inspector who has an office in the town, but the availability of his services is not advertised. The medical social worker and the colliery social welfare organizer who would deal with pit compensation claims are based twelve miles away, and the Ministry of Social Security Office is six miles away. The mental welfare officer works from an office nine miles distant and under a reorganization scheme is soon to move very much further away. Family service units at Sheffield can be contacted through the offices of the Children's Department which are eleven miles away, but the child care officer for the town has, at the time of writing, moved to take up another appointment and a replacement has not yet been found.

The town of which I am writing has a population of about twelve thousand and it is unrealistic to suppose that a town of this size can have major services of all the kinds which have been mentioned based upon it. But the problem here is not simply the perennial one of services being spread too thinly. The real problem is that so far as the residents of the town are concerned most of the normal counselling and advisory services I have mentioned might just as well not exist at all.

People cannot avail themselves of services they know nothing about.

In such circumstances it is surely undesirable that any additional counselling services should be narrowly based. Somebody whose main concern is counselling might be the best person to bring about conditions of greater co-operation and greater effectiveness among the existing services. The counsellor is a specialist by virtue of his skill, but he does not specialize in any particular kind of human problem. He is not over-anxious to post elsewhere those clients who do not fit into any particular niche, yet he is very conscious of the need to refer clients so that they may receive the best possible help. Thus agencies which have never been in contact with each other might find a common contact through the work of a counsellor. They do not seem to fit into each other's patterns of work yet properly he fits into both.

I can well imagine that the kind of community developmental role which I would ascribe to the counsellor would be totally alien to many. Yet in the township which I have described above the needs are very plain. Normal counselling services need to be known about and need to be more readily available. In this situation how does the counsellor behave? Does he attempt to plug the gap and pick up the pieces and wait for the day when things will be different? or does he take the bull by the horns and dirty his hands with community work? If he adopts this second course the boundaries of his job may extend alarmingly. He is likely to become involved in public education about rights and services. He may find that he is not simply concerned with helping clients to agencies but also in helping agencies to reach prospective clients. Referral may come to mean not an address on a slip of paper and a preparatory telephone call, but indulging in organizational manoeuvres, perhaps with a variety of voluntary agencies, which make it possible for clients to reach distant offices at the right time of day. More dangerously, to embark on such work is likely to mean that the counsellor becomes the person through which complaints about the deficiencies and inadequacies of existing services are likely to be channelled and the use of this information involves him in yet more complicated and delicate developmental work.

Though this may not be a very easy path it may be very necessary that someone treads it. That that someone should be a counsellor concerned primarily with 'young' people is perhaps a highly contentious suggestion, but it is not a nonsensical one. He is the person on the scene whose concerns cut across those of the individual helping agencies who as part of their work may be involved in counselling. What I suggest is that the youth counsellor's job may be seen as having two main parts. Partly he is concerned with the direct practice of counselling and this may be mainly an institution based job, though I would hope not entirely so. Partly also he may be concerned with the availability of normal counselling services in his area. This is not an institution based job and may in some circumstances demand of him a very positive community work role.

Community work

My main interest in non-institutional work is in its possibilities for youth and community work.

So far as the younger age groups are concerned there seem so many interesting possibilities which have never received the same level of encouragement and support as has the main stream club-based youth service. Adventure playgrounds have a tremendous amount to offer and yet are comparatively few in number despite the fact that they are relatively cheap to initiate and maintain. That they do not only appeal to very young children is very well illustrated by Turner's account in his book *Something Extraordinary*.[10] The playleader scheme is youthwork without the youth club and helps thousands of young people make the best use of leisure in public parks; and yet the scheme is very little known by those who do not come into direct contact with it. In many areas a playleader on a school campus throughout the summer holiday period could make a vital contribution to the leisure lives of young people during a period when many youth clubs close completely. There are of course many adventurous schemes and experiments taking place, but in the main youthwork and clubwork are synonymous, and a limited view of the possibilities tends to be reinforced by some training and administrative bodies.

So far as the over-eighteens are concerned there is scope for certain kinds of non-institutional community work. In this context my thesis would be that a community worker is somebody who applies his skill to the development of a locality in accordance with the wishes of some of the people of the locality and within the limits imposed by his employing agency. Such a definition is perhaps impossibly wide though I have included in it some curtailments with which not all would agree. For example, I have said that the employing agency imposes limits and would maintain that for this reason the field is rarely as wide open as it seems. Whatever is done has to be justified to someone, and while this process has its dangers and its limitations it also is a process of information and education. Also I have said that the community worker works in accordance with the wishes of only some of the community with which he is involved. Practically I would maintain that this is bound to be the case and I have a profound mistrust of phrases which make reference to 'working with the whole community'. The worker may have the unification of the community as an ideal and of course it is only by the corporate action of some groups of people that he can help them achieve anything at all, but during the course of his work he is by virtue of his association with particular groups, for some people and against others, and in favour of some things and opposed to others.

The questions are what help can he give and where does he start? So far as working with young adults is concerned some possible answers to these questions are given by the account of the project in Moortown. While the situation there had some special features it was, in its fundamentals, far from uncommon. Here was a small town in which the immediately available leisure provision did not meet the needs of some of the resident young people and where the young people lacked the group cohesion, imaginative stimulation and faith in their own abilities to do much about the situation for themselves. The worker provided some of the missing ingredients with the results which I have already described at some length in Chapter 8.

It is necessary to place the Moortown project into some kind of perspective. It was a project manned by a part-time worker and which perhaps made demands of a part-timer which under other circumstances it would be desirable to avoid. The project was initiated in an atmosphere of experiment and was thus able to benefit from the willingness of the L.E.A. to bend the rules in its favour. In other circumstances and in many other local education areas such a project would have been impossible. One of the attractions of the project which undoubtedly influenced the sponsoring authority was that it all cost so little. Total running costs amounted to less than ten pounds per week and this is rather less than the heating and lighting costs of many youth centres.

Certainly I would not present the project in Moortown as a model of what ought to happen, but rather as a project which illustrates some of the possibilities of non-institutional work. Ideally one would want more money to work with, a small team of workers and very well organized supervision and support resources. And it is worth pointing out that even this might be had for less money than is needed to run many youth clubs.[11]

However, the point about towns like Moortown is not simply that there are a few young adults in the town who do not know how to spend their leisure time and thus may be 'a problem' as a result. The real issue is that the young are the tip of the iceberg. The lack of social and recreational provision and the lack of stimulation towards an activist or participative leisure life effects all ages and not just the young. For example, the work in nearby Minton showed that in some cases marriage was the road to still greater boredom for some of the young women. The obvious symptoms of the problem disappear with marriage because marriage, like youth clubs, 'keeps them off the streets', but the problem of an uninteresting, unstimulating leisure may in fact become more acute because of the ties of the home and the comparative poverty of the early years of marriage.

All this is not so judgmental as may at first sight appear. There is nothing wrong with the staple leisure activities of the communities which I have described in this book and it is not the job of the community worker to manipulate people towards leisure activities which on some grounds or other are considered more desirable. But I have been writing about depressed communities; communities where many people are poor by comparison with people in more prosperous areas, communities from which many leisure opportunities are missing completely, from which many kinds of stimulation are absent and where the range of real choice is very much more limited than it is elsewhere. In this situation the community worker's job was to widen the area of choice and to help people carry their choices into action. The stimulation and encouragement which he was able to provide helped to break down some of the cultural factors inhibiting the exercise of choice and to create new outlets for the skills and abilities of the people with whom he worked. In the event some of the things which the young people chose to do came in for a good deal of criticism. Running a semi-commercial discotheque is not the ideal of all adults of a 'worthwhile activity' for young people, but it was what the group wanted to do at that particular time and it was a new and exciting choice for them.

In the case of Moortown, the worker deliberately set out to work with young people in the town, because he was a youth worker engaged on a project sponsored by the youth service. But it is possible to see his work in community work terms in that the logical extensions of his work lead to the enrichment of the whole community and not simply to continuing work with certain age groups. This is best illustrated by giving three simple examples.

First, there was the involvement of adults in the town, and the adults here can be divided into two groups who might be described as council and businessmen. There was a relationship between some of the council and some of the young people in the town which did not previously exist and one practical outcome of this relationship was a Sunday afternoon pop concert which attracted a number of people over a very wide age range. There was a new relationship with some businessmen which led to practical help in providing for the leisure of young people. But also the action of one group of young people challenged some of the adults who run commercial concerns to think about the provision they make and has led some of them to consider making new forms of provision. One publican has approached the group with a very attractive proposition simply because he thought that with their help his pub could become a very much more attractive place.

Second, there were ventures like the art exhibition which involve school children, art teachers and local artists. What criteria of success should be applied here is very difficult to say, but in the long term something may come simply from the meeting of people with a common interest.

Third, there was the stimulation which an active group of young people provided for the community. Some of the group organized a sea fishing trip from Bridlington. When they came back they talked about it and one of the pubs in the town organized its own trip. Two of the group were able to help with this because they knew the ropes, but this was not an activity of the group, nor was the worker in any way involved, nor the trip confined to people of any particular age group. It was a good idea which spread.

Again it is necessary to remember that what is being discussed is the work of one part-timer over a period of two years. It would be silly to pretend that Moortown has been greatly changed by the project or that wonders have been achieved in so short a time. The work with the central group was solid, accountable and, to my mind, remarkable. The rest is much more tenuous, but one can see at least the beginning of change and the possibility of more change. There were some new opportunities for some people. There has been some enrichment of the environment.

I would hesitate to draw many direct lessons from the Moortown experience, but it does indicate some possibilities and if the current 'youth and community' worker phrase is to mean anything perhaps it should be taken to include work of this nature. There is room here to experiment and explore. The method of work is not applicable to every kind of situation, but it is applicable to those barren environments with little leisure provision, and to those groups who are alienated from such provision as exists. It does not solve all the problems, but it does offer a rational approach to working with young adults. It can both help their development and help them to help the development of the community in which they live. This contribution from the young is not something many communities can afford to be without.

However, if this sort of work has its advantages it also has its dangers and difficulties. Some of these I have already mentioned in Chapter 8 and I have no reservations about saying that the Moortown project sailed close to the wind on a number of occasions. It would be easy to advocate widescale experiment, but it might also be irresponsible to do so. Not all education, social or community work is necessarily better than none. Bad practice cannot be defined simply in the passive sense of lacking the ingredients of the good, it may be in an active sense harmful and destructive. This is a truism for all work involving people, but where the work involves particularly intensive relationships with individuals or small groups the potential for certain kinds of damage is heightened and it is easy to see that people could be hurt. In Chapter 8 I stressed the need to protect the worker, and all workers in exposed situations need the opportunity of supportive supervision. The employers' responsibility is to provide this opportunity.

The people on the receiving end also need some protection; protection from being damaged by the relationship they enter into with the worker. This protection can only come from the worker being as aware as he can be of all the implications of what he is about. Again supervision should help by demanding from the worker an analysis of all that is happening and other training should enable the worker to interpret the events in which he is involved as well as helping him to act effectively.

All this makes the business sound very difficult and provides a number of reasons for doing nothing whatever about it. But this should not be the case. The work itself need not be technically very difficult. Like most jobs there is room for people with varying degrees and kinds of ability, and like most jobs difficulties arise when a worker strays into fields in which he is not competent. There is a special difficulty in that this 'straying' is difficult to control because the worker is in an exposed and vulnerable position. However, there is no mystique about this. The factors in any given situation at any given moment of time are to some extent assessable and their development to some extent calculable. Risk in some measure is unavoidable, but what is avoidable is a foolhardy, uncaring blundering into people's lives with no thought for the consequences. In this respect imagination and sensitivity are more useful than good intentions.

There is no need any longer to manage without signposts. Detached youth work in this country has been going on for more than ten years with over a dozen major projects and many more minor ones. Experience in Europe and America is substantial and often well documented and relevant. Community work which has to do with young people[12] is not new and there is a great deal of experience on which to draw. Not all this information is as readily available or as detailed as one would wish, but much which may be helpful is there for the finding and there are a growing body of people with experience in this field from whom advice may be sought.

Finally therefore, so far as non-institutional work is concerned what is needed is not a blind leaping into the dark, but responsible exploration of the possibilities. Projects need not be big or expensive or dramatic, but they do need thought, preparation, planning and continued guidance if they are to function effectively. In this field, as in any other, the orientation of 'experts' will differ and their advice on some points may conflict, but the broad path is much too well trodden and established to allow excuse for the worst errors of thoughtless experiment.

Appendix

RELEASE

50A PRINCEDALE ROAD
LONDON W 11

Facts from Judges' Rules and Administrative Directions to the Police 1964:
1. You are entitled to telephone your friends or your solicitor. 7(a)
2. You need never make any statement unless you wish to do so. 11
3. You should not be harrassed by the police to make a statement. (e)
4. Reasonable arrangements should be made for your comfort and refreshment. 3

EMERGENCY (24 hours)
01-603 8654

OFFICE for general enquiries
(10 am to 6 pm weekdays, late nights Mondays and Thursdays 10 pm.)
01-229 7753

If you are arrested, you are advised:
1. To insist on telephoning the emergency number on this card for assistance.
2. To make no statements.
3. Not to discuss the matter with which you are charged.
4. To request that any property taken from you is packaged and sealed in your presence.
5. To be polite to police officers.

References

1 Education for leisure

1 Joffre Dumazedier, *Toward a Society of Leisure*, Free Press, New York, 1967.
2 Mr Salter-Davies, then chief HMI, used a form of words similar to this during an address he gave to the Department of Education Summer School in, I believe, 1967. He is not of course responsible for what is said here other than in that what he said then helped me to formulate this statement of aim.
3 HMSO, *Half Our Future*, 1963, para 75.
4 *Toward a Society of Leisure*, p. 87.
5 *Half our Future*, para. 81.
6 *Half our Future*, para. 265.
7 Government Social Survey, *Young School Leavers*, HMSO, 1968.
8 John Partridge, *Life in a Secondary Modern School*, Penguin Books, 1968.
9 *Sociology of Education*, Vol. 41, No. 3.

2 The youth service

1 *Youth and Community Work in the 70s*, Proposals by the Youth Service Development Council, HMSO, 1969.
2 B. D. Davies and Alan Gibson, *The Social Education of the Adolescent*, University of London, 1967.
3 National Council of Social Service, *Young People Today*, 1960.
4 Dr Cyril Smith, 'Organisations or Movements', *Youth Review*, No 6, June 1966.
5 *The Youth Service in England and Wales*, HMSO, 1960.
6 *Ibid.*, paragraph 134.
7 See J. R. Watts and T. A. Whitworth, *The Professional Youth Leader's*

View of His Career and Role, p. 11, 'Nearly all of them saw their work as socializing or educational.'

8 Conversely, of course, expectations about social education and expectations about the mainstream of work being concerned with 'normal' young people are what get in the way of social work programmes in youth clubs. My assumption here is simply that the main functions of the service are most commonly seen as being recreational provision and social education for 'ordinary reasonably well behaved' young people. In this context expectation that the youth leader can also conduct a side lines campaign for the reformation of delinquents just confuses the issue. I am not saying that present priorities and allocation of resources within the service is necessarily right. That is a different argument.

9 M. Blandy, *Razor Edge*, Gollancz, 1967.

10 *Youth Service*, October 1967.

11 J. R. Watts and T. A. Whitworth, *The Professional Youth Leader's View of His Career and Role*, pp. 7-8.

12 *Youth and Community Work in the 70s*, Appendix 3.

13 See 'Social Needs and Satisfactions of Some Young People', F. Musgrove, *British Journal of Educational Psychology*, Vol. XXXVI, February 1966.

14 I would not personally argue in favour of a total club democracy and suggest that the opportunity for self-governing and self-programming activity groups might be more useful and more pertinent.

15 Peter Terson, *Zigger-Zagger*, scene 25, Penguin Modern Playwrights, Penguin, 1970.

16 Apologies to Byron's *Don Juan*.

3 Education in leisure time

1 *The Youth Service in England and Wales*, HMSO, 1960, para 135.

2 *Ibid.*, para. 135.

3 B. D. Davies and Alan Gibson, *The Social Education of the Adolescent*.

4 R. S. Peters, *Education as Initiation*, University of London Institute of Education, 1963.

5 Dennis Gabor, for example.

6 *Towards a Society of Leisure*, p. 286.

4 The leisure organizations of some young adults

1 For statistical information relating to Young Farmers' Clubs see: Membership Survey Report, National Federation of Young Farmers' Clubs 1966.

2 *Disinherited Youth*, Carnegie Trust, 1939.
3 See Appendix.
4 *The Release Report on Drug Offenders and the Law*, Cardine Coon and Rufus Harris, Sphere, 1969.

5 Young adults, work and leisure in Minton: part I

1 Norman Dennis, Fernando Henriques and Clifford Slaughter, *Coal is Our Life, An Analysis of a Yorkshire mining community*, Eyre & Spottiswoode, 1956.
2 B.B.C. Audience Research Department, *The People's Activities*, B.B.C., 1965.
3 T. Cauter and J. S. Downham, *The Communication of Ideas*, Chatto & Windus, 1954.

6 Young adults, work and leisure in Minton: part II

1 For one published example see W. M. Morley, *New Town Youth*, Easington R.D.C. and Peterlee Development Corporation, 1966.

7 Young adults, work and leisure in Minton: some conclusions

1 See Reyner Banham, Paul Barber, Peter Hall, Cedric Price, 'Non-Plan: An Experiment in Freedom', *New Society*, 20 March 1969.
2 Some teachers I talked with claimed that discotheques led to beer being consumed by children as young as thirteen on licensed premises. I never saw this, but would agree that under-age drinking was commonplace throughout the area as a whole.
3 Still in the main under fifteen thousand population.
4 Cyril S. Smith, University of Manchester, December 1966 (a report on Bury). *Young People at Leisure*, Pearl Jephcott, *Time of One's Own*, Oliver & Boyd, 1967 (leisure and young people).

8 The project in Moortown

1 Seagate Worker's Report, p. 19; Mary Morse, *The Unattached*, Penguin, 1965.

195

2 Reference to training in this context may be misleading. With the exception of a short course organized by the Department of Youth Work at Manchester University, I know of no specific training for detached youth work. Most detached work projects have, however, involved the workers in some form of in-service training.

3 *The Unattached*, p. 88.

4 See G. W. Goetschius and J. M. Tash, *Working with Unattached Youth*, Routledge & Kegan Paul, 1967.

5 *Ibid.*, pp. 233 and 234.

9 Providing for the leisure of young adults

1 Lord Robertson of Oakbridge, opening the debate on Youth and the Nation in the House of Lords on 21 February 1968, 'rose to call attention to the need for a more comprehensive policy towards the youth of the nation, and to the desirability of creating further opportunities for young people to play a full part in every aspect of our national life.' Hansard, Vol. 289, No. 43.

2 *Half Our Future* HMSO, 1963.

3 This is also the line taken in *Youth and Community Work in the 70s*. The report states: '...in practice we see the change of emphasis in youth work at about the age of 16 or 17.

Work among the younger age groups should be mainly the responsibility of the schools and voluntary organizations, working either in unison or independently.'

Summary and Recommendations for Action, p. 1.

4 See Chapter 3, p. 40.

5 Statistics. pp. 168-70 *Youth and Community Work in the 70s*, HMSO, 1969.

6 *The Youth Service in England and Wales*, HMSO, 1960, para. 134.

7 The first of the main proposals of *Youth and Community Work in the 70s* reads: 'A Youth and Community Service should be established which will get away from the club-is-the-youth-service approach, meet the needs of young people by making contact with them *wherever* they are to be found, and recognise them as part of the community.' p. 1.

However, the club-is-the-youth-service approach is well entrenched and change will not be achieved very easily. Ten years ago the Albemarle committee recommended that the service should concern itself with the encouragement of self programming groups (paras 173-6 and 193-5, *The Youth Service in England and Wales*), but with very little practical effect. The report also gave powerful encouragement to experimental work with the 'unattached' (para. 356) with the result, very largely, that it got only what it asked for: 'experiment'. But even with experiments the local education authorities have, with a few notable exceptions, played very little part and the experience of the experiments has done little to modify the traditional clubwork approach of either statutory or voluntary bodies.

8 See the reports of the surveys conducted by the Regional Councils for Sport.

9 For this information I am grateful to Mr D. Anthony.

10 H. S. Turner, *Something Extraordinary*, Michael Joseph, 1961.

11 This does not mean that non-institutional work is something which can be bought cheaply. It is not. Skill is an expensive commodity wherever it is to be exercised. Crude comparisons of costs between institutional and non-institutional work or even between the work of different institutions are not very helpful because so much depends upon the people worked with and what is being achieved. The only point I want to make here is that many of the commonly accepted forms of work are, if all the 'hidden' costs are taken into account, very expensive. A considerable investment in non-institutional work might be made for less than the *total* running costs of some youth clubs.

12 For one well documented example see John Spencer with Joy Tuxford and Norman Dennis, *Stress and Release in an Urban Estate*, Tavistock, 1964.

Bibliography

ABERCROMBIE, M. L. JOHNSON, *The Anatomy of Judgement*, Hutchinson, 1960.

ANTHONY, E. J. and FOULKES, S. H., *Group Psychotherapy*, Penguin, 1957.

BALES, R. F., and PARSONS, T., *Family, Socialization and Interaction Process*, Routledge & Kegan Paul, 1956.

BAR, R. (ed.), *Curriculum Innovation in Practice*, Edge Hill College of Education, 1969.

BARNES, D., *Language, the Learner and the School*, Penguin, 1969.

BATTEN, T. R., in collaboration with BATTEN, M., *The Non-Directive Approach in Group and Community Work*, Oxford University Press, 1967.

B.B.C. Audience Research Department, *The People's Activities*, B.B.C., 1965.

BERNSTEIN, B., 'Education Cannot Compensate for Society', *New Society* No. 387.

BION, W. R., *Experiences in Groups*, Tavistock, 1961.

BLANDY, M., *Razor Edge*, Gollancz, 1967.

Boy Scouts Association, *The Advance Party Report '66*, BSA, 1966.

BREW, J. MACALISTER, *Youth and Youth Groups*, Faber, 1957.

Bristol Association of Youth Clubs, *The Ninepins Coffee Bar Experiment*, B.A.Y.C., *n.d.*

BUTTON, L., *Friendship Patterns in Older Adolescents*, University College of Swansea Education Department 1965.

CALDER, N. (ed.), *The World in 1984, I & II*, Penguin, 1965.

CARTER, M., *Home, School and Work*, Pergamon, 1962.

CARTER, M. *Into Work*, Penguin, 1966.

CAUTER, T., and DOWNHAM, J. S., *The Communication of Ideas*, Chatto & Windus, 1954.

CLEGG, A., *Children in Distress*, Penguin, 1968.

COATES, K., and SILBURN, R., *Poverty, Deprivation and Morale*, University of Nottingham, 1967.

DAVIES, B., Activity in Youth Work, *Youth Review*, No. 14.

DAVIES, B. D., and GIBSON, A., *The Social Education of the Adolescent*, University of London Press, 1967.

DENNIS, N., HENRIQUES, F., and SLAUGHTER, C. *Coal is Our Life*, Eyre &

Spottiswoode, 1956.

Derbyshire Education Committee, *Professional Youth Leadership*, Derbyshire Education Committee, 1965.

DOLLARD, J., and MILLER, N. E., *Personality and Psychotherapy*, McGraw Hill, 1950.

DUMAZEDIER, J., *Toward a Society of Leisure*, Collier Macmillan, 1967.

EDWARDS, H. J., *The Evening Institute*, National Institute of Adult Education, 1961.

EPPEL, E. M., and EPPEL, M., 'Teenage Values', *New Society*, No. 59.

EPPEL, E. M., and EPPEL, M., 'Teenage Idols', *New Society*, No. 60.

ETZIONI, A., *The Active Society*, Free Press, New York, 1968.

EVANS, W., *Young People in Society*, Blackie, 1965.

EWEN, J., Keep them Out of Here, unpublished account of the Freebooters Project.

FARNDALE, J., and LEICESTER, J. H., (eds), *Trends in the Service for Youth*, Pergamon, 1967.

FARRANT, M. R., 'The Contribution of Research to the Youth Service', *Youth Review*, No. 17.

FRANKENBURG, R., *Communities in Britain*, Penguin, 1966.

FROMM, E., *The Sane Society*, Routledge & Kegan Paul, 1956.

FYVEL, T. R., *The Insecure Offenders*, Chatto & Windus, 1961.

GABOR, D., *Inventing the Future*, Penguin, 1963.

GAVRON, H., *The Captive Wife*, Routledge & Kegan Paul, 1966.

GOETSCHIUS, G. W., and TASH, J. M., *Working with Unattached Youth*, Routledge & Kegan Paul, 1967.

GOSLING, R., *Lady Albemarle's Boys*, Young Fabian, 1961.

HALL, P., and PRICE, C., 'Non-Plan: An Experiment in Freedom', *New Society*, 20 March 1969.

HAMBLETT, C., and DEVERSON, J., *Generation X*, Gibbs & Phillips, 1964.

HARRISON, J., 'A Report on the Efficacy of 'Out-Reach' Counselling Services on the South Okendon/Belhus Estate', unpublished.

HAYWOOD, H., *Partners with the Young*, The tenth M.A.Y.C. King George VI memorial lecture, Methodist Youth Department, 1970.

HERBERT, R., *Youth Service—Has it a Future?* Church of England Youth Council, 1969.

Herder Correspondence, *Adolescent Sub-culture: Myth or Reality*, Herder, 1968.

HOGAN, J. M., *The Future of the Youth Service*, University of Leeds Institute of Education, 1965.

HOGGART, R., *The Uses of Literacy*, Penguin, 1968.

HOLDEN, H. M., and WARD, B., *Soho Project Report 1967/68*, Soho Project, 1970.

HMSO, *The Youth Service in England and Wales*, 1960.

HMSO, *Half Our Future*, 1963.

HMSO, *Report of the Committee on the Age of Majority*, 1967.

HMSO, *Youth and Community Work in the 70s*, 1969.

Schools Council: *Enquiry I: Young School Leavers*, 1968.

Cross'd with Adversity, Working Paper No. 27, 1970.

Counselling in Schools, Working Paper No. 15, 1967.

JAMES, W., 'People and the Youth Service—The Satisfaction and Frustration of Human Needs' (In Service Training of Youth Leaders in Derbyshire 1967), unpublished.

JEPHCOTT, P., *Time of One's Own*, Oliver & Boyd, 1967.

JONES, M., *Social Psychiatry in Practice*, Penguin, 1968.

KEEBLE, R. W. J., *A Life Full of Meaning*, Pergamon, 1965.

KERR, M., *The People of Shipp Street*, Routledge & Kegan Paul 1958.

KLEIN, J., *The Study of Groups*, Routledge & Kegan Paul, 1958.

KLEIN, J., *Working with Groups*, Hutchinson, 1963.

KONOPKA, G., *Social Group Work*, Prentice Hall, 1963.

KUENSTLER, P., *Social Group Work in Great Britain*, Faber, 1955.

Lancashire Education Committee, *Like Us—But Younger*, (Report of Working Party of Division 7.), Lancashire Education Committee, 1966.

LAURIE, P., *The Teenage Revolution*, Anthony Blond, 1965.

LEIGH, M., 'An Experiment in Supervision', *Youth Review*, No. 17.

MACLEOD, I., *The Macleod Report*, The Young Conservative and Unionist Organisation, 1965.

MANN, P. H., *Young Men and Work*, University of Sheffield Department of Sociological Studies, 1966.

MARJORAM, J., 'I was One of the Unattached', *Anarchy* 55 (Vol. 5, No. 9), 1965.

MARTIN, D., 'A Charter for the Unfree Child', *Anarchy* 21, 1962.

MATHEWS, J., *Professional Skill*, N.A.Y.C., 1960.

MATHEWS, J. E., *Working with Youth Groups*, University of London Press, 1966.

MAYS, J. B., *The Young Pretenders*, Michael Joseph, 1965.

Methodist Youth Department, *Young Adults and the Church*, Methodist Youth Department, 1965.

MILSON, F., *Youth at the Centre*, Westhill College of Education, 1965.

MILSON, F., 'What Kind of People are Youth Leaders', *Youth Review*, No. 6, 1966.

MORELY, W. M., *New Town Youth*, Easington R.D.C. and Peterlee Development Corporation, 1966.

MORSE, M., *The Unattached*, Penguin, 1965.

MUSGROVE, F., *Youth and the Social Order*, Routledge & Kegan Paul, 1964.

MUSGROVE, F., 'The Social Needs and Satisfactions of Some Young People', *British Journal of Educational Psychology*, Vol. xxxvi, 1966.

National Association of Youth Clubs, *Report of the Industrial Youth Project*, N.A.Y.C., 1968.

National Council of Social Service, *Young People Today*, N.C.S.S., 1960.

National Federation of Young Farmers' Clubs, *Membership Survey Report*, N.F.Y.F.C., 1966.

New York City Youth Board, *Reaching the Unreached*, New York, 1952.

New York City Youth Board, *Reaching the Fighting Gang*, New York, 1960.

PARTRIDGE, J., *Life in a Secondary Modern School*, Penguin, 1968.

PEDLER, M., *In a Town Like Alfreton*, Alfreton Workers Educational Association, 1969.

PETERS, R. S., *Education as Initiation*, University of London Institute of

Education, 1963.

PETTES, D. E., *Supervision in Social Work*, Allen & Unwin, 1967.

PHILLIPS, M., *Small Groups in England*, Methuen, 1965.

PYKETT, P., *Schools and Youth Service in the Community*, Church of England Youth Council, 1970.

RAYBOULD, S. G. (ed.), *Trends in English Adult Education*, Heinemann, 1959.

RAYBOULD, S. G., *University Extramural Education in England*, Michael Joseph, 1964.

RIESMAN, D., DENNEY, R., and GLAZER, N., *The Lonely Crowd*, Yale University Press, 1952.

RICHARDSON, E., *Group Study for Teachers*, Routledge & Kegan Paul, 1967.

RYLAND, G., and WILSON, G., *Social Group Work Practice*, Houghton Mifflin, 1949.

SCHOFIELD, M., *The Sexual Behaviour of Young People*, Longmans, 1965.

SMITH, C. S., *Young People at Leisure*, University of Manchester, 1966.

SMITH, C. S., 'Organisations or Movements?', *Youth Review*, No. 6., 1966.

SMITH, C. S., 'Social Work Method and the Youth Service', *Trends in Education*, No. 10, 1968.

SPIEGEL, J. P., 'The Resolution of Role Conflict within the Family' *A Modern Introduction to the Family* (ed.) Bell, N. W., and Vogel, E. F., Routledge & Kegan Paul, 1960.

SPROTT, W. J. H., *Human Groups*, Penguin, 1958.

Surrey Educational Research Association, *Attitudes and Aspirations of Surrey School Leavers towards Youth Service, Further Education and Training*, S.E.R.A., 1964.

TASH, J. M., *Supervision in Youth Work*, National Council of Social Service, 1967.

United Nations, Department of Economic and Social Affairs, *The Prevention of Delinquency in Selected European Countries*, United Nations, 1955.

VANESS, T., *School Leavers*, Methuen, 1962.

VENABLES, E., *The Young Worker at College*, Faber, 1965.

WARD, B., 'The Soho Project', *Youth Review*, No. 17, 1970.

WARE, E., *Right at 18?* British Youth Council, 1966.

WATTS, J. R., and WHITWORTH, T. A., *The Professional Youth Leader's view of his Career and Role*, University of Bradford Department of Educational Research, 1968.

WHYTE, W. H., *The Organisation Man*, Cape, 1959.

WILLIAMS, J. E., *The Derbyshire Miners*, Allen & Unwin, 1962.

WILMOTT, P., *Adolescent Boys of East London*, Routledge & Kegan Paul, 1966.

WOOTTON, B., *Social Science and Social Pathology*, Allen & Unwin, 1959.

YOUNG, M., *Innovation and Research in Education*, Routledge & Kegan Paul, 1965.

Youth and the Nation, Hansard, Vol. 289, Nos 43 and 44.

Youth Service Association, *Survey on Tutor/Teacher/Youth Leader Appointments*, Y.S.A., 1965.

BIBLIOGRAPHY

Youth Service Information Centre, *Experiments and Development Projects in Work with Young People.*

Youth Service Information Centre, *Youth Work Project Summaries,* Y.S.I.C.

Index

The International Library of
Sociology
and Social Reconstruction

Edited by W. J. H. SPROTT
Founded by KARL MANNHEIM

ROUTLEDGE & KEGAN PAUL
BROADWAY HOUSE, CARTER LANE, LONDON, E.C.4

CONTENTS

PRINTED IN GREAT BRITAIN BY HEADLEY BROTHERS LTD
109 KINGSWAY LONDON W C 2 AND ASHFORD KENT

GENERAL SOCIOLOGY

Brown, Robert. Explanation in Social Science. *208 pp. 1963. (2nd Impression 1964.) 25s.*

Gibson, Quentin. The Logic of Social Enquiry. *240 pp. 1960. (3rd Impression 1968.) 24s.*

Homans, George C. Sentiments and Activities: Essays in Social Science. *336 pp. 1962. 32s.*

Isajiw, Wsevelod W. Causation and Functionalism in Sociology. *165 pp. 1968. 25s.*

Johnson, Harry M. Sociology: a Systematic Introduction. *Foreword by Robert K. Merton. 710 pp. 1961. (5th Impression 1968.) 42s.*

Mannheim, Karl. Essays on Sociology and Social Psychology. *Edited by Paul Keckskemeti. With Editorial Note by Adolph Lowe. 344 pp. 1953. (2nd Impression 1966.) 32s.*

Systematic Sociology: An Introduction to the Study of Society. *Edited by J. S. Erös and Professor W. A. C. Stewart. 220 pp. 1957. (3rd Impression 1967.) 24s.*

Martindale, Don. The Nature and Types of Sociological Theory. *292 pp. 1961. (3rd Impression 1967.) 35s.*

Maus, Heinz. A Short History of Sociology. *234 pp. 1962. (2nd Impression 1965.) 28s.*

Myrdal, Gunnar. Value in Social Theory: A Collection of Essays on Methodology. *Edited by Paul Streeten. 332 pp. 1958. (3rd Impression 1968.) 35s.*

Ogburn, William F., and **Nimkoff, Meyer F.** A Handbook of Sociology. *Preface by Karl Mannheim. 656 pp. 46 figures. 35 tables. 5th edition (revised) 1964. 45s.*

Parsons, Talcott, and **Smelser, Neil J.** Economy and Society: A Study in the Integration of Economic and Social Theory. *362 pp. 1956. (4th Impression 1967.) 35s.*

Rex, John. Key Problems of Sociological Theory. *220 pp. 1961. (4th Impression 1968.) 25s.*

Stark, Werner. The Fundamental Forms of Social Thought. *280 pp. 1962. 32s.*

FOREIGN CLASSICS OF SOCIOLOGY

Durkheim, Emile. Suicide. A Study in Sociology. *Edited and with an Introduction by George Simpson. 404 pp. 1952. (4th Impression 1968.) 35s.*

Professional Ethics and Civic Morals. *Translated by Cornelia Brookfield. 288 pp. 1957. 30s.*

Gerth, H. H., and **Mills, C. Wright.** From Max Weber: Essays in Sociology. *502 pp. 1948. (6th Impression 1967.) 35s.*

Tönnies, Ferdinand. Community and Association. *(Gemeinschaft und Gesellschaft.) Translated and Supplemented by Charles P. Loomis. Foreword by Pitirim A. Sorokin. 334 pp. 1955. 28s.*

SOCIAL STRUCTURE

Andreski, Stanislav. Military Organization and Society. *Foreword by Professor A. R. Radcliffe-Brown. 226 pp. 1 folder. 1954. Revised Edition 1968. 35s.*

Cole, G. D. H. Studies in Class Structure. *220 pp. 1955. (3rd Impression 1964.) 21s. Paper 10s. 6d.*

Coontz, Sydney H. Population Theories and the Economic Interpretation. *202 pp. 1957. (3rd Impression 1968.) 28s.*

Coser, Lewis. The Functions of Social Conflict. *204 pp. 1956. (3rd Impression 1968.) 25s.*

Dickie-Clark, H. F. Marginal Situation: A Sociological Study of a Coloured Group. *240 pp. 11 tables. 1966. 40s.*

Glass, D. V. (Ed.). Social Mobility in Britain. *Contributions by J. Berent, T. Bottomore, R. C. Chambers, J. Floud, D. V. Glass, J. R. Hall, H. T. Himmelweit, R. K. Kelsall, F. M. Martin, C. A. Moser, R. Mukherjee, and W. Ziegel. 420 pp. 1954. (4th Impression 1967.) 45s.*

Jones, Garth N. Planned Organizational Change: An Exploratory Study Using an Empirical Approach. *About 268 pp. 1969. 40s.*

Kelsall, R. K. Higher Civil Servants in Britain: From 1870 to the Present Day. *268 pp. 31 tables. 1955. (2nd Impression 1966.) 25s.*

König, René. The Community. *232 pp. Illustrated. 1968. 35s.*

Lawton, Denis. Social Class, Language and Education. *192 pp. 1968. (2nd Impression 1968.) 25s.*

McLeish, John. The Theory of Social Change: Four Views Considered. *About 128 pp. 1969. 21s.*

Marsh, David C. The Changing Social Structure in England and Wales, 1871-1961. *1958. 272 pp. 2nd edition (revised) 1966. (2nd Impression 1967.) 35s.*

Mouzelis, Nicos. Organization and Bureaucracy. An Analysis of Modern Theories. *240 pp. 1967. (2nd Impression 1968.) 28s.*

Ossowski, Stanislaw. Class Structure in the Social Consciousness. *210 pp. 1963. (2nd Impression 1967.) 25s.*

SOCIOLOGY AND POLITICS

Barbu, Zevedei. Democracy and Dictatorship: Their Psychology and Patterns of Life. *300 pp. 1956. 28s.*

Crick, Bernard. The American Science of Politics: Its Origins and Conditions. *284 pp. 1959. 32s.*

Hertz, Frederick. Nationality in History and Politics: A Psychology and Sociology of National Sentiment and Nationalism. *432 pp. 1944. (5th Impression 1966.) 42s.*

Kornhauser, William. The Politics of Mass Society. *272 pp. 20 tables. 1960. (3rd Impression 1968.) 28s.*

Laidler, Harry W. History of Socialism. Social-Economic Movements: An Historical and Comparative Survey of Socialism, Communism, Co-operation, Utopianism; and other Systems of Reform and Reconstruction. *New edition. 992 pp. 1968. 90s.*

Lasswell, Harold D. Analysis of Political Behaviour. An Empirical Approach. *324 pp. 1947. (4th Impression 1966.) 35s.*

Mannheim, Karl. Freedom, Power and Democratic Planning. *Edited by Hans Gerth and Ernest K. Bramstedt. 424 pp. 1951. (3rd Impression 1968.) 42s.*

Mansur, Fatma. Process of Independence. *Foreword by A. H. Hanson. 208 pp. 1962. 25s.*

Martin, David A. Pacificism: an Historical and Sociological Study. *262 pp. 1965. 30s.*

Myrdal, Gunnar. The Political Element in the Development of Economic Theory. *Translated from the German by Paul Streeten. 282 pp. 1953. (4th Impression 1965.) 25s.*

Polanyi, Michael. F.R.S. The Logic of Liberty: Reflections and Rejoinders. *228 pp. 1951. 18s.*

Verney, Douglas V. The Analysis of Political Systems. *264 pp. 1959. (3rd Impression 1966.) 28s.*

Wootton, Graham. The Politics of Influence: British Ex-Servicemen, Cabinet Decisions and Cultural Changes, 1917 to 1957. *316 pp. 1963. 30s.*
Workers, Unions and the State. *188 pp. 1966. (2nd Impression 1967.) 25s.*

FOREIGN AFFAIRS: THEIR SOCIAL, POLITICAL AND ECONOMIC FOUNDATIONS

Baer, Gabriel. Population and Society in the Arab East. *Translated by Hanna Szöke. 288 pp. 10 maps. 1964. 40s.*

Bonné, Alfred. State and Economics in the Middle East: A Society in Transition. *482 pp. 2nd (revised) edition 1955. (2nd Impression 1960.) 40s.*
Studies in Economic Development: with special reference to Conditions in the Under-developed Areas of Western Asia and India. *322 pp. 84 tables. 2nd edition 1960. 32s.*

Mayer, J. P. Political Thought in France from the Revolution to the Fifth Republic. *164 pp. 3rd edition (revised) 1961. 16s.*

CRIMINOLOGY

Ancel, Marc. Social Defence: A Modern Approach to Criminal Problems. *Foreword by Leon Radzinowicz. 240 pp. 1965. 32s.*

Cloward, Richard A., and **Ohlin, Lloyd E.** Delinquency and Opportunity: A Theory of Delinquent Gangs. *248 pp. 1961. 25s.*

5

Downes, David M. The Delinquent Solution. A Study in Subcultural Theory. *296 pp. 1966. 42s.*

Dunlop, A. B., and McCabe, S. Young Men in Detention Centres. *192 pp. 1965. 28s.*

Friedländer, Kate. The Psycho-Analytical Approach to Juvenile Delinquency: Theory, Case Studies, Treatment. *320 pp. 1947. (6th Impression 1967). 40s.*

Glueck, Sheldon and Eleanor. Family Environment and Delinquency. *With the statistical assistance of Rose W. Kneznek. 340 pp. 1962. (2nd Impression 1966.) 40s.*

Mannheim, Hermann. Comparative Criminology: a Text Book. *Two volumes. 442 pp. and 380 pp. 1965. (2nd Impression with corrections 1966.) 42s. a volume.*

Morris, Terence. The Criminal Area: A Study in Social Ecology. *Foreword by Hermann Mannheim. 232 pp. 25 tables. 4 maps. 1957. (2nd Impression 1966.) 28s.*

Morris, Terence and Pauline, assisted by **Barbara Barer.** Pentonville: A Sociological Study of an English Prison. *416 pp. 16 plates. 1963. 50s.*

Spencer, John C. Crime and the Services. *Foreword by Hermann Mannheim. 336 pp. 1954. 28s.*

Trasler, Gordon. The Explanation of Criminality. *144 pp. 1962. (2nd Impression 1967.) 20s.*

SOCIAL PSYCHOLOGY

Barbu, Zevedei. Problems of Historical Psychology. *248 pp. 1960. 25s.*

Blackburn, Julian. Psychology and the Social Pattern. *184 pp. 1945. (7th Impression 1964.) 16s.*

Fleming, C. M. Adolescence: Its Social Psychology: With an Introduction to recent findings from the fields of Anthropology, Physiology, Medicine, Psychometrics and Sociometry. *288 pp. 2nd edition (revised) 1963. (3rd Impression 1967.) 25s. Paper 12s. 6d.*

The Social Psychology of Education: An Introduction and Guide to Its Study. *136 pp. 2nd edition (revised) 1959. (4th Impression 1967.) 14s. Paper 7s. 6d.*

Homans, George C. The Human Group. *Foreword by Bernard DeVoto. Introduction by Robert K. Merton. 526 pp. 1951. (7th Impression 1968.) 35s.*

Social Behaviour: its Elementary Forms. *416 pp. 1961. (3rd Impression 1968.) 35s.*

Klein, Josephine. The Study of Groups. *226 pp. 31 figures. 5 tables. 1956. (5th Impression 1967.) 21s. Paper 9s. 6d.*

Linton, Ralph. The Cultural Background of Personality. *132 pp. 1947. (7th Impression 1968.) 18s.*

Mayo, Elton. The Social Problems of an Industrial Civilization. With an appendix on the Political Problem. *180 pp. 1949. (5th Impression 1966.) 25s.*

Ottaway, A. K. C. Learning Through Group Experience. *176 pp. 1966. (2nd Impression 1968.) 25s.*

Ridder, J. C. de. The Personality of the Urban African in South Africa. A Thematic Apperception Test Study. *196 pp. 12 plates. 1961. 25s.*

Rose, Arnold M. (Ed.). Human Behaviour and Social Processes: an Interactionist Approach. *Contributions by Arnold M. Rose, Ralph H. Turner, Anselm Strauss, Everett C. Hughes, E. Franklin Frazier, Howard S. Becker, et al. 696 pp. 1962. (2nd Impression 1968.) 70s.*

Smelser, Neil J. Theory of Collective Behaviour. *448 pp. 1962. (2nd Impression 1967.) 45s.*

Stephenson, Geoffrey M. The Development of Conscience. *128 pp. 1966. 25s.*

Young, Kimball. Handbook of Social Psychology. *658 pp. 16 figures. 10 tables. 2nd edition (revised) 1957. (3rd Impression 1963.) 40s.*

SOCIOLOGY OF THE FAMILY

Banks, J. A. Prosperity and Parenthood: A study of Family Planning among The Victorian Middle Classes. *262 pp. 1954. (3rd Impression 1968.) 28s.*

Bell, Colin R. Middle Class Families: Social and Geographical Mobility. *224 pp. 1969. 35s.*

Burton, Lindy. Vulnerable Children. *272 pp. 1968. 35s.*

Gavron, Hannah. The Captive Wife: Conflicts of Housebound Mothers. *190 pp. 1966. (2nd Impression 1966.) 25s.*

Klein, Josephine. Samples from English Cultures. *1965. (2nd Impression 1967.)*
  1. Three Preliminary Studies and Aspects of Adult Life in England. *447 pp. 50s.*
  2. Child-Rearing Practices and Index. *247 pp. 35s.*

Klein, Viola. Britain's Married Women Workers. *180 pp. 1965. (2nd Impression 1968.) 28s.*

McWhinnie, Alexina M. Adopted Children. How They Grow Up. *304 pp. 1967. (2nd Impression 1968.) 42s.*

Myrdal, Alva and **Klein, Viola.** Women's Two Roles: Home and Work. *238 pp. 27 tables. 1956. Revised Edition 1967. 30s. Paper 15s.*

Parsons, Talcott and **Bales, Robert F.** Family: Socialization and Interaction Process. *In collaboration with James Olds, Morris Zelditch and Philip E. Slater. 456 pp. 50 figures and tables. 1956. (3rd Impression 1968.) 45s.*

Schücking, L. L. The Puritan Family. *Translated from the German by Brian Battershaw. 212 pp. 1969. About 42s.*

7

THE SOCIAL SERVICES

Forder, R. A. (Ed.). Penelope Hall's Social Services of Modern England. *288 pp. 1969. 35s.*

George, Victor. Social Security: Beveridge and After. *258 pp. 1968. 35s.*

Goetschius, George W. Working with Community Groups. *256 pp. 1969. 35s.*

Goetschius, George W. and **Tash, Joan.** Working with Unattached Youth. *416 pp. 1967. (2nd Impression 1968.) 40s.*

Hall, M. P., and **Howes, I. V.** The Church in Social Work. A Study of Moral Welfare Work undertaken by the Church of England. *320 pp. 1965. 35s.*

Heywood, Jean S. Children in Care: the Development of the Service for the Deprived Child. *264 pp. 2nd edition (revised) 1965. (2nd Impression 1966.) 32s.*

An Introduction to Teaching Casework Skills. *190 pp. 1964. 28s.*

Jones, Kathleen. Lunacy, Law and Conscience, 1744-1845: the Social History of the Care of the Insane. *268 pp. 1955. 25s.*

Mental Health and Social Policy, 1845-1959. *264 pp. 1960. (2nd Impression 1967.) 32s.*

Jones, Kathleen and **Sidebotham, Roy.** Mental Hospitals at Work. *220 pp. 1962. 30s.*

Kastell, Jean. Casework in Child Care. *Foreword by M. Brooke Willis. 320 pp. 1962. 35s.*

Morris, Pauline. Put Away: A Sociological Study of Institutions for the Mentally Retarded. *Approx. 288 pp. 1969. About 50s.*

Nokes, P. L. The Professional Task in Welfare Practice. *152 pp. 1967. 28s.*

Rooff, Madeline. Voluntary Societies and Social Policy. *350 pp. 15 tables. 1957. 35s.*

Timms, Noel. Psychiatric Social Work in Great Britain (1939-1962). *280 pp. 1964. 32s.*

Social Casework: Principles and Practice. *256 pp. 1964. (2nd Impression 1966.) 25s. Paper 15s.*

Trasler, Gordon. In Place of Parents: A Study in Foster Care. *272 pp. 1960. (2nd Impression 1966.) 30s.*

Young, A. F., and **Ashton, E. T.** British Social Work in the Nineteenth Century. *288 pp. 1956. (2nd Impression 1963.) 28s.*

Young, A. F. Social Services in British Industry. *272 pp. 1968. 40s.*

SOCIOLOGY OF EDUCATION

Banks, Olive. Parity and Prestige in English Secondary Education: a Study in Educational Sociology. *272 pp. 1955. (2nd Impression 1963.) 32s.*

Bentwich, Joseph. Education in Israel. *224 pp. 8 pp. plates. 1965. 24s.*

Blyth, W. A. L. English Primary Education. A Sociological Description. *1965. Revised edition 1967.*

1. Schools. *232 pp. 30s. Paper 12s. 6d.*
2. Background. *168 pp. 25s. Paper 10s. 6d.*

Collier, K. G. The Social Purposes of Education: Personal and Social Values in Education. *268 pp. 1959. (3rd Impression 1965.) 21s.*

Dale, R. R., and **Griffith, S.** Down Stream: Failure in the Grammar School. *108 pp. 1965. 20s.*

Dore, R. P. Education in Tokugawa Japan. *356 pp. 9 pp. plates. 1965. 35s.*

Edmonds, E. L. The School Inspector. *Foreword by Sir William Alexander. 214 pp. 1962. 28s.*

Evans, K. M. Sociometry and Education. *158 pp. 1962. (2nd Impression 1966.) 18s.*

Foster, P. J. Education and Social Change in Ghana. *336 pp. 3 maps. 1965. (2nd Impression 1967.) 36s.*

Fraser, W. R. Education and Society in Modern France. *150 pp. 1963. (2nd Impression 1968.) 25s.*

Hans, Nicholas. New Trends in Education in the Eighteenth Century. *278 pp. 19 tables. 1951. (2nd Impression 1966.) 30s.*
Comparative Education: A Study of Educational Factors and Traditions. *360 pp. 3rd (revised) edition 1958. (4th Impression 1967.) 25s. Paper 12s. 6d.*

Hargreaves, David. Social Relations in a Secondary School. *240 pp. 1967. (2nd Impression 1968.) 32s.*

Holmes, Brian. Problems in Education. A Comparative Approach. *336 pp. 1965. (2nd Impression 1967.) 32s.*

Mannheim, Karl and **Stewart, W. A. C.** An Introduction to the Sociology of Education. *206 pp. 1962. (2nd Impression 1965.) 21s.*

Morris, Raymond N. The Sixth Form and College Entrance. *231 pp. 1969. 40s.*

Musgrove, F. Youth and the Social Order. *176 pp. 1964. (2nd Impression 1968.) 25s. Paper 12s.*

Ortega y Gasset, José. Mission of the University. *Translated with an Introduction by Howard Lee Nostrand. 86 pp. 1946. (3rd Impression 1963.) 15s.*

Ottaway, A. K. C. Education and Society: An Introduction to the Sociology of Education. *With an Introduction by W. O. Lester Smith. 212 pp. Second edition (revised). 1962. (5th Impression 1968.) 18s. Paper 10s. 6d.*

Peers, Robert. Adult Education: A Comparative Study. *398 pp. 2nd edition 1959. (2nd Impression 1966.) 42s.*

Pritchard, D. G. Education and the Handicapped: 1760 to 1960. *258 pp. 1963. (2nd Impression 1966.) 35s.*

Richardson, Helen. Adolescent Girls in Approved Schools. *Approx. 360 pp. 1969. About 42s.*

Simon, Brian and **Joan** (Eds.). Educational Psychology in the U.S.S.R. *Introduction by Brian and Joan Simon. Translation by Joan Simon. Papers by D. N. Bogoiavlenski and N. A. Menchinskaia, D. B. Elkonin, E. A. Fleshner, Z. I. Kalmykova, G. S. Kostiuk, V. A. Krutetski, A. N. Leontiev, A. R. Luria, E. A. Milerian, R. G. Natadze, B. M. Teplov, L. S. Vygotski, L. V. Zankov. 296 pp. 1963. 40s.*

9

SOCIOLOGY OF CULTURE

Eppel, E. M., and **M.** Adolescents and Morality: A Study of some Moral Values and Dilemmas of Working Adolescents in the Context of a changing Climate of Opinion. *Foreword by W. J. H. Sprott. 268 pp. 39 tables. 1966. 30s.*

Fromm, Erich. The Fear of Freedom. *286 pp. 1942. (8th Impression 1960.) 25s. Paper 10s.*

The Sane Society. *400 pp. 1956. (4th Impression 1968.) 28s. Paper 14s.*

Mannheim, Karl. Diagnosis of Our Time: Wartime Essays of a Sociologist. *208 pp. 1943. (8th Impression 1966.) 21s.*

Essays on the Sociology of Culture. *Edited by Ernst Mannheim in co-operation with Paul Kecskemeti. Editorial Note by Adolph Lowe. 280 pp. 1956. (3rd Impression 1967.) 28s.*

Weber, Alfred. Farewell to European History: or The Conquest of Nihilism. *Translated from the German by R. F. C. Hull. 224 pp. 1947. 18s.*

SOCIOLOGY OF RELIGION

Argyle, Michael. Religious Behaviour. *224 pp. 8 figures. 41 tables. 1958. (4th Impression 1968.) 25s.*

Nelson, G. K. Spiritualism and Society. *313 pp. 1969. 42s.*

Stark, Werner. The Sociology of Religion. A Study of Christendom.
Volume I. Established Religion. *248 pp. 1966. 35s.*
Volume II. Sectarian Religion. *368 pp. 1967. 40s.*
Volume III. The Universal Church. *464 pp. 1967. 45s.*

Watt, W. Montgomery. Islam and the Integration of Society. *320 pp. 1961. (3rd Impression 1966.) 35s.*

SOCIOLOGY OF ART AND LITERATURE

Beljame, Alexandre. Men of Letters and the English Public in the Eighteenth Century: 1660-1744, Dryden, Addison, Pope. *Edited with an Introduction and Notes by Bonamy Dobrée. Translated by E. O. Lorimer. 532 pp. 1948. 32s.*

Misch, Georg. A History of Autobiography in Antiquity. *Translated by E. W. Dickes. 2 Volumes. Vol. 1, 364 pp., Vol. 2, 372 pp. 1950. 45s. the set.*

Schücking, L. L. The Sociology of Literary Taste. *112 pp. 2nd (revised) edition 1966. 18s.*

Silbermann, Alphons. The Sociology of Music. *Translated from the German by Corbet Stewart. 222 pp. 1963. 32s.*

SOCIOLOGY OF KNOWLEDGE

Mannheim, Karl. Essays on the Sociology of Knowledge. *Edited by Paul Kecskemeti. Editorial note by Adolph Lowe. 352 pp. 1952. (4th Impression 1967.) 35s.*

Stark, W. America: Ideal and Reality. The United States of 1776 in Contemporary Philosophy. *136 pp. 1947. 12s.*

The Sociology of Knowledge: An Essay in Aid of a Deeper Understanding of the History of Ideas. *384 pp. 1958. (3rd Impression 1967.) 36s.*

Montesquieu: Pioneer of the Sociology of Knowledge. *244 pp. 1960. 25s.*

URBAN SOCIOLOGY

Anderson, Nels. The Urban Community: A World Perspective. *532 pp. 1960. 35s.*

Ashworth, William. The Genesis of Modern British Town Planning: A Study in Economic and Social History of the Nineteenth and Twentieth Centuries. *288 pp. 1954. (3rd Impression 1968.) 32s.*

Bracey, Howard. Neighbours: On New Estates and Subdivisions in England and U.S.A. *220 pp. 1964. 28s.*

Cullingworth, J. B. Housing Needs and Planning Policy: A Restatement of the Problems of Housing Need and "Overspill" in England and Wales. *232 pp. 44 tables. 8 maps. 1960. (2nd Impression 1966.) 28s.*

Dickinson, Robert E. City and Region: A Geographical Interpretation. *608 pp. 125 figures. 1964. (5th Impression 1967.) 60s.*

The West European City: A Geographical Interpretation. *600 pp. 129 maps. 29 plates. 2nd edition 1962. (3rd Impression 1968.) 55s.*

The City Region in Western Europe. *320 pp. Maps. 1967. 30s. Paper 14s.*

Jackson, Brian. Working Class Community: Some General Notions raised by a Series of Studies in Northern England. *192 pp. 1968. (2nd Impression 1968.) 25s.*

Jennings, Hilda. Societies in the Making: a Study of Development and Redevelopment within a County Borough. *Foreword by D. A. Clark. 286 pp. 1962. (2nd Impression 1967.) 32s.*

Kerr, Madeline. The People of Ship Street. *240 pp. 1958. 28s.*

Mann, P. H. An Approach to Urban Sociology. *240 pp. 1965. (2nd Impression 1968.) 30s.*

Morris, R. N., and Mogey, J. The Sociology of Housing. Studies at Berinsfield. *232 pp. 4 pp. plates. 1965. 42s.*

Rosser, C., and Harris, C. The Family and Social Change. A Study of Family and Kinship in a South Wales Town. *352 pp. 8 maps. 1965. (2nd Impression 1968.) 45s.*

RURAL SOCIOLOGY

Chambers, R. J. H. Settlement Schemes in Africa: A Selective Study. *Approx. 268 pp. 1969. About 50s.*

Haswell, M. R. The Economics of Development in Village India. *120 pp. 1967. 21s.*

Littlejohn, James. Westrigg: the Sociology of a Cheviot Parish. *172 pp. 5 figures. 1963. 25s.*

Williams, W. M. The Country Craftsman: A Study of Some Rural Crafts and the Rural Industries Organization in England. *248 pp. 9 figures. 1958. 25s.* (*Dartington Hall Studies in Rural Sociology.*)
The Sociology of an English Village: Gosforth. *272 pp. 12 figures. 13 tables. 1956.* (*3rd Impression 1964.*) *25s.*

SOCIOLOGY OF MIGRATION

Humphreys, Alexander J. New Dubliners: Urbanization and the Irish Family. *Foreword by George C. Homans. 304 pp. 1966. 40s.*

SOCIOLOGY OF INDUSTRY AND DISTRIBUTION

Anderson, Nels. Work and Leisure. *280 pp. 1961. 28s.*

Blau, Peter M., and Scott, W. Richard. Formal Organizations: a Comparative approach. *Introduction and Additional Bibliography by J. H. Smith. 326 pp. 1963.* (*4th Impression 1969.*) *35s. Paper 15s.*

Eldridge, J. E. T. Industrial Disputes. Essays in the Sociology of Industrial Relations. *288 pp. 1968. 40s.*

Hollowell, Peter G. The Lorry Driver. *272 pp. 1968. 42s.*

Jefferys, Margot, with the assistance of Winifred Moss. Mobility in the Labour Market: Employment Changes in Battersea and Dagenham. *Preface by Barbara Wootton. 186 pp. 51 tables. 1954. 15s.*

Levy, A. B. Private Corporations and Their Control. *Two Volumes. Vol. 1, 464 pp., Vol. 2, 432 pp. 1950. 80s. the set.*

Liepmann, Kate. Apprenticeship: An Enquiry into its Adequacy under Modern Conditions. *Foreword by H. D. Dickinson. 232 pp. 6 tables. 1960.* (*2nd Impression 1960.*) *23s.*

Millerson, Geoffrey. The Qualifying Associations: a Study in Professionalization. *320 pp. 1964. 42s.*

Smelser, Neil J. Social Change in the Industrial Revolution: An Application of Theory to the Lancashire Cotton Industry, 1770-1840. *468 pp. 12 figures. 14 tables. 1959.* (*2nd Impression 1960.*) *50s.*

Williams, Gertrude. Recruitment to Skilled Trades. *240 pp. 1957. 23s.*

Young, A. F. Industrial Injuries Insurance: an Examination of British Policy. *192 pp. 1964. 30s.*

ANTHROPOLOGY

Ammar, Hamed. Growing up in an Egyptian Village: Silwa, Province of Aswan. *336 pp. 1954.* (*2nd Impression 1966.*) *35s.*

Crook, David and Isabel. Revolution in a Chinese Village: Ten Mile Inn. *230 pp. 8 plates. 1 map. 1959.* (*2nd Impression 1968.*) *21s.*
The First Years of Yangyi Commune. *302 pp. 12 plates. 1966. 42s.*

Dickie-Clark, H. F. The Marginal Situation. A Sociological Study of a Coloured Group. *236 pp. 1966. 40s.*

Dube, S. C. Indian Village. *Foreword by Morris Edward Opler. 276 pp. 4 plates. 1955. (5th Impression 1965.) 25s.*
India's Changing Villages: Human Factors in Community Development. *260 pp. 8 plates. 1 map. 1958. (3rd Impression 1963.) 25s.*

Firth, Raymond. Malay Fishermen. Their Peasant Economy. *420 pp. 17 pp. plates. 2nd edition revised and enlarged 1966. (2nd Impression 1968.) 55s.*

Gulliver, P. H. The Family Herds. A Study of two Pastoral Tribes in East Africa, The Jie and Turkana. *304 pp. 4 plates. 19 figures. 1955. (2nd Impression with new preface and bibliography 1966.) 35s.*
Social Control in an African Society: a Study of the Arusha, Agricultural Masai of Northern Tanganyika. *320 pp. 8 plates. 10 figures. 1963. (2nd Impression 1968.) 42s.*

Ishwaran, K. Shivapur. A South Indian Village. *216 pp. 1968. 35s.*
Tradition and Economy in Village India: An Interactionist Approach. *Foreword by Conrad Arensburg. 176 pp. 1966. (2nd Impression 1968.) 25s.*

Jarvie, Ian C. The Revolution in Anthropology. *268 pp. 1964. (2nd Impression 1967.) 40s.*

Jarvie, Ian C. and **Agassi, Joseph.** Hong Kong. A Society in Transition. *396 pp. Illustrated with plates and maps. 1968. 56s.*

Little, Kenneth L. Mende of Sierra Leone. *308 pp. and folder. 1951. Revised edition 1967. 63s.*

Lowie, Professor Robert H. Social Organization. *494 pp. 1950. (4th Impression 1966.) 50s.*

Mayer, Adrian C. Caste and Kinship in Central India: A Village and its Region. *328 pp. 16 plates. 15 figures. 16 tables. 1960. (2nd Impression 1965.) 35s.*
Peasants in the Pacific: A Study of Fiji Indian Rural Society. *232 pp. 16 plates. 10 figures. 14 tables. 1961. 35s.*

Smith, Raymond T. The Negro Family in British Guiana: Family Structure and Social Status in the Villages. *With a Foreword by Meyer Fortes. 314 pp. 8 plates. 1 figure. 4 maps. 1956. (2nd Impression 1965.) 35s.*

DOCUMENTARY

Meek, Dorothea L. (Ed.). Soviet Youth: Some Achievements and Problems. *Excerpts from the Soviet Press, translated by the editor. 280 pp. 1957. 28s.*

Schlesinger, Rudolf (Ed.). Changing Attitudes in Soviet Russia.
2. The Nationalities Problem and Soviet Administration. Selected Readings on the Development of Soviet Nationalities Policies. *Introduced by the editor. Translated by W. W. Gottlieb. 324 pp. 1956. 30s.*

13

Reports of the Institute
of Community Studies

(*Demy 8vo.*)

Cartwright, Ann. Human Relations and Hospital Care. *272 pp. 1964. 30s.*

Patients and their Doctors. A Study of General Practice. *304 pp. 1967. 40s.*

Jackson, Brian. Streaming: an Education System in Miniature. *168 pp. 1964.* (*2nd Impression 1966.*) *21s. Paper 10s.*

Jackson, Brian and **Marsden, Dennis.** Education and the Working Class: Some General Themes raised by a Study of 88 Working-class Children in a Northern Industrial City. *268 pp. 2 folders. 1962.* (*4th Impression 1968.*) *32s.*

Marris, Peter. Widows and their Families. *Foreword by Dr. John Bowlby. 184 pp. 18 tables. Statistical Summary. 1958. 18s.*

Family and Social Change in an African City. A Study of Rehousing in Lagos. *196 pp. 1 map. 4 plates. 53 tables. 1961.* (*2nd Impression 1966.*) *30s.*

The Experience of Higher Education. *232 pp. 27 tables. 1964. 25s.*

Marris, Peter and **Rein, Martin.** Dilemmas of Social Reform. Poverty and Community Action in the United States. *256 pp. 1967. 35s.*

Mills, Enid. Living with Mental Illness: a Study in East London. *Foreword by Morris Carstairs. 196 pp. 1962. 28s.*

Runciman, W. G. Relative Deprivation and Social Justice. A Study of Attitudes to Social Inequality in Twentieth Century England. *352 pp. 1966.* (*2nd Impression 1967.*) *40s.*

Townsend, Peter. The Family Life of Old People: An Inquiry in East London. *Foreword by J. H. Sheldon. 300 pp. 3 figures. 63 tables. 1957.* (*3rd Impression 1967.*) *30s.*

Willmott, Peter. Adolescent Boys in East London. *230 pp. 1966. 30s.*

The Evolution of a Community: a study of Dagenham after forty years. *168 pp. 2 maps. 1963. 21s.*

Willmott, Peter and **Young, Michael.** Family and Class in a London Suburb. *202 pp. 47 tables. 1960.* (*4th Impression 1968.*) *25s.*

Young, Michael. Innovation and Research in Education. *192 pp. 1965. 25s. Paper 12s. 6d.*

Young, Michael and **McGeeney, Patrick.** Learning Begins at Home. A Study of a Junior School and its Parents. *About 128 pp. 1968. 21s. Paper 14s.*

Young, Michael and **Willmott, Peter.** Family and Kinship in East London. *Foreword by Richard M. Titmuss. 252 pp. 39 tables. 1957.* (*3rd Impression 1965.*) *28s.*

The British Journal of Sociology. *Edited by Terence P. Morris. Vol. 1, No. 1, March 1950 and Quarterly. Roy. 8vo., £3 annually, 15s. a number, post free. (Vols. 1-18, £8 each. Individual parts £2 10s.*

All prices are net and subject to alteration without notice

1268 H.B.